The Grass Roots of English History

The Grass Roots of English History

Local Societies in England before the Industrial Revolution

DAVID HEY

Bloomsbury Academic
An imprint of Bloomsbury Publishing Plc

B L O O M S B U R Y
LONDON • OXFORD • NEW YORK • NEW DELHI • SYDNEY

Bloomsbury Academic
An imprint of Bloomsbury Publishing Plc

50 Bedford Square	1385 Broadway
London	New York
WC1B 3DP	NY 10018
UK	USA

www.bloomsbury.com

BLOOMSBURY and the Diana logo are trademarks of Bloomsbury Publishing Plc

First published 2016

British Library Cataloguing-in-Publication Data
A catalogue record for this book is available from the British Library.

ISBN:	HB:	978-1-4742-6251-4
	PB:	978-1-4742-8164-5
	ePDF:	978-1-4742-6253-8
	ePub:	978-1-4742-6252-1

Library of Congress Cataloging-in-Publication Data
Names: Hey, David.
Title: The grass roots of English history : local societies in England before the Industrial Revolution / David Hey.
Description: London : Bloomsbury Academic, an imprint of Bloomsbury Publishing Plc, 2016. | Includes bibliographical references and index.
Identifiers: LCCN 2015043337| ISBN 9781474262514 (hardback) | ISBN 9781474281645 (paperback) | ISBN 9781474262538 (ePDF) | ISBN 9781474262521 (ePub)
Subjects: LCSH: England—Social life and customs. | England—History, Local. | England—Rural conditions. | Country life—England—History. | Community life—England—History. | Families—England—History. | Landscapes—Social aspects—England—History. | Social change—England—History. | BISAC: HISTORY / Europe / Great Britain. | HISTORY / Social History.
Classification: LCC DA115 .H49 2016 | DDC 942–dc23 LC record available at http://lccn.loc.gov/2015043337

Cover design: Sharon Mah
Cover image: The Luttrell Psalter: Psalm 97 © The British Library Board

Typeset by RefineCatch Limited, Bungay, Suffolk
Printed and bound in Great Britain

For my darling wife, Pat

David sadly passed away during the production of this book.

He was a lovely man with many interests but History was his main passion.

This is the final book written by David. We know how much he enjoyed writing it.

He was a wonderful Husband, Dad, Grandad and friend to many and will be sadly missed.

CONTENTS

ILLUSTRATIONS

All images author's own.

PREFACE

Over the last 50 years or so, I have been much involved in the study of English local and family history at both the professional and amateur level and I have seen how the local approach – now sometimes labelled 'micro-history' to give it academic respectability – has helped to transform our understanding of the history of the nation at large. In the last few decades local history in one form or another has become accepted as part of the mainstream of historical research. Local historians are no longer as defensive about their subject as they used to be. By looking at a restricted geographical area, however it is defined, they have the opportunity to differ from most of their colleagues by extending their chronological range and by using not just documentary records but also a wide range of different types of evidence, including that provided by archaeology, architecture, botany, cultural studies, linguistics, genetics and historical demography. No historian can be an expert in all these things, but he or she can be receptive to an inter-disciplinary approach in co-operation with experts from other areas.

The essential starting points for a local study are an understanding of the administrative framework of either a parish, township, manor or borough, and a familiarity with the natural surroundings. Landscape history has blossomed since William Hoskins wrote *The Making of the English Landscape* (1955). It includes the study of farms and field systems, woodland management, the pattern of highways and lanes, the layout and buildings of towns, the interpretation of place-names, and the study of vernacular architecture as well as of great palaces and country houses, cathedrals, monasteries and parish churches. Yet all the while, we must have at the forefront of our minds the people who inhabited these landscapes: the ordinary English families as well as the high and the mighty. The present popular interest in family history is a very welcome development that reinforces the value of the local approach.

The emphasis in this book is on the differing nature of the various local societies that were found throughout England. People used to refer to the neighbourhood with which they were familiar as their 'country', by which they meant not the whole of England but the local district that stretched as far as the nearest market towns. The core groups of families that remained rooted in these neighbourhoods were the ones that shaped local culture and passed on their traditions. They often bore distinctive surnames that were unique to their particular 'country', a characteristic feature that is still evident today despite the mobility of modern times. The use of 'country' in this sense is now largely forgotten, but it was used commonly up to about the First World War. We will start by exploring its old meaning, for this is how most English people once viewed the world in which they lived.

Local history is a co-operative venture. The friends who have helped me over the past 50 years are far too numerous to list here, but many of their publications are quoted. I thank the anonymous referees who commented on the original text, and I welcome the many thoughts that they and their colleagues suggested. I am particularly grateful to Emily Drewe, Frances Arnold and Emma Goode of Bloomsbury Publishing and to Veronica Lyons for her helpful copyediting.

David Hey

CHAPTER ONE

Introduction:

The countries of England

A sense of belonging to a particular place – a town or a rural parish – within a wider district was once stronger than it is now. Before the increased mobility of the later twentieth century, most people lived in a world with limited mental horizons. Although some gentry families thought of themselves as belonging to a county community long before the Industrial Revolution, ordinary people did not regard themselves as, say, Lancashire folk or Devonians until well into the nineteenth century. In Yorkshire, the cutlers of the Sheffield district had little in common with the weavers of the West Riding textile towns and countryside to the north, and they knew nothing about the farmers of the Vale of York or of the Wolds and Holderness further east, nor did they have any contact with the lead miners of the Yorkshire Dales.

Instead of regarding provincial England as a group of counties, we need to think in terms of the much smaller neighbourhoods that people used to refer to as their 'country'. One of the definitions of 'country' in the *Oxford English Dictionary* is: 'A tract or district having more or less definite limits in relation to human occupation, e.g. owned by the same lord or proprietor, or inhabited by people of the same race, dialect, occupation, etc.' The term is a useful one, for most of us share a sense of belonging to both a particular place and to a wider district in which families had friends and relations and people with whom they did business. We no longer call this a 'country' but it often corresponds to the neighbourhood that was familiar to our ancestors.

When Daniel Defoe visited Lincoln in the early eighteenth century, he found that the city stood 'in a most rich, pleasant, and agreeable country'.[1] A century earlier in 1614, when Robert Smyth, a successful London merchant tailor, founded a market hall and grammar school in his native town of Market Harborough, he explained in his will that, as a young man, 'I came out of my country and from my father's house with my cuppe empty' and that with his staff he crossed the river Welland, before heading for the capital city.[2] The river seems to have formed a mental barrier at the edge of his particular 'country'.

Victorian novelists used the term regularly. George Eliot and Thomas Hardy were very conscious of this usage, and Anthony Trollope supplied a map of 'The Barchester Country' to accompany his set of ecclesiastical novels. In Eliot's *Silas Marner*, for instance, Silas says to Dolly, 'But your ways are different: my country was a good way off.' In the preface to *The Mayor of Casterbridge*, which he set in Dorchester, Hardy referred to 'the real history of the town called Casterbridge and the neighbouring country', and one of his characters says, 'We will leave Casterbridge as quietly as we have come, and go back to our own country.'[3]

It has long been a commonplace of social history that in the Tudor and Stuart era the great majority of English people – men and women, country dwellers as well as those living in towns – moved from their place of birth at some stage of their lives. The composition of early modern communities was constantly changing. Yet it seems that much of this movement across parish boundaries did not affect the stability of the groups of families that formed the core of local societies within a wider 'country'. For instance, it was common for young farm servants or domestic servants to move beyond their parish boundary in search of employment, but their movement was generally confined to the district bounded by the nearest market towns, and most people found their marriage partners from within the same district.

When Richard Gough wrote the history of his native parish of Myddle in Shropshire in 1701, he used phrases such as 'He was a person well reputed in his country' or 'She did much good in the country', for although he concentrated on the personal histories of every family in the parish, he knew that their movements were not confined by the parish boundary but by the nearest market towns of Shrewsbury, Ellesmere and Wem. Remarkably, the 1901 census returns reveal exactly the same picture of stability and restricted mobility 200 years later. Of the 135 male householders in the parish, 35 had been born in Myddle and 76 in neighbouring places. In other words, 82 per cent of the householders came from the 'country' that Gough knew so well. Only one man came from south of the river Severn, a few miles away, and very few had ventured from beyond the Shropshire boundary. In an age before family cars became common, people still lived in local worlds.[4]

It can be argued that the character of a local community was determined not so much by all the coming and going but by the families that stayed put, even though at any one time they may have been outnumbered by those who had recently moved in. In tracing the individual pedigrees of all the people in his parish, from the gentry down to the humblest cottager, Gough was particularly conscious of those families – such as his own – that had been resident in Myddle for several generations, the ones who formed the core of his community and who provided it with a sense of continuity. He frequently remarked in passing: 'We have a tradition'; 'I have heard by ancient persons'; and 'I have been credibly informed by ancient persons'.

Country folk then, as now, delighted in talking about the family histories of their neighbours, recounting their triumphs, dwelling on their misfortunes, and attributing common characteristics to successive generations and even to distant cousins. Thomas Bewick, the eighteenth-century artist, spoke of this interest in family histories amongst the old inhabitants of the cottages scattered around the edges of the commons on the south bank of the Tyne in the 1750s and 1760s:

> After I left the country, I always felt much pleasure in revisiting them, and over a tankard of ale to listen to their discourse. It was chiefly upon local biography, in which they sometimes traced the pedigrees of their neighbours a long way back.[5]

The core groups of families who remained rooted in their 'country' were the ones that shaped local culture and passed on their traditions. They were as vital as were the nature of the work and the appearance of the local landscape in determining the special characteristics of their neighbourhood. In *Anna of the Five Towns* (set in the Potteries in 1902), Arnold Bennett wrote:

> Mynors belonged to a family now otherwise extinct in the Five Towns – one of those families, which by virtue of numbers, variety, and personal force seem to permeate a whole district, to be a calculable item of it, an essential part of its identity.[6]

Networks of long-resident families were formed and repeatedly strengthened by intermarriage. Many of these old urban dynasties continued to run provincial towns over several generations, while in the countryside farming clans set the standards for local society. Whenever a dispute arose over local customs or practices, the contending parties turned to old people who had lived locally all their lives. Newcomers learned to conform to the accepted ways of the natives.

We still speak of the difference between chalk and cheese, a phrase derived from the two 'countries' of Wiltshire. In the seventeenth century John Aubrey wrote, rather extravagantly, that the 'chalk country' lay on the downs, 'where 'tis all tillage, and where the shepherds labour hard, their flesh is hard, their bodies strong, being weary after hard labour, they have not leisure to read or contemplate of religion'. In the 'dirty, clayey country' to the north, by contrast, the people

> speak drawling; they are phlegmatic, skins pale and livid, slow and dull, heavy of spirit; herebout is but little tillage or hard labour, they only milk the cows and make cheese; they feed chiefly on milk meats, which cools their brains too much, and hurts their inventions.[7]

Speech is the most distinctive characteristic that separates one local society from another, and is the one that is still immediately apparent. Nowadays, accents and rhythms of speech rather than the use of dialect words provide the clues, though the unconscious use of dialect may betray a speaker's origins. In the days when crafts such as the making of pots, knives or hosiery were the major occupations of well-defined districts, the terminology of the workplace helped to set people apart from each other. The decline of traditional industries has meant that distinctive vocabularies have been lost. Accents continue to flourish, however. Most people can quickly recognize a Geordie or a Brummie accent or grasp that a speaker is from somewhere in the North of England, but the identification can be much more precise than that. An informed listener can place a speaker within a restricted area that corresponds to the old idea of a 'country'. The persistence of local patterns of speech can be explained only by the immobility of the core families who set the standards to which newcomers, or their children, eventually conformed. It is very noticeable that the children of Commonwealth or European immigrants into English cities in recent years have learned that the best way to become accepted is to speak as the natives do.

Most of the immigrants who looked for employment in the growing industrial towns travelled only short distances. On visiting Yorkshire in the early eighteenth century, Daniel Defoe referred to 'the country called Hallamshire', a district that contained the ancient lordship which had been centred on Sheffield Castle and which was defined by its distinctive topography, the overwhelming importance of the cutlery and allied trades, the dialect of the inhabitants, and a dense network of family ties and friendships. The apprenticeship registers of the Hallamshire Cutlers' Company from 1624 to 1799 show that two out of every three boys came from places that were within 21 miles of the centre of Sheffield and that fewer than one in ten came from places more than 41 miles away.[8] This pattern was typical of provincial neighbourhoods across England. Throughout the land, the labour force remained essentially local in origin even when the population started to grow rapidly.

In Victorian times, people thought of their 'country' as being the district that attracted locals to stay there: 'a cultural, a working area, a migration area, an ambit for hiring fairs, a market-orientated area, a dialectal zone, a district of certain core families, a style-defined area of built culture', and so on. We are the recipients of a much older thought process that places inhabitants in a fixed region. Nowadays, the term tends to be associated with artists and writers. We speak of 'the Constable country' and 'the Brontë country'. The term remains a useful one in understanding how people conceptualized their own world. Just as the inhabitants of Tudor and Stuart England spoke of yeomen and husbandmen rather than peasants, so they and their descendants in the eighteenth and nineteenth centuries spoke of 'countries' and not of regions.

The local nature of English surnames

Each 'country' in England had its distinctive collection of surnames that were formed locally in the Middle Ages. East Lancashire had its Cleggs, its Kershaws and its Ramsbottoms. In the West Riding the Calder Valley textile district was the home of the Amblers, the Gaukrogers and the Murgatroyds, whereas the Broomheads, Creswicks and Dungworths lived in the south of the riding in the metalworking district of Hallamshire, centred on Sheffield. Such examples can be multiplied from every part of the land. They show that, until modern times, although people were prepared to move from their place of birth, they did not go far unless they ventured to London or migrated overseas. Life was still lived at an intensely local level. Even now, a person's surname can still be a badge of identity, as clear an indication of the family's place of origin as his or her way of speaking.

The study of surnames was once a specialist task that was left to linguists with expertise in old languages. *A Dictionary of English Surnames* by P.H. Reaney (first edition, 1958) still stands prominently on the shelves of public libraries. Reaney offered explanations of the meaning of surnames from the earliest recorded examples that he could find in printed sources throughout England. This was the commendable technique that had long been used by place-name scholars, but it is now recognized that his method took little or no account of how very many names changed their form over the centuries. As Reaney did not consider the present distributions of surnames, he often quoted records of a name from places for which there is no later evidence and which lay well away from the districts where these names are now concentrated. Many of these early names were merely by-names that never became hereditary, and many others disappeared after the calamity of the Black Death reduced the national population drastically. D.K. Tucker has calculated that no less than 2,972 names in the current edition of Reaney's dictionary, that is 11 per cent of the total, no longer existed at the time of the national census of 1881.[9]

A new approach to the study of surnames began in 1965 when Richard McKinley was appointed Director of the English Surnames Survey in the Department of (now the Centre for) English Local History at the University of Leicester. The survey concentrated on the historical origins, evolution and spread of surnames in local contexts. McKinley produced a steady stream of county studies, covering Norfolk, Suffolk, Oxfordshire, Lancashire and Sussex and *A History of British Surnames* (1990), which demonstrated the Leicester approach.[10] As part of the same project, George Redmonds' volume on the West Riding was the first to champion the idea that very many English surnames have a single-family origin, and in *Surnames and Genealogy: A New Approach* (1997), he argued that each family name, including the common ones as well as the rare, should be treated as having a unique history that must be traced back in time step by step.[11] Only by this methodical approach can we be certain whether a name has retained its early form or has been altered, either subtly or out of recognition, over the centuries.

In recent years, the case for the single-family origins of many surnames has been strengthened by Turi King's DNA analysis of the male Y chromosome of men bearing the same surname. Her methods and findings are summarized in George Redmonds, Turi King and David Hey, *Surnames, DNA and Family History* (2011),[12] a multidisciplinary approach which recognizes that DNA alone does not always produce a definite conclusion, for the results are often frustrated by illegitimacy or changes of name. The results of DNA investigations have to be considered alongside those of linguistic, genealogical and historical research.

One of the most important advances in the study of surnames has been the mapping of their geographical distribution at various points of time. By far the best maps are those that show the distribution of the surnames that were recorded in the national census of 1881 and which are available on Stephen Archer's CD, *The British 19th Century Surname Atlas*.[13] These maps are arranged by the former poor law unions, which were usually the same as the census and civil registration districts. Their message is that in 1881 the great majority of distinctive surnames – those that appear to have had a single-family origin – were still decidedly local in character. Families throughout England have tended to remain settled near the place where their surname was first recorded. In 1881 the most common 500 surnames in Britain were shared by 40 per cent of the population, yet at the same time over 30,000 British surnames were borne by only 10 per cent of the inhabitants. These maps have shown that standard dictionaries such as Reaney's are very often mistaken in their explanations of the origins and meanings of names.

Staffordshire provides many examples of surnames that have remained concentrated in their county of origin.[14] The most obvious ones are those that were derived from local place-names. Wedgwood, appropriately, was the name of a small place in the parish of Wolstanton in the northern part of the Potteries. In the national census of 1881 only 279 men, women and children bore this name. The 131 Wedgwoods who lived in Staffordshire included 67 in the Wolstanton district and 36 in neighbouring Stoke-on-Trent. The surname is found in Staffordshire records in much earlier times. Amongst the 51,000 names in 'A List of Families in the Archdeaconry of Stafford, 1532–3'[15] are those of John Wedgwood and his family at Horton, and William Wedgwood and his family in the adjacent township of Biddulph. A William Wedgwode of Tunstall was recorded in a subsidy roll of 1327.[16] We cannot be certain that the surname had become fixed and hereditary by then, but it is possible that this William is the ancestor of all the Wedgwoods, perhaps even the first bearer of the name.

Some other surnames of the type that we call locative are clearly derived from north Staffordshire settlements. They include Swinnerton, Burslem, Tunstall and Sneyd. The 1881 census listed 294 Sneyds, of whom 106 were living in Staffordshire, including 37 in Stoke and 25 in Wolstanton. Many other distinctive surnames were derived from small places, names such as Chell (386 of whose 669 representatives in 1881 lived in Staffordshire), Podmore (with 425 Staffordshire residents amongst 1,074 in the whole of Britain) or Wooliscroft (with 130 Staffordshire people amongst a total of 246). Some surnames came from lonely farmsteads such as Gradbach, which has given us the surname Greatbach (with 43 of the 85 people of this name in 1881 living in Staffordshire). Other Staffordshire surnames developed a slightly different form from the place-name from which they are derived, but these can be recognized quickly. Thus, Dillon comes from Dilhorne, and Brunt is derived from Brund. Surnames that now differ radically from the place-name are more difficult to identify. Yates's map of Staffordshire (1775)[17] marks Humpidge Green, which is now known as Humbage Green, but the surname is written as Huntbach or Huntbatch. Only 134 people with these names were listed in the 1881 census, 60 of them in Staffordshire, and 54 in neighbouring Cheshire and Shropshire.

Some of the Staffordshire surnames that were derived from personal names are just as distinctive. Raybould, which was derived from an old personal name, appears to have had a single-family origin in what became known as the Black Country. The 903 Rayboulds in 1881 included 306 in Dudley and 259 not far away in Stourbridge. Some surnames that came from pet names, or diminutive forms of old personal names, also have striking distribution patterns. Elkin, for example, a diminutive form of the common medieval name Elias, was clearly a north Staffordshire name in origin.

Arnold Bennett was well aware of the value of using local surnames in giving his novels an authentic appeal. In *Anna of the Five Towns*, he introduced his character Ephraim Tellwright with an explanation (in a footnote) that the surname was derived from tile-wright, 'a name specially characteristic of, and possibly originating in, this clay-manufacturing district'. The 1881 national census recorded only 32 people with this name and all of them lived in Staffordshire: 30 in the Potteries and just 2 in Leek. In the Staffordshire hearth tax returns of 1666[18] the Samuel Tellright who was recorded at Sneade in the township of Tunstall was the only person with this surname. It looks as if Tellwright had a single-family origin. Arnold Bennett also knew of another form of the name that was in local use. Later in his novel, Ephraim Tellwright was addressed by 'a hardy old potato woman' as 'Mester Terrick'. Bennett tells us (again, in a footnote) that Terrick is a corruption of Tellwright. This is a remarkable folk memory, for the shortened version of the name was in use hundreds of years earlier. The list of people in the Archdeaconry of Stafford in 1532–3 records the families of Richard Telryk at Newcastle-under-Lyme, John Teryk at Tunstall, and Jeffrey and Thomas Teryk at Wolstanton. No Tellwrights were recorded in this particular list. Three-and-a-half centuries later, people in and around the Potteries were apparently still aware that Terrick was a shortened form of Tellwright.

Maps of surname distributions at the time of the 1881 national census are a matchless source of information about names in every part of the United Kingdom. We have nothing as accurate or as comprehensive in earlier times, but useful comparisons with these Victorian lists are provided by the various county hearth tax returns of the 1660s and 1670s, which come from about half way between the period of surname formation and the present day. These returns usually narrow the distribution patterns of the surnames that were recorded in 1881 and they provide strong clues as to where names originated in the Middle Ages. Hearth tax returns have long been used by historians for assessing population levels and social structure at both national and local levels and in the study of vernacular architecture, but in the past most editions of hearth tax returns ignored or underplayed their usefulness for the study of surnames.[19]

The survival of hearth tax returns is uneven across the land, but an increasing number of counties now have at least one return in print, often as a publication of a county record society, such as those for Bedfordshire, Derbyshire or Nottinghamshire. In the year 2000 Professor Margaret Spufford launched the University of Roehampton Hearth Tax Centre as a long-term project to publish the fullest returns for every county that did not already have a printed edition. The substantial volumes that have been produced by the British Record Society now emphasize the value of this source for the study of surnames.[20]

The listings of those householders or cottagers who were exempt from the tax on the grounds that they either received parish relief or that they paid less than 20 shillings a year rent are inconsistent, so in some cases many names have not been recorded. Nevertheless, this imperfect set of records provides our most comprehensive list of surnames at a particular point of time in post-Restoration England and Wales. We are not yet able to provide national distribution maps, as we can for 1881, but that day will come.

A third important source for mapping the distribution of surnames is provided by the three substantial volumes listing the poll tax returns of 1377–81, edited by Carolyn C. Fenwick.[21] These contain lists of taxpayers that are arranged by townships or parishes, in a similar manner to the hearth tax, but unfortunately a few counties have no returns and others have only incomplete ones. Nevertheless, the long lists of names that do survive provide essential information about surnames close to the time when they were being formed. The poll tax returns often record surnames that were confined to a particular country. Many belonged to just a single taxpayer and his or her family.

Essex provides us with suitable examples of the various types of surnames that can be traced back from the national census of 1881 to the county's hearth tax returns of 1670 (which the British Record Society published in 2012)[22] and then to the poll tax returns of 1377–81. Surnames derived from towns, villages, hamlets or isolated farmsteads, which account for about a quarter of English surnames, are usually the easiest to identify. For example, the village of Ardleigh, northeast of Colchester, is the obvious source of the surname Ardley. In 1881 only 327 men, women and children in the whole of Britain bore this name, with 52 in the Braintree district and 18 in and around Halstead, a little further west. Two centuries earlier, six householders with this name were taxed on one to four hearths: two in Messing, two in Bocking, and one each in Halstead and further south at Burnham on Crouch. We find the Ardleys much earlier in the 1377 poll tax returns for Colchester, where Robert, Henry and Thomas Ardleigh were grouped together, and another Thomas Ardleigh lived in a separate part of the town. Their names were spelt in the same way as the village, but four years later the poll tax returns for Boreham record John Ardeleye, a butcher, and John Ardeleye junior.

Boreham is another obvious example of a place-name that became used as a surname. The 1881 census noted 1,190 Borehams, overwhelmingly in Essex and neighbouring parts of Suffolk. The name was a common one in Essex two centuries earlier when 30 Boreham households were scattered thinly and widely within the county. Ten of these were amongst those exempted from payment because of their poverty, but one family was taxed on five hearths. The 1377 poll tax return for Colchester records two Thomas Borhams and two John Borhams.

The next group of surnames gathers together those that were derived from personal names, including pet forms and diminutives. They were often just as concentrated in their distribution as were the locative names, and sometimes they were so rare as to suggest that they had a single-family origin. Aylett seems to be derived from an Old English personal name. In the national census of 1881, 657 men, women and children bore this name, mainly in and just beyond Essex. In the hearth tax returns of 1670, Essex had 42 Aylett households, a large number, led by a gentleman with ten hearths at White Roding, and other prosperous householders with six to nine hearths elsewhere. Only two Ayletts had exemption certificates. Yet these families declined in number during the next two centuries. Further back in time, in 1377, John Aylet senior paid his poll tax at Broomfield, just north of Chelmsford.

It is perhaps more surprising that the Biblical name, Eve, should have such a striking distribution in 1881, with the greatest concentration in Chelmsford. In the national census, 357 of the 1,127 bearers of this name lived in Essex, with 234 in Middlesex, 172 in Surrey and 104 in Kent. Many of these, of course, were living in Greater London. In Essex, 95 were found in Chelmsford, 43 in Romford, 42 in Braintree and 42 in West Ham. Two centuries earlier, in 1670, the surname Eve was borne by 49 Essex householders. A man with the eccentric name of Adam Eve was taxed on one hearth at Colchester. Back in the fourteenth century, the record of the John Ene, who was taxed at Great Easton in 1381, may be a mistranscription of Eve.

Nicknames, too, sometimes had such a tight distribution as to suggest a single-family origin. Root is thought to have been a nickname for a bright, cheerful person, though the possibility remains that it denoted a player of a musical instrument known as a rote. In 1881, 977 British householders bore this surname, with 367 in Essex and 229 in Middlesex. The variants Roote (57) and Rootes (133) bring this total up to 1,160, though Essex had only eight householders called Roote, and no Rootes. In 1670 the Essex hearth tax returns listed 14 householders named Root(e), who were concentrated in the northeastern parts of the county. Joanna Root of Sible Hedingham had seven hearths, and Thomas Root of Great Maplestead and his namesake at Tolleshunt Knights each had four, but six other householders with this name had exemption certificates. In the 1377 poll tax returns, William Rote was the constable of Stapleford Abbotts, and John Rutte was the constable of Quendon. Four years later, John Rowth and John Routh of Felsted and John Rote and Marion Rote of Lambourne paid their poll tax.

The final category of names is that derived from occupations. This includes some of our most common surnames, such as Smith, Taylor and Wright, but occasionally we come across names that are rare and restricted in their distribution and which seem to have had a single-family origin. Kellogg is an occupational name, not for a manufacturer of cornflakes, but for a pork butcher, literally a 'kill hog'. In 1381 William Kelhog paid poll tax at Magdalen Laver. The earliest recorded examples of the name are from Essex: Geoffrey Kyllehog in 1277 and Walter Kelehoog in 1369. But in 1881, only seven Kelloggs (with four spellings) were recorded in the national census, at Holborn, Southwark, Fareham (Hampshire) and Liverpool. Two centuries earlier, in 1670, Essex had four householders with this name, each of them in the lowest ranks of society: James Skillogg (1 at Little Hallingbury), Thomas Killhog (1 exempt, Waltham Holy Cross), Thomas Killhogg (1 exempt, Waltham Holy Cross), and Grace Killhogg (1 exempt, Manuden). Joseph Kellogg of Great Leighs moved to Connecticut in 1651. Emigration to America may well explain the virtual disappearance of rare names such as this.

The Derbyshire hearth tax returns of the same year, 1670, provide a suitable comparison with Essex. The county's most distinctive surnames arose in the isolated parts of the Peak District. The surname Heathcote or Hethkett, for instance, is derived from a sheep farm that was founded by the monks of a Leicestershire Cistercian abbey high above Hartington and the Dove Valley. The surname was recorded in the Buxton and Tideswell poll tax returns in 1381. Thirty Heathcotes were listed in the Derbyshire hearth tax returns of 1670, mostly in the northwest (including five in Hartington), but also in and around Chesterfield (where they had arrived by the fifteenth century). Another four householders were recorded in Staffordshire and two in Nottinghamshire, but the Heathcotes had not yet moved into Yorkshire.

The distribution of the Needhams in 1881 rules out an origin from Needham in Suffolk and points to another Cistercian grange not far from Heathcote. No less than 50 Needhams were recorded in the Derbyshire hearth tax returns of 1670. The poll tax returns for the High Peak in 1381 record Needhams in Bowden, Castleton and Derby.

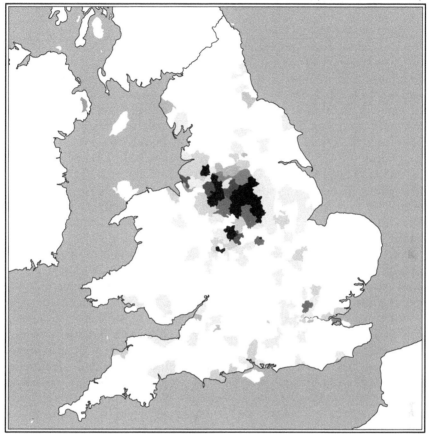

Heathcote

Based on actual numbers in each
Poor Law Union (Source: 1881 Census)

FIGURE 1 *The distribution of the Heathcotes in 1881 points to the origin of their Peak District surname.*

Ronksley Moor is still marked on Ordnance Survey maps, high in the Derwent Valley, but the old farm known as Ronksley was demolished when the Derwent and Howden reservoirs were constructed about a hundred years ago. A John de Ronkeslai was recorded there in 1366,[23] and just one man with this name was recorded on the other side of the river in the Chapelry of Bradfield in the West Riding poll tax returns of 1379. In the late 1980s only 35 Ronksleys were listed in the national telephone directories, 23 of them in the Sheffield directory. It remains a rare name that is largely confined to the country of its origin.

The identification of place-names that have given rise to surnames is not always as straightforward as these examples. Adam of Cartlache was recorded in Holmesfield manor in 1327,[24] so the hamlet of Cartedge, half a mile down the lane from Holmesfield, is one source of the surname, but there is another small place called Cartledge, near Macclesfield, which also produced a surname at the other side of the Peak District.

Some surnames that were derived from personal names are just as distinctive as the locative ones. Dictionaries mistakenly attribute the surname Levick to the French *l'éveque*, meaning 'bishop'. Sometimes, it was simply a sloppy pronunciation of Levitt, a surname that is found in many parts of England. In north Derbyshire, Levitt and Levick are alternative spellings of the name in the Norton parish register. However, the surname Levick also developed from an Old Norse personal name, Leathwick, which was recorded in the adjoining parish of Eckington from 1350 onwards. The poll tax returns for 1377–81 do not survive for northeast Derbyshire, but in 1670 Francis Leathwicke paid for two hearths at Eckington, Robert Levicke paid hearth tax on two hearths at Newbold, near Chesterfield, and William Lethwicke was taxed on one hearth at Barlbrough, all within a few miles of each other. As late as 1769, a man was described in an Eckington manor court roll as 'William Levick otherwise Leathwick'.[25]

Pet forms or diminutives of personal names that end in *-cock* or *-kin* often have multiple origins, but some are so rare as to suggest a single-family origin. The etymology of Burdekin, a Peak District name that has spread a little into Yorkshire and Lancashire, is problematic, as the first record is to a John Burdikan in Castleton in 1381. By 1670, his descendants were living in Hope, Edale, Tideswell and Charlesworth and just across the Yorkshire border. Soon, they had found their way to Sheffield and Wigan, then in the early nineteenth century Thomas Burdekin sought his fortune as a merchant in Australia; his wife had a river named after her in Queensland and their son became Mayor of Sydney.[26] We need to keep these long-distance migrants in mind when we emphasize the point that most members of a family did not move very far.

Nicknames, too, sometimes had such a tight distribution as to suggest a single-family origin. Wildgoose is a name that was perhaps bestowed on a shy, retiring person, but we have no way of telling. The name was found mainly in Derbyshire in 1881, but the John Wildegos who was recorded just across the Staffordshire border at Bradnop in 1327 may have been the ancestor of all the present bearers of this name. In the Derbyshire hearth tax returns of 1670, Richard Wilgouse paid tax on two hearths at Darley, and his neighbour John Wilgouse paid on one, while a Widdow Wilgoose was taxed on one hearth at Stainsby or Heath.

Occupational surnames form the final category. Names such as Smith, Taylor, Wright and Turner are amongst the most common in the land, but some rare crafts have produced a group of surnames that have a distinctive regional flavour. A Boler was not someone who made bowls, which was the job of the Turner, but someone who smelted lead on a windy escarpment known as a Bole Hill. A Ralph le Bolere held land in Eyam in 1299–1301.[27] Men named Boler were recorded in the High Peak poll tax returns of 1381 at Ashford, Baslow, Darley, Tideswell and Wormhill. In 1670 Derbyshire had twelve households of Bolers, and in the national census of 1881 most of the 173 bearers of this rare surname lived within the county's borders.

The pull of London

London was the great exception to the rule that most migrants did not travel very far. In the medieval and early modern centuries, London was a magnet for young people from all parts of England, just as it is today. Its population growth was fuelled by immigration from a much wider area than was usual for English towns. In the thirteenth century, as the national population rose to unprecedented levels, London became by far the largest city in England with 80,000–100,000 inhabitants and 126 parish churches. In 1334 Londoners paid £11,000 in tax, whereas the inhabitants of the next largest city, Bristol, paid £2,200.[28] Even so, at that time London was smaller than the leading cities in Continental Europe.

London's first advantage over other towns was that, following William the Conqueror's decision to be crowned at Westminster, it replaced Winchester as the centre of royal government. The Roman walls of the City were rebuilt and the White Tower was erected high above them in the eastern corner. Old St Paul's, too, was reconstructed on a massive scale in Romanesque style. When it was finished, this cathedral was the longest in England, and its timber spire was the tallest in Europe. On the south bank of the Thames, the Archbishop of Canterbury built Lambeth Palace, the Bishop of Winchester, whose diocese extended as far as Southwark, erected a palace there, and the Bishops of Ely and Rochester had palaces nearby. The Greyfriars erected the second-largest church in London, just to the north of St Paul's, but London's great monastic houses and hospitals were mainly founded in the suburbs.

London was not only the centre of civil and ecclesiastical power and authority; it also flourished as the country's leading port, the hub of the national road network, and the leading centre of manufacture. The river Thames was a major natural route with links to the Continent. A new road, known as Thames Street, was constructed along the top of a bank that overlooked the waterfront, and a fresh set of narrow lanes and alleys, such as Bull Wharf Lane, Swan Lane, Trig Lane and Vintners Place, ran down to the Thames and its landing places. Wharfs were extended well out into the river.[29]

The medieval London Bridge, constructed under the direction of Peter de Colechurch, was built with stone from Dorset and Kent, with 19 arches and a drawbridge across the central span. It provided the only crossing of the Thames other than by ferry. By 1358 it was lined with 138 shops, and Cheapside had become the commercial heart of the City, where craftsmen had shops fronting on each side of the wide street, market traders set up their stalls to sell bread, corn, fish and meat, leather goods, and wool and linen cloth, and hawkers wandered around calling their wares. In the adjoining lanes, numerous other craftsmen, of all kinds, worked at their trades. In many a family business the husband was employed at a craft while his wife managed the shop. Women were cooks and bakers, brewers and sellers of ale, and managers of taverns. Fortunes, or at least a decent living, could be made in London, but for many people the City's rapid growth resulted in overcrowding, a shortage of work, intense competition and poverty.

By 1127 the City was divided into 24 wards, each with its own aldermen, and in 1189 London had acquired its first mayor, Henry Fitz Ailwyn. Craft associations, known as livery companies because of their distinctive dress, protected the interests of their members like an early trade union. They insisted that only freemen of the City should be allowed to practise their craft or trade and to sell their goods according to the companies' rules and regulations. Each livery company was associated with a religious fraternity; the Worshipful Company of Blacksmiths, for instance, formed one dedicated to St Eloy, the patron saint of smiths.[30] In 1319 Edward II granted the Corporation of the City of London a charter that confirmed its ancient liberties and insisted that nobody should pursue a trade within the City unless he was a freeman through his company. The 'Great Twelve' companies emerged as leaders of the London business world towards the end of his reign. The Mayor and Corporation thrived on their independence, and by 1422 the city had 111 livery companies representing the separate trade and craft guilds, with jurisdiction extending four miles beyond the city walls.

London did not suffer as badly as the leading provincial towns in the decades of recession following the Black Death. Indeed, it grew wealthier at their expense. In 1534–5 Londoners contributed as much tax as all the other English towns put together. Twelve years earlier, London's contribution to King Henry VIII's enforced loan was nearly equal to that of the rich counties of Norfolk and Suffolk combined, and it accounted for about one-eighth of the total levy.[31]

The combined population of the City of London and Southwark was nevertheless only 3 per cent of that of medieval England as a whole. In other words, 97 per cent of English people lived in the provinces. The lack of surviving poll tax returns for London in 1377–81 means that we have no early evidence about migration from surnames that were derived from places, such as we have for provincial cities, but there is no reason to doubt that the city's rapid population growth was the result of massive immigration from a much wider area than was usual in English towns. These native immigrants far outnumbered those from Flanders, France and Italy, whose names stand out in the records because of their unusual nature.

London's rate of growth in these decades was far higher than that of the rest of England. In 1550 only about 4 per cent of the national population lived in the capital city; by 1700 nearly 10 per cent were Londoners.[32] At any one time, only a minority of the city's inhabitants had been born there. Population levels in the towns of provincial England were modest in comparison. In the late seventeenth century, Norwich was the next largest city, with about 30,000 inhabitants. The cathedral cities and county towns attracted immigrants only from a restricted area that was often no larger than the 'countries' that surrounded them. The pull of London was truly exceptional.

Contemporary maps show that while most people were huddled together within the City's walls, many other inhabitants, rich and poor alike, lived in the spreading suburbs.[33] Across London Bridge, in Southwark, the palaces of the bishops of Winchester and Rochester were set amongst bear gardens, theatres and brothels, and the hovels of the poor. Westminster remained legally separate, but it was in effect a western suburb, connected to the City by ribbon development along the Strand and around the Palace of Whitehall, the Inns of Court, and the huge mansions of the nobility. Poor or alien immigrants often took up work in the liberties or suburbs that lay outside civic jurisdiction, where the livery companies found it difficult to enforce their ordinances and where the first playhouses were built to perform the works of Christopher Marlowe, William Shakespeare and Ben Jonson.

The City and its suburbs accounted for half the increase in the English urban population during the later sixteenth and seventeenth centuries. It grew at an astonishing rate, from about 120,000 inhabitants in 1550 to 200,000 in 1600, and 375,000 by 1650. Yet the number of recorded burials in London's surviving parish registers was consistently greater than the number of recorded baptisms. The city's growth must have been brought about by immigration, for the people who died there each year outnumbered those who were born within its boundaries.[34]

Five major outbreaks of plague occurred in London between 1563 and 1665, and other killer diseases kept mortality rates high. The City was a notoriously unhealthy place where the pestilence was endemic. The last, and most horrific, outbreak of the disease started in the slums of St Giles-in-the-Fields and spread to the parishes inside the northwestern walls of the City. At its peak, over 50 people were buried each day in several of the larger parishes.[35]

The 'Great Fire' of 1666 was the most momentous event in London's long history. It started at a bakery in Pudding Lane in the early hours of Sunday 2 September 1666 and spread rapidly west. Strong winds from the east soon turned the fire into a conflagration. By Wednesday, seven out of every eight buildings in the City, and all those immediately to the west of the medieval walls, had been gutted. The surviving houses and public buildings were huddled together just inside the northern wall. Altogether, about 13,200 houses, 87 parish churches, St Paul's Cathedral, and all the halls of the City's livery companies were destroyed. Some 65,000 Londoners were left homeless, more than double the population of any other English city.[36]

Yet by 1670 most of the houses and shops had been rebuilt in brick; a remarkable testimony to London's wealth and economic resilience.

London soon recovered from these disasters. Tony Wrigley has estimated that the huge rise in its population between 1650 and 1750 can be accounted for only if the annual number of immigrants numbered at least 8,000.[37] Social historians have shown that most of the migrants who arrived there were in their late teens.[38] Most of them did not work independently, nor did they serve as apprentices, and they commonly moved from one job to another. Young men far outnumbered young women.

Those boys who did serve apprenticeships are recorded in the archives of the various livery companies. Apprenticeship registers provide a wealth of information about the origins of many of the youngsters who were attracted to London from all parts of England. For example, the 1,895 entries in the apprenticeship books of the Worshipful Company of Blacksmiths between 1632 and 1652 show that boys came to learn the trade from every English county except Northumberland.[39] Most of them were the sons of farmers or labourers, particularly those who lived in the small towns and countryside of the Midlands. The largest number from a single county came from Northamptonshire, which contributed 199 boys, that is 10.5 per cent of the total, during this period. Next came the neighbouring counties of Leicestershire with 88 boys, Oxfordshire (84), Warwickshire (84), Buckinghamshire (78), Gloucestershire (74), Berkshire (74), Wiltshire (64), Herefordshire (53) and Cambridgeshire (48). Surprisingly few came from the counties to the south of the Thames, even those such as Kent (28) and Sussex (15) that were not far away. These migrant boys found masters with the help of 'friends', that is men who were relatives or godparents, or who were sometimes connected with the father socially or through business. Most provincial families had at least one friend in London who would negotiate on their behalf, and some had several.[40]

At some stage or other in their lives, numerous people from the provinces settled in London, but it is difficult to measure this movement and it is not easy to estimate how many of them eventually returned to their native 'country'. Richard Gough, the author of a history of his Shropshire parish of Myddle at the close of the seventeenth century, mentioned nineteen local families that had at least one son or daughter who went to live in London; some of these families had several members who settled there. The Shropshire hearth tax returns of 1672 record 91 households in Myddle, 15 of which had at least one member who, at one time or another, had lived in London. This is a minimum figure, for Gough often referred incidentally to the capital as if it were a commonplace that people from his parish should be there, even though the two places are some 160 miles apart. For instance, when describing Richard Woulf he wrote, 'I met with him in London about forty yeares ago', and on another occasion he mentioned that he had bought Mrs Mary Corbett's wedding ring from Richard Watkins, a London goldsmith, who was the son of William Watkins, a gentleman who lived in Myddle parish.[41]

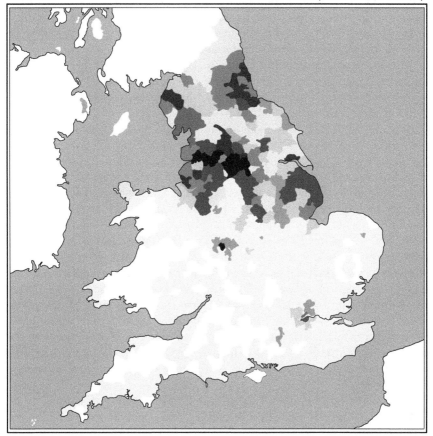

Wilkinson

Based on actual numbers in each
Poor Law Union (Source: 1881 Census)

FIGURE 2 *Wilkinson is a northern name with multiple origins, but London was an attraction for some.*

Adam Eyre, a yeoman farmer in a remote part of the moorland parish of Penistone in southwest Yorkshire, is well known to social historians of the early modern period because of his diurnal, or diary, which he kept from 1647 to 1649. He had been a captain of a troop of horses in the Parliamentary army during the Civil War and a minor bureaucrat afterwards. He was well connected to the Puritan gentry families that dominated his parish and he played a key role in local government. He travelled widely in his 'country' and made occasional visits to London. Everyone has assumed that he continued to live in much the same way after 1649, but Andrew Hopper has cast an entirely new light on him. During the 1650s, Eyre became a civil servant in The Strand, styled himself as a gentleman of London, and eventually an esquire, and undertook the second-largest purchase of Crown lands in Yorkshire for the staggering sum of £5,996 7s. 6d. He served the Protectorate regime in minor local offices until the Restoration of King Charles II in 1660, when he returned to his moorland home. He was buried at Penistone in 1661, and the will that was proved was the one he had made in 1648, before his adventures in the capital city.[42]

The sheer size and sophistication of London and the high wages that could be earned there made the capital city the major market for provincial goods such as Hallamshire metalware. Until the early eighteenth century, London merchants controlled the sales, in the capital and abroad, of the cutlery and tools that were made in and around Sheffield. Before then, the Sheffield factors who wished to expand their businesses did not branch out on their own but joined the system by moving to London and setting up in the Minories. Hallamshire's links with London were not restricted to those who sold cutlery. News of national events reached Sheffield within a few days, brought by word of mouth or by newspapers. London was important, too, in the ideological and financial support it gave to the Dissenting cause in Sheffield. The Revd Timothy Jollie and the bookseller Nevill Simmons were amongst those who came from the capital to settle in the town. The strength of the London link is also evident from deeds enrolled in the West Riding land registry; between 1710 and 1736, 33 deeds relating to the parish of Sheffield mention at least one party from London. Most, if not all, of these Londoners had family connections with Sheffielders and had acquired property in the parish through inheritance or marriage. We are left with the firm impression that in the early modern period Sheffield had closer links with the capital than with any other urban centre beyond the most immediate market towns.[43]

The pull of London helped to give the English a sense of national unity. Since at least the early seventeenth century, and probably from well before, London had been connected to smaller cities and market towns in every part of the kingdom by weekly carrying services. John Taylor's *Carriers Cosmographie* of 1637 gives an account of the London inns where provincial carriers arrived and departed. We read, for instance, that: 'The Carrier of Lincolne doth lodge at the White Horse without Cripplegate, he commeth every second Friday . . . The carriers of Stampford doe lodge at the Bell in Aldersgate-street, they do come on wednesdaies and thursdaies.'

Our next major source of information about these long-distance journeys is from 1685, when Thomas Delaune published *The Present State of London*, which included the names of 645 carriers and 212 coachmen, a total of 805 individuals (for some served as both). Dorian Gerhold has calculated that about 205 waggons and 165 gangs of packhorses entered and left London every week, carrying a total of about 460 tons of goods each way.[44] Direct services were available from as far north as Kendal, as far west as Denbigh, Oswestry and Monmouth, and as far southwest as Bideford and Exeter. Of course, the network of carrying services was densest near London, and direct services were much less common 80 miles beyond, but the long-distance routes were linked to regional and local services that between them covered all parts of England. By 1715, regular carrying services by road in and out of London had more than doubled since 1637 and coach services to most provincial centres numbered nearly a thousand a week.

The longest route to London at the time of Delaune's list was the 263 miles from Kendal, where four partners in the long-distance carrying business had a combined stock of 50 to 60 packhorses. Carriers had to calculate whether to use packhorses, which were quicker, or waggons, which could carry larger loads and were therefore more economical. The further the distance from London, the more likely was the use of packhorses. The Kendal partners carried cloth, stockings and other goods from Kendal and brought back 'choice wares' from London. When Richard Greenwood, one of the partners, was robbed on his return journey in 1665, he was carrying 'silk, tabby, tafatta, ribbon, lace, cambrick, holland, diaper, stuffs, hats, some plate, and many more mercers' and haberdashers' wares and gentlemen's goods'. A weekly service was maintained in an arrangement whereby each partner set off to London every four weeks. They left Kendal on Monday mornings and arrived in the capital ten days later (a little longer in winter), including Sunday as a rest day. Their route took them through Kirkby Lonsdale, Keighley, Wakefield, Rotherham, Mansfield, Loughborough, Welford, Northampton and Stony Stratford, though sometimes they travelled instead via Preston, Warrington, Holmes Chapel, Lichfield, Coventry and Towcester to rejoin the route at Stony Stratford. Each partner paid all his costs and kept all the income. The return journey began on Friday at noon and they got back to Kendal the following week on Tuesday or Wednesday, at an average of about 25 miles per day of travel.[45]

The hearth tax returns for London and Middlesex in 1666 capture some of the drift of migrants from the provinces and abroad over the centuries by recording surnames that were formed from distinctive place-names. The picture is far from complete, of course, for most immigrants bore common names and we do not know when they or their ancestors arrived; some families may have settled in London much earlier. Nevertheless, the surname evidence allows us to paint a broad picture of movement over time.[46]

The Peak District surname Greatorex provides a clear example of how a surname that otherwise remained concentrated close to its point of origin three or four centuries earlier had nevertheless migrated to London. The name undoubtedly has a single-family origin from a farm in the 'great valley' at Wormhill, not far from Buxton. A William of Greterakes paid poll tax at Wormhill in 1381, and a Robert Greterakes witnessed a deed at Greterakes in 1423. The Derbyshire hearth tax returns for Michaelmas 1670 recorded 20 households of Greatorexes. At that time, the surname appears to have been confined to Derbyshire, except for those seven householders who had set up home in the northern suburbs of London, where the tax collectors had difficulty in spelling their name.

Only 113 householders with distinctive locative surnames from Cumberland and Westmorland were recorded in the London and Middlesex returns, but they indicate that some determined people from the remote North West had travelled 263 miles along the route that was taken by the Kendal carriers. The same tax return records at least 723 householders with distinctive names from Lancashire and the West Riding of Yorkshire. About 45 per cent of these northern names were housed outside the City walls in the western and northwestern suburbs, with another 12 per cent in Middlesex. The rest were scattered within the square-mile of the City, with about 18 per cent in the eastern and northeastern suburbs.

These distinctive surnames provide only part of the picture. Another method is to gather all the surnames that end in -*son*, for this was a northern method of name-making that extended from lowland Scotland as far south as Leicestershire and Norfolk but which was particularly pronounced in Yorkshire and Lancashire and virtually absent in the southern half of England. The London and Middlesex hearth tax returns record 1,960 such names. A similar exercise can be carried out with the Welsh surnames that are found in large numbers in seventeenth-century London. Welsh migrants settled mostly in the western, northwestern and northern suburbs or further out in Middlesex, though 22 per cent lived in the eastern and northeastern suburbs outside the walls. Patronymic surnames that were formed by adding the suffix -*s* to a personal name provide a broader picture of migration from both Wales and the English counties immediately beyond the border. The London and Middlesex hearth tax returns contain 2,342 such names. Historians had paid less attention to these native migrants than they had to the 'aliens' who came from across the Channel and the North Sea. The distinctive names of the members of 'alien' communities were much smaller in number than those from the various regions of England and Wales.

Immigrants from overseas gave London a very different character from urban societies in provincial England, except in those towns where they had been allowed to settle. Immigration on a much larger scale than hitherto had started in the sixteenth century, when French Huguenots came to escape religious persecution, especially after the massacre on St Bartholomew's Day in 1572, and Dutch, Flemish and Walloon refugees fled from Spanish oppression. Between 1540 and 1600, over 50,000 settlers moved from France and the Low Countries to work as silk weavers and in other textile crafts, or as market gardeners. They found homes in London and the towns of eastern and southeastern England, especially Norwich, Canterbury, Sandwich, Maidstone and Southampton, and they made a significant contribution to the introduction of new craft skills. When the Edict of Nantes, which had granted religious freedom to French Protestants in 1598, was revoked in 1685, another wave of refugees was attracted to the same towns. They founded their own churches and tended to live in particular neighbourhoods, notably Spitalfields, a centre of the silk trade, but in time most of them or their descendants became assimilated in the native population.[47]

London continued to attract youngsters in droves. In 1680 the Yorkshire squire, Sir John Reresby, complained in the House of Commons that 'London drained all England of its people'.[48] At any one time, only a minority of Londoners had been born there. London was a cosmopolitan city with a babble of dialects and a constant stream of immigrants. In this, it remained very different from the cities in the provinces.

In *Jude the Obscure*, Thomas Hardy's character Arabella says to Sue: 'I've left London now, you know, and at present I am living at Alfredston, with my friend Anny, to be near my old country.' After attending the Hay-on-Wye Flower Show in August 1870, the Revd Francis Kilvert wrote in his diary, 'There was an excursion train from Builth . . . for the occasion. The town was hung with flags. The whole country was there.'[49] Clearly, he did not mean that everybody in England was present. Well away from London, people were still using the word to mean the district to which they felt that they belonged, one that could evoke sentimental feelings amongst those who have moved away: 'Oh, the oak and the ash and the bonny ivy tree,' they sang. 'They flourish at home in my own country.'

CHAPTER TWO

The people of England

Ancient origins

Who are the English and where did they come from? Many of the old myths can now be tested by scientific techniques. Isotope analysis of the enamel in the teeth of ancient skeletons can tell us where a person lived as a child. Studies of the Y-chromosome in modern male populations and of mitochondrial DNA, which is passed down by mothers, suggest that the majority of modern Britons are the descendants of people who came to live in these islands in two great waves from the Continent of Europe, starting in prehistoric times once the last Ice Age was over. One wave, which originated in the Iberian Peninsula, gradually moved up the Atlantic coast to Brittany and then across the English Channel to the western parts of the British Isles. The other came from across the North Sea, stretching from France as far north as Scandinavia. People have come and gone from these shores throughout our long history, usually in small numbers but from time to time in much larger groups.[1]

The first humans who lived in what is now the southern half of England during warm periods between the various protracted Ice Ages had no direct genetic links with us. Most signs of their activities were obliterated when the ice returned. Then, about 12,000 years ago, summer temperatures started to rise until they were 2–3 °C higher than they are at present, and the winters became much milder. In these favourable conditions, birch, hazel and pine trees began to grow on the open tundra land; then oak, ash, elm and native lime trees became established on the new, rich soils, with willow and alder in the wetlands. Wild cattle, deer, horses, pigs and smaller animals began to attract hunters, armed with flint weapons, who followed them, according to season, over extensive hunting grounds. The finds at Creswell Crags in 2003–4 by an international team of archaeologists in the dramatic Magnesian Limestone gorge that separates Derbyshire from Nottinghamshire included no fewer than 90 engravings of deer, horses, bison, bears and birds, most of them following the natural curves of the rocks on the ceiling of the entrance chamber of Church Hole. This prehistoric rock art here is similar in style to that found in caves in France and Spain and is thought to be as old.[2]

By about 6000 BCE, sea levels had risen to such an extent that Britain was separated from the Continent by the North Sea. The earliest hunter-gatherers have left only faint marks on the landscape, but towards the end of the fifth millennium BC a way of life based on settled farming spread from Western Asia across Europe to Britain during the period known to prehistorians as the Neolithic or New Stone Age. Whether this dramatic change of lifestyle was the result of immigration rather than just the gradual spread of ideas is a question that is hotly debated, but a genetic study at Leicester University concluded that the new agricultural techniques were indeed brought by new men who chose native women as their partners.[3] A more settled way of life and a regular food supply encouraged population growth. We can make no more than an educated guess that about 100,000 people occupied the British Isles at the start of the New Stone Age and perhaps about a quarter of a million at the end.

Prehistoric cultural identities and boundaries were not fixed over very long periods of time. The large tribes that emerged in the late Iron Age were known to the Romans as the Catuvellauni, whose territory lay north of the Thames Estuary in present-day Hertfordshire and Essex; the Trinovantes of northern Essex and Suffolk; the Cantiaci, who gave their name to Kent; and the Atrebates, whose lands lay south of the Thames in Hampshire and Surrey. Further west were the Durotriges, whose heartland was in Dorset, the Dumnonii of Devon and Cornwall, the Dobunni of the Severn Valley and neighbouring districts, and the Cornovii of Shropshire and beyond. The Iceni were based in Norfolk, the Corieltauvi in the East Midlands, and the Brigantes in the North. Each of these tribes probably incorporated numerous smaller ones.[4]

The various divisions of what is now England were organized in their own distinctive ways. Whereas the territory of the Durotriges was dominated by hill-forts, that of the Catuvellauni consisted of small villages and farmsteads controlled from a few sprawling defended sites. That at *Camulodunum* (Colchester) was spread over 12 square miles and was defined by deep ditches and high banks. Here were temples and the substantial houses of the tribal leaders, set amongst numerous roundhouses and industrial buildings. The massive defences of *Verlamion* (the native predecessor of Roman Verulamium and medieval St Albans) can still be seen in Prae Wood, Beech Bottom Dyke and the Devil's Dyke. At Stanwick in North Yorkshire, the Brigantes tribe enclosed 750 acres with great banks and ditches. Some of these Late Iron Age strongholds are the first settlements that are known to us by their contemporary names. They were market centres but they were not planned towns. *Calleva Atrebatum* (Silchester) is the only place that has revealed firm evidence of a tightly packed settlement with a street plan before the Roman conquest.[5]

In the late Iron Age, people in these parts of present-day southern England were well aware of the Roman Empire. Indeed, they had more in common with the tribes immediately across the Channel than with British tribes further west and north. Iron Age Britain had no unity. It was peopled by tribes whose ways of life differed from each other in their customs, the form of their settlements, the nature of their economies, and in the artefacts that have been discovered from excavations. The Roman writer Tacitus was shrewdly observant when he commented:

> Who the original inhabitants of Britain were is impossible to be certain, as is common with barbarians; we do not know whether they were aboriginal or immigrant. Nevertheless, their physical characteristics vary a good deal, and that in itself is evidence. The people of Caledonia have large limbs and reddish hair, which indicates a Germanic origin; the Silures have darker skins and tend to have curly hair, and the fact that their land lies opposite Spain makes it probable that they originated from the Iberian peninsula. Those closest to the Gauls resemble them, whether because original characteristics of race persist, or because lands that come close together have similar climates. On the whole, however, we may assume that it was the Gauls who occupied the island opposite them.[6]

Modern genetics has refined these generalizations, but Tacitus was broadly correct.

The prehistory of England ends with the arrival of the Romans. From that time we enter the age of history with written evidence, albeit scant and partial. Our literary sources are brief, biased and often baffling, so we remain largely reliant upon archaeological finds that usually cannot be dated precisely. Attempts to match early written records to the physical evidence are rarely successful. Historians were once unanimous in seeing the Romans as the bringers of order and civilization, for there seemed to be strong parallels with the history of the British Empire, but nowadays the trend is in the opposite direction with the Roman army being regarded more as an occupying force that acted purely out of self interest. The slim evidence at our disposal can be and is interpreted in different ways.

The Romans portrayed the Ancient Britons as barbarians who fought naked in battle; it is from Roman sources that we derive our image of woad-stained brutes. Around 90–120 CE, a couple of generations after the Roman conquest, a Roman soldier at Vindolanda, near Hadrian's Wall, contemptuously dismissed his opponents as *Brittunculi*, roughly translated as 'wretched, little Brits'. But is this pejorative view justified?[7] For centuries before the Roman invasion, the native people had wheeled vehicles, iron tools, effective farming systems, brightly dyed clothes, and works of art that equalled those of Greece and Rome. The English Channel and the North Sea hindered invaders but did not cut off communications. The tribal kingdoms of southern and eastern England had regular contacts with continental Europe, and their leaders imported Roman luxury goods and wine. The Ancient Britons were not the savage barbarians that Roman writers would have us believe.

Julius Caesar wrote a memoir of what he had found or had heard:

The interior portion of Britain is inhabited by those of whom they say that it is handed down by tradition that they were born in the island itself: the maritime portion by those who had passed over from the country of the Belgae for the purpose of plunder and making war . . . The number of the people is countless, and their buildings exceedingly numerous, for the most part very like those of the Gauls . . . The most civilised of all these nations are they who inhabit Kent, which is entirely a maritime district, nor do they differ much from the Gallic customs. Most of the inland inhabitants do not sow corn, but live on milk and flesh, and are clad with skins.[8]

By 'the most civilised', Caesar meant 'most like the Romans'. The tribes whose territories lay within easy reach of the Continent already had strong political, cultural and commercial contacts with the Roman Empire. Some of the tribal leaders in the south found the Roman way of life attractive and they looked upon the Roman army as a potential ally against their aggressive neighbours. The Ancient Britons had no concept of a united country before the Romans imposed their rule. Tacitus thought that the Ancient Britons' failure to combine their forces against the invaders was their greatest weakness: 'Rarely do two or three tribes join for averting a common danger; and so while they fight as individuals, they are overcome as a whole.'[9]

The pace of the Roman advance was not sustained; tribes in the highland zone of Britain offered prolonged resistance. The newly conquered land had to be heavily garrisoned, with about 16,000 legionaries and the same number of auxiliary troops, who came from all over the empire and spoke many different languages. Most of them had been recruited in Spain, France, Germany and other parts of Europe; relatively few were born and bred in Rome. These soldiers added to the genetic stock by sometimes having families with local women even though it was not until the third century that they were officially allowed to marry. The Roman conquest made little difference to the ancient way of life in highland parts of Britain. Our evidence is limited to a tiny proportion of the population and we know little about the poorest sections of society, either in the towns or the countryside, though we can note that as slavery was commonplace in the Roman Empire, thousands of Britons must have been enslaved as prisoners of war during the different phases of the Roman conquest.

The Romans brought Christianity to *Britannia*, but it made little progress before Constantine was proclaimed emperor at York in 306. In 313, his Edict of Milan announced total religious toleration throughout the empire, with Christianity as the favoured choice. The main support for the Christian church in the fourth century seems to have been amongst the owners of villas. The best evidence comes from Lullingstone in Kent, where in the late fourth century a self-contained suite of rooms at the eastern end of the villa was decorated with wall paintings that include the Chi-Rho symbol and human figures praying with outstretched arms in the manner of the time.[10]

For most native people, the retreat of the Romans in the early fifth century must have made very little difference to their lives. In large parts of Britain, even in some districts in the South East, Roman culture had been absorbed only at a superficial level. The Romans must be credited with the introduction of writing and written laws, the Latin language, the erection of superior buildings and public amenities, the development of industries, particularly the large-scale production of pottery, and the bringing into cultivation of extensive areas of new land and the encouragement of markets for agricultural produce. They left an impressive legacy, but their invasion was undertaken for their own benefit.

The Romans regarded *Britannia* as a barbarian outpost of their empire on the edge of the known world. It required a strong military presence to enforce the veneer of a superior civilized society. The Romans preserved tribal identities in the administrative districts, for they lacked the manpower to rule otherwise. When men from the south of England were stationed on Hadrian's Wall in the fourth century, they referred to themselves in inscriptions as members of the Durotriges and Dumnonii tribes.[11] This persistence of tribal loyalties and rivalries led to the breakdown of law and order when the Romans withdrew in the early fifth century. When the Anglo-Saxons arrived they found a deeply divided country, just as the Romans had done a few centuries before.

The creation of England

It is popularly believed that the English are different from the other nations of the British Isles because they are the descendants of Anglo-Saxon warriors and settlers from northwest Europe who drove the native British out of their land into Wales, Ireland and Scotland. England does indeed take its name from the Angles, who came from the Schleswig-Holstein peninsula between modern Germany and Denmark and from further north. The Saxons came from northwest Germany. At first sight, the ultimate triumph of the English language and the widespread adoption of Anglo-Saxon place-names seem to support foundation myths based on legendary characters such as Hengist and Horsa. Nevertheless, the reality of what happened after the Roman withdrawal is far more complicated and contentious than the traditional story would have us believe.[12]

The fragile unity that the Romans had enforced upon Britain disintegrated rapidly when the army left. The central administration broke down, the country soon became divided amongst regional tribes, and the economy suffered badly. No new coins were struck, and within a few decades even such basic skills as making pottery seem to have been lost; the continued manufacture of kitchenware in York until well into the fifth century was unusual. Roman towns and rural villas decayed and eventually fell into ruin. By the middle of the fifth century, *Britannia* was a divided and a poorer country.

We can only speculate about conditions in the second and third decades of the fifth century in Britain, as there is little reliable archaeological evidence to go on. The great majority of people lived in the countryside, where life continued in much the old manner at a lower level of profitability as the money-based market economy had collapsed. No British leader had sufficient authority to rule the whole of the province that had been abandoned by the Romans.

Into this political vacuum stepped the Anglo-Saxons. The contradictory and biased accounts in our earliest historical sources, which were written long after the events they purport to describe, suggest that they took over much of England in the 440s. The tale was told that, after the Roman withdrawal, a British warlord called Vortigern invited mercenaries from across the North Sea to help him in the tribal wars and that these foreigners soon took advantage of the troubled times to seize territories for themselves in the East and South East. The Romans had used Saxon mercenaries in a similar manner, so there may be some truth behind this legend, but archaeological investigations suggest a much slower process of Anglo-Saxon occupation, which was often halted and sometimes reversed. Other legends, such as those about King Arthur, can be readily dismissed as tales that were invented much later.[13]

The Angles, Saxons, and smaller groups of Jutes and Frisians from northwest Europe eventually occupied those lowland and fertile parts of central and southern England that had once been fully Romanized. They settled in a landscape that was not very different from their homelands. Their earliest cemeteries were in the South and the East, where a large number of fifth- and sixth-century burials and cremations, accompanied by grave goods of a southern Scandinavian and northern Germanic character, have been found. But the contrasts between different local communities within this zone were marked; for example, the Scandinavian-style early cremation cemeteries of parts of East Anglia are very different from those in a district extending eastwards from the Upper Thames along the Chilterns. Anglo-Saxon warriors advanced rapidly in these districts in the late fifth century, but they moved no further west during the next 60 or 70 years. This was a period of consolidation that saw the emergence of different Anglian and Saxon cultures. The country long continued as a collection of different tribes before it eventually became known as England.[14]

The few surviving historical sources cannot take us much further. New knowledge about the origins of the Anglo-Saxons must come mainly from fresh archaeological discoveries and from scientific enquiries, notably genetics and the stable isotope analysis of teeth. Archaeologists have confirmed a change of culture from the Roman period, but they usually find it difficult to distinguish the settlements and cemeteries of the invaders from those of the natives. The styles of dress, brooches, pottery and aisled halls that are associated with the early Anglo-Saxons do not necessarily prove that everybody who adopted them had travelled across the North Sea.

Changes may have been cultural, with native people gradually adopting the new fashions, some of which had appeared much earlier at late fourth-century sites in eastern England, long before the retreat of the Roman army. Many of the finds cannot be dated precisely.

The eventual adoption of the English language and the widespread replacement of British place-names by Old English ones was once thought to support the idea that the native population of Britain had been driven out by tens of thousands of Anglo-Saxon soldiers and settlers, for neither the Romans nor the Normans made such an impact when they came to England. But the parallel experience of the British Empire in modern times shows that a relatively small ruling elite and army can enforce such changes, and the triumph of the Portuguese language in Brazil or of Spanish in Central America points to the same conclusion. English names for our villages and hamlets do not prove that these settlements were founded by the Anglo-Saxons, for many sites have provided archaeological evidence of earlier occupation, sometimes stretching back into the prehistoric era.[15]

DNA studies have proved that while a large number of Anglo-Saxons settled in southeastern and central England, the continued presence of Ancient British families was more substantial. There was no genocide. The people of the North and the West, who had hardly altered their lifestyles during the Roman occupation, continued to resist change in later times. The Angles did not conquer the northern and western British kingdoms until well into the seventh century, and the Saxon penetration of the South West was not much quicker. The Anglo-Saxons became the new rulers, but the great majority of the people who farmed the land were descended from the native inhabitants.

The Peoples of the British Isles project, based on the DNA of modern-day populations, has concluded that the genetic differences between people were subtle but nonetheless real. The researchers were struck by how clear the patterns of regional differences were and by how families had stayed in their geographic regions over the centuries. The county boundary between Cornwall and Devon along the river Tamar remains a genetic divide, and the descendants of the people of the ancient kingdom of Elmet are still found mainly on the Pennine edges of West Yorkshire and east Lancashire. As yet, however, no clear timescale has been established for genetic markers; we can see only broad patterns. The maps that mark the settlements of people from northwest Europe in lowland England do not differentiate between the Anglo-Saxons and their predecessors who migrated in prehistoric and Roman times. Today, the white, indigenous English share about 40 per cent of their DNA with the French, about 26 per cent with the Germans, 11 per cent with the Danes and about 9 per cent with the Belgians.[16]

During the late sixth and seventh centuries, the most-successful warlords were able to enforce the merger of small tribal groups into the first Anglo-Saxon kingdoms. Richly furnished barrow burials for kings and princes date from this time, not only in England but also in southern Scandinavia and the

Rhineland. The great ship burial in one of the mounds on a spur overlooking the estuary of the river Deben at Sutton Hoo (Suffolk) is thought to have been that of Raedwald, king of East Anglia and overlord of the English until his death in 625, such is the splendour of the gold ornaments and other treasures that have been found there. This is one of the richest graves that has been excavated in the whole of Europe. The Deben estuary was an obvious point of entry for invaders from the North Sea in the fifth century, and several major early Anglo-Saxon settlements were founded nearby. Ipswich became a long-distance trading port in the late sixth or early seventh century, and Bede noted that Rendlesham was the site of a royal palace in the seventh century. Sutton Hoo had great significance as a high-status burial ground between about 570 and 630 for the Wuffingas, the tribe that came to dominate East Anglia. Eastern and southeastern England formed part of a larger North Sea community, where skilled craftsmen produced sophisticated jewellery and other high-quality products, including spoons and bowls made in Byzantine workshops in the eastern Mediterranean.[17]

The earliest surviving written records of English settlement date from about 670, more than two centuries after the first warriors crossed the North Sea. Margaret Gelling showed that the largest group of place-names that was recorded before Bede's history was completed came from features of the landscape, such as hills, valleys, fords and springs.[18] This is true of Celtic names from the Romano-British era, of names where the earliest Anglo-Saxon archaeological material has been found, and of places of major administrative importance in this and later periods.

The difficulties of interpreting Anglo-Saxon place-names are illustrated by -ingas names such as Hastings and Reading, which were once thought to have denoted the followers of tribal leaders from the earliest period of Anglo-Saxon settlement. As the distribution of such names does not tally with archaeological evidence such as pagan cemeteries, it is now accepted that folk names such as these belong to a later stage of settlement.[19] For example, a group of eight ecclesiastical parishes in central Essex, which are called the Rodings (pronounced Roothings) because they each bear this place-name element, marked the territory of 'the people of Hrotha'. The shape of the original estate was determined by the natural topography and the need to contain a cross-section of all the available local resources. It was already fragmented by the time of the first reference in Domesday Book, but as late as the eighteenth century Daniel Defoe thought of the Rodings as a distinct 'country'.[20] Similar-sized districts took their names from topographical features. For example, a line of Worcestershire villages named Lenchwick, Sheriff's Lench, Atch Lench, Church Lench, Abbots Lench and Rous Lench stretch for five miles along the *hlenc*, an 'extensive hill-slope' north of Evesham, but we cannot put a precise date to their foundation.[21]

The majority of English villages and towns were not founded until long after the original settlers had arrived on these shores. Documentary evidence for most places is usually lacking before the Domesday Book of 1086. This means that we cannot date the origins of settlements with any confidence, nor can we be certain of the original forms of their names.

The notion that the Continental invaders and settlers were known collectively as the English first appears in historical records much later, at the end of the seventh century in the law codes of King Ine of Wessex, then famously in Bede's *Ecclesiastical History of the English People* (731), but it was not developed fully until the late ninth century when King Alfred embraced the concept to stir his followers to resist the Danes. Until then, the Anglo-Saxons lived in small kingdoms that were often at war with each other. We have no written sources for Anglo-Saxon kingdoms before the seventh century, and nothing much until the eighth. Although the various peoples known as the Anglo-Saxons shared a basic language and some aspects of a common culture, they were not a unified group. The different origins of these Germanic warriors and settlers are reflected in the individual characters of the various territories that were merged into a unified England several centuries later. The earliest Anglo-Saxon kingdoms were naturally in the East and the South East: Lindsey, East Anglia, Essex, Kent and Sussex. Occasionally, the ruler of the most powerful kingdom at the time was acknowledged as Bretwalda or 'over-king', but Anglo-Saxon England did not become a united political force until the triumph of Wessex late in the first millennium.[22]

Kent had been an Iron Age and Romano-British territory long before the Germanic invasions. Bede wrote that the Jutes took over Kent, parts of Hampshire, and the Isle of Wight, whose name is derived from a British word of uncertain origin and meaning, but he was describing events of long ago in a distant place, so he may have over-simplified the situation. Close links with the Continent meant that Kent became the first English kingdom to convert to Christianity, the first to mint its own coins, and the one that has by far the largest surviving number of seventh- and eighth-century royal diplomas.[23] Likewise, the names of the kingdom of Lindsey and its capital Lincoln pre-date the Anglian invasions and indeed the Romans. The second element of Lindsey is Old English *-eg*, 'an island or raised land in a wet area', for the kingdom was defined on all sides by rivers, fens or the sea.[24]

Bede noted that the Saxons were divided into three groups that formed kingdoms in the east, south and west of England, which is how the names of Essex, Sussex and Wessex arose, though he did not mention Middlesex. The West Saxon kingdom originated in the upper Thames Valley, but by the seventh century it was centred in Hampshire and Wiltshire and it was expanding into Somerset and Dorset. By the eighth century much of the former British kingdom of Dumnonia had been subdued.[25] Devon retained its British name, and Cornwall was named after the British tribe, the Cornovii, with the Saxon suffix *-wealh*, a disparaging term for the British 'foreigners'. Wales and villages such as the numerous Waltons acquired their names in the same way. In the North West, the British word *Cymri* was used to describe the Cumbrians, and Carlisle retained its Romano-British name.[26]

The Angles settled in the Midlands and the North, away from the Saxons. The East Angles were divided between the north-folk and the south-folk, whose names are preserved in the present counties of Norfolk and Suffolk, in what had once been the rich lands of the Iceni tribe, while the various peoples who sailed up the Humber and its great tributaries, the Trent and the Ouse, eventually merged into the two major kingdoms of Mercia and Northumbria. The Mercians were the 'boundary folk', and the general consensus now is that they took their name from the border that they shared with the British to the west. Their original heartland extended over most of modern Staffordshire, Leicestershire, Nottinghamshire, south Derbyshire and north Warwickshire. Mercia became a major power in the first half of the seventh century under Penda and reached its widest extent under Offa, its ruler from 757 to 796, whose famous 120-mile dyke that marked the border with Wales (or perhaps just the kingdom of Powys) is the longest linear earthwork of its kind in Europe, but only in its central section is its military nature obvious.[27]

At its greatest extent, Northumbria stretched from the river Humber into lowland Scotland. It combined two ancient territories, Bernicia and Deira, both of which had British names. By the end of the eighth century, the various Anglo-Saxon kingdoms controlled all the area south of the Forth and as far west as Wales and Cornwall. They spoke a common language but with strong regional dialects. Warfare was endemic and extolled as heroic, for land and plunder to reward the king's warriors for their loyalty could be acquired only through battle. The competition between Northumbrian and Mercian kings for control of midland England was savage.[28]

We know far less about the smaller territories that survived. A list known as the Tribal Hidage, which provides the names of some of the small kingdoms that existed in the seventh century, records the territory of the tribe that occupied the northern edge of the Mercian heartland as *Pecsaetna lond*, 'the land of the settlers of the Peak'. The Pecsaete seem to have been British, like their northern neighbours, the inhabitants of Elmet, who were conquered by the Northumbrians in 617 but whose territory kept its name long afterwards. In 920, the *Anglo-Saxon Chronicle* referred to Bakewell as being in *Peac lond*, and in 963 a charter described Ballidon, near Ashbourne, as being 'in the district of' the Pecsaete. These tribal lands seem to have extended over the whole of what is now known as the Peak District.[29] The memory of other small kingdoms that lost their independence but retained a group identity is preserved by district names such as Lindrick and Hatfield on the Yorkshire-Nottinghamshire border, or Balne and Ashfield nearby.[30]

Meanwhile, Christianity was imposed on the population from above once a king had been converted, for it helped to bolster his authority. The leading figures were appointed from the local elite. Once Sussex and the Isle of Wight had been converted during the 670s and 680s, all the English kings were baptized in the Christian faith. The conversion of their subjects followed quickly. Theodore of Tarsus, who was Archbishop of Canterbury from 669 to 690, vigorously enforced the dominance of Christianity. It has recently become clear that the pagan practice of furnished burials came to an abrupt end during his time.[31]

From the late eighth century onwards, bands of warriors from Scandinavia crossed the North Sea in speedy longships in search of plunder. The *Anglo-Saxon Chronicle* recorded the horror that was felt in 793 when Viking raiders sacked the famous Northumbrian monastery at Lindisfarne. Danish raids intensified in the 830s, then in 865 a 'great army' led by Halfdan sailed up the Humber; the following year saw them established in York. These Danish Vikings quickly became the rulers of much of those parts of northern and eastern England that the Angles had conquered in earlier times. This is unsurprising because they came on the same routes across the North Sea and their genes can hardly be distinguished from those of their predecessors. One of the most common questions asked of geneticists by those who are tested is, 'Can you prove that I'm a Viking?' The answer usually turns out to be 'No'.[32]

The victorious armies settled in Yorkshire (876), eastern Mercia (877) and East Anglia (879), and were soon joined by farming families from their

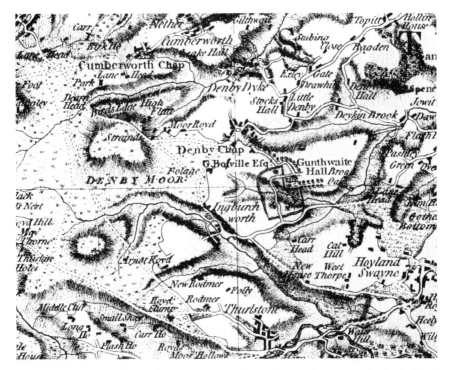

FIGURE 3 *The Viking place-names Denby and Gunthwaite and the hybrids Thurlstone and Hoyland Swaine are shown close together on Jefferys' map of Yorkshire (1772).*

native lands. A second wave of settlement occurred from 902 onwards when groups of Norwegian Vikings from Ireland, Wales and western Scotland settled in the Wirral, west Lancashire, Westmorland and Cumberland, and then on marginal land across the Pennines in parts of Yorkshire.

The size of the original Danish armies and the number of subsequent Viking settlers are matters of much debate. In the absence of sufficient literary sources, we have to depend on the interpretation of place-names, which survive in great numbers, but, as with the Anglo-Saxons, this evidence is not as straightforward as it might seem. The Danish equivalent of Anglo-Saxon place-name suffix -*tun* was -*by*, as in Derby, Grimsby or Selby. Such names have long been regarded as the earliest form while those ending in -*thorpe* were outlying farmsteads or hamlets, but it has been argued recently that the -*bys* were devoted to livestock farming and the -*thorpes* to arable cultivation. The variety of Scandinavian words for topographical features and different types of fields that are found widely in eastern England is striking; names such as beck (brook), carr (marsh), dale (valley), gate (road), lathe (barn), holme (meadow), and different pronunciations such as kirk (church), brigg (bridge) and rigg (ridge). When I was a boy in South Yorkshire, we used to 'lake' at football, not 'play', unaware that we were using a word that is still in use in Norway.[33]

The density of Danish words is particularly evident in Lincolnshire, where Domesday Book recorded 225 settlements with names ending in -*by*, compared with only 22 in Nottinghamshire and 10 in Derbyshire. Gillian Fellows Jensen has shown that no less than 140 of the 220 landowners recorded in the Lincolnshire folios of Domesday Book had Danish personal names. This contrasting geographical pattern is also seen within Yorkshire. In the North Riding, 223 out of the 649 names that were recorded in Domesday Book were of Scandinavian origin, and a further 66 were hybrids or English names that were influenced by Scandinavian speech. Similar numbers were recorded in the East Riding, but the Viking presence further inland in the West Riding was much less pronounced. In Yorkshire as a whole, 70 per cent of the recorded personal names in Domesday Book were of Scandinavian origin.[34]

The river Tees appears to have been a major cultural barrier, for the relative absence of Scandinavian place-names and the distribution of the distinctive sculpture that was developed by the new settlers show that the Vikings did not penetrate far into County Durham and Northumberland. In Norfolk, Scandinavian place-names are far fewer and are restricted to certain districts, while Rutland, which was surrounded by counties that formed part of what became known as the Danelaw, including Lincolnshire, seems to have remained outside Danish control, for it has very few Scandinavian place-names and none at all derived from -*by*. It is clear from these distribution patterns that Viking settlements had a profound and lasting influence that contributed a great deal to the regional diversity of England.

It has long been argued that the abundance of place-names and field-names of Scandinavian origin and the lasting influence of Danish and Old Norse speech on the dialects of northern England imply that large numbers of immigrant farmers sailed across the North Sea once the conquest was complete. But an alternative view is that these place-names simply demonstrate that a Viking elite took over existing estates and created smaller units, which in time became manors. In many cases it is likely that Viking place-names replaced older ones; it is known, for example, that Whitby was once known as Streoneshalh, and Derby as Northworthy. Elsewhere, many a village has a name that is partly Anglian and partly Viking. Neither archaeological investigations nor genetic studies support the idea of a massive invasion and settlement. The Viking contribution to the population of the places where they settled appears to have been similar to that of their Anglian predecessors.[35]

The Vikings conquered most of the territories of the Angles but were unable to defeat the Saxon kingdom of Wessex. The Danish army was reduced in size once many of the soldiers had become farmers or settlers, and Alfred's troops managed to hang on by resorting to guerrilla warfare in the Somerset Levels. In May 878 Alfred defeated Guthrum at the Battle of Edington, near Westbury, a turning point in English history. The Treaty of Wedmore in 886 required the Danes to abandon their stronghold in Wessex (at Chippenham) and Guthrum was made to convert to Christianity and withdraw to East Anglia. England was now divided between Wessex and the Danelaw along a boundary that ran from the Essex side of the Thames Estuary as far as the river Lea, up the river to its source, then across to Bedford and along the river Ouse to Watling Street, the Roman road that took the boundary through the Midlands. The effectiveness of this boundary is shown by the presence of very few Scandinavian place-names to the south of it.

Alfred made an alliance with the ruler of what remained of the kingdom of Mercia and started to call himself 'King of the Angles and Saxons'. Alfred was a charismatic and able ruler, whose achievements were deemed heroic in Asser's influential biography. He became a patron of the arts and architecture, founded a school at his court, translated Christian texts from Latin into English and encouraged the monks of his abbeys to record events in English in the *Anglo-Saxon Chronicle*, established a code of law to be used throughout his realm, and fostered economic development, notably with the creation of mints where coins were struck in some of his burhs. By the time of his death in 899, Wessex had been transformed into the leading Anglo-Saxon kingdom and the bulwark against the Vikings. A sense of Englishness was promoted to new levels in Alfred's Wessex. Since his time, national politics has been centred in the south of England.[36]

Alfred's son, Edward the Elder, King of Wessex (899–924) and of Mercia (c.918–24), and Alfred's daughter, Aethefleda, Lady of the Mercians, pushed the Danes back to the Humber, and Edward's supremacy was acknowledged by those who ruled further north. Edward the Elder created new burhs within Mercia, notably at Bedford, Chester, Gloucester, Hereford, Manchester and Nottingham, but those that occupied former Roman sites paid scant regard to their predecessors. Colchester had declined into a one-street village, but Edward repaired the Roman walls in 917 and laid out new streets and new properties, including two churches. By the time that Domesday Book was compiled in 1086, Colchester had grown piecemeal into a borough. The Five Boroughs of the Danelaw – Derby, Leicester, Lincoln, Nottingham and Stamford – each had an earlier history, but after 910 they were re-modelled in the style of Alfred's burhs. Located on navigable rivers and major roads, they perhaps became proper towns only under Edward the Elder.[37]

Aethelstan, Edward's son, was the first king to rule the whole of England. His legendary victory over an invading force of Vikings, Scots and Irishmen at the Battle of Brunanburh in 937 was commemorated in numerous early sources and folk tales. The site of the battle is much debated.[38] The supremacy of Edgar, his successor, was highlighted at Chester, where he was rowed on the river Dee by kings from north Wales, Scotland and the Isle of Man. During his reign, Edgar introduced new law codes and standard coinage and he was a strong supporter of monastic reform.

Under these Wessex kings, England was divided into shires, which in turn were subdivided into hundreds. The earliest shires, or counties as they became known later, were Berkshire, Dorset, Hampshire, Somerset and Wiltshire, which were formed in eighth- and ninth-century Wessex. Berkshire and Dorset had Celtic roots, whereas Hampshire, Somerset and Wiltshire took their names from their administrative centres: Southampton, Somerton and Wilton, respectively. The West Midland counties were created during the tenth-century campaigns of Edward the Elder into the kingdom of Mercia; for example, Shropshire was formed by the union of two tribal districts and named after its capital, Shrewsbury. The East Midland shires were created under the Danelaw during the ninth or tenth centuries and were named after the military centres that became their county towns: Derby, Nottingham, Leicester, Northampton, Huntingdon, Bedford and Cambridge. Lincolnshire united the two Danish armies based on Lincoln and Stamford. North of the Humber, the only county that was created before the Norman Conquest was Yorkshire, the area controlled from Jorvik. By the tenth century the mixed cultural origins of Yorkshire's inhabitants meant that they were markedly different from people who lived further south.[39]

In the first half of the eleventh century, the Vikings made a major contribution to the concept of a united England under one monarch. In 1013 the Danish King Svein Forkbeard, who had ruled Denmark from about 985 and who had long been involved in persistent raids on England, landed in the Humber estuary and sailed up the river Trent to Gainsborough, where he was acknowledged as king by most of the rulers within the old

Danelaw. His forces then moved south and west, where he took Oxford and Winchester rapidly and London by the end of the year. King Aethelred was forced into exile, but Svein died on 3 February 1014. His younger son Cnut had hard-fought battles with Aethelred's son, Edmund Ironside, before he was crowned King of England in 1016. At a great assembly at Oxford in 1018, after the murder of his opponents, Cnut promised to adhere to the laws of King Edgar; his reign over England and subsequently over Denmark (1019) and Norway (1028) ushered in two decades of peace. He developed the national economy and recognized that regular taxation, or geld, was essential for maintaining stability. But he died young in 1035 and was buried in the Old Minster, Winchester. His two sons both died in their twenties, so the throne returned to the Saxon line in the person of Edward the Confessor (1042–66).[40]

The Saxon and Danish kings who created the unified kingdom laid the foundations of law and order throughout the realm and ensured that England would be a Christian country. But the struggle for the succession to the throne in 1066 was not a simple matter of Englishmen fighting Normans. King Harold's mother was Danish and his father had been created an earl by Cnut; Edward the Confessor's mother was a Norman; and the Normans were originally Vikings who had settled in northern France in the ninth century but who had soon learned to speak French.

The Norman Conquest

The Battle of Hastings in 1066 turned out to be the last invasion of England by a conquering army and the most traumatic of all. The Normans created powerful lordships up and down the land and set much of the countryside aside as private hunting forests, some of whose names, such as the New Forest, Epping Forest, or the Forest of Bowland, resonate with us today. They were responsible for much of what we now regard as our heritage: castles, cathedrals, monasteries and many of our parish churches. Words in current use, such as 'table', 'bacon' or 'cutlery', and popular personal names, such as William, Henry, Robert and Thomas, or Margaret and Joan, were Norman French in origin. The impact of the Norman Conquest was felt in every part of the land.

William's decision to invade had been taken by an inner circle of friends and relations and he attracted support from the Church and from lords in Normandy, Brittany, Picardy, Boulogne, Flanders and other nearby provinces who each supplied contingents of kinsmen and followers. During the twelfth century it became a common boast amongst Anglo-Norman landowners that an ancestor had fought at Hastings, but the identities of only fifteen warriors in the battle are certain, another four are almost certain, and a few others have serious claims. Descents can be proved in the female line to the present day from some of these names, but in the male line only the descendants of William Malet have a provable claim. Some of the most eminent baronial families arrived in England long after the Conquest.[41]

The number of people who crossed the English Channel from France and the Low Countries formed a small minority, yet victory at Hastings led to the largest transfer of property ever seen in English history. Virtually all the members of the Anglo-Danish aristocracy, including the senior clergymen, were removed. Sometimes, all the lands of an English lord were granted to a newcomer; in other cases, the scattered estates of several previous owners were brought together to form a new barony, such as those centred on the castles at Richmond and Tickhill in Yorkshire. Almost all the major landowners who were named in Domesday Book were men who came from northern France, but they included some who had arrived after the battle of Hastings. Henry of Huntingdon, writing in the third decade of the twelfth century, noted: 'In the twenty-first year of King William's reign there was hardly a nobleman of English descent left in England, but all were reduced to servitude and mourning, so that it was a disgrace to be called an Englishman.'[42]

The Norman Conquest elevated some men to unaccustomed wealth and power and many of those in the king's service were 'raised from the dust', to use Orderic Vitalis's memorable phrase.[43] Other Norman and Breton families became landowners shortly after the Conquest, but subsequent immigration occurred on a relatively small scale. The rate of turnover in many of the Norman baronial families that held the major lordships was rapid. Families were sometimes dispossessed for backing an unsuccessful claimant to the throne, but the main reason for change of ownership was the failure to produce male heirs. It has been calculated that 54 out of the 189 English baronies that were in existence by 1166 descended in the female line in the hundred years after the Conquest, six of them twice. Where descent from a Norman baronial family to the present day can be proved, it is usually through younger branches.[44]

Norman French long remained the language of the elite and it strongly influenced the development of Middle English. Yet England has relatively few place-names of French origin, except where the name of a lord has been added as a suffix, as in Kingston Bagpuize in Oxfordshire or Ashby-de-la-Zouch in Leicestershire. But by the end of the thirteenth century, nearly all Old English and Scandinavian personal names had fallen out of use and had been replaced by Norman ones.[45]

The Norman barons introduced the fashion for surnames into England, though only a few families had fixed and hereditary ones before the Conquest. The most common practice was to take the name of the place that was the family's chief residence, either in Normandy or from their newly acquired estates in England. English people often found these French names difficult to pronounce, so a name such as Beaufour became Boffey, and Sémerville was twisted into Somerfield. Other surnames that differ considerably from the present forms of the place-names from which they were derived include Challis, Pinkney and Samper, which come respectively from Eschalles, Picquigny and various places in northern France named Saint-Pierre.[46]

Names such as these show that by the time the Domesday Book was compiled in 1086, most of the invaders had come from the départements of Seine-Maritime and Calvados in upper Normandy and that many others were from Manche in west Normandy and from further south in Eure and Orne. The rest of the invading army originated from further afield in Brittany, Flanders, Anjou, Poitou, Paris and the Gatinais. The lack of documentary evidence before the late twelfth century often frustrates attempts to locate the homes of family names, and the pioneering study by Lewis C. Lloyd warned of the danger of assuming that all Normans in England bearing the same name came from the same place.[47] The easy assumption that all the people with French surnames who appear in medieval records were descended from men who had fought at Hastings must be resisted.

New settlers, from various levels of society, continued to arrive in England from northern France and the Low Countries over the next few centuries. Some of them are immediately recognizable from surnames such as Fleming and Flanders. Those named Bremner, Brabner, Brabazon, Brabson, Brabyn and Brabham all came from the duchy of Brabant; those called Burgoyne, Burgin, Burgon and Burgan from Burgundy. Chamness and Champney are derived from Champagne, and Wasteneys is a corruption of Gatinais.

The poll tax returns of 1377–81 are our main source of information about the surprisingly wide distribution of names such as these by the late fourteenth century. The surnames French, France and Frenchman are found in each of the counties for which returns have survived. Many a farmer, craftsman or labourer of French origin was described thus by his neighbours. We cannot tell how many generations had passed between the bestowal of the surname and the recording of a descendant when he paid his poll tax, but some of those who were listed in 1377–81 seem to have been the first bearers of the name. In Lancashire, where many surnames were newly formed at that time, taxpayers included Gylowe le Frencheman and Janyn le Frencheman, two farmers in Rixton-with-Glazebrook, and fourteen others labelled le Frensh, de Fraunce, Franch, de Franse or Alice Frenshewyf.[48]

We have no way of knowing how people of French descent had come to live in remote villages such as Eyam in the Peak District or in Cheselbourne, Iwerne Courtenay, Osmington, Pulston, Tyneham and Waterston in Dorset. In Berkshire, five people named Fraunch or Franch were taxed in East Challow, and single others named French were recorded in ten other places in the county. Most of these people lived deep in the countryside.

Some farmers and workers from Brabant had also settled in parts of the English countryside. Five were listed in Lancashire and fourteen in Leicestershire. They seem to have been no different from their neighbours except for their distinctive surnames. More surprisingly, three men from

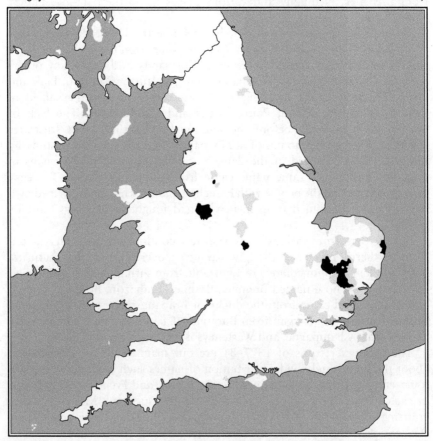

Mingay

Based on actual numbers in each
Poor Law Union (Source: 1881 Census)

FIGURE 4 *The surname Mingay is derived from a Breton personal name. Its tight distribution in 1881 suggests a single-family origin on the Suffolk-Norfolk border.*

Brabant had settled in Kirkby Stephen in Westmorland, where they were recorded as a tailor, shoemaker and dyer.

The Flemings had a more concentrated pattern. The printed poll tax returns for Derbyshire, Dorset, Gloucestershire, Herefordshire and Lancashire contain no householders with this surname, and Leicestershire had only John Flemyng at Bagworth. Four Flemings lived modestly in the Isle of Wight; one was based in Rochester, and another four were taxed in the Berkshire towns of Faringdon, Newbury and Reading. Their numbers were small compared with the nineteen Flemings who were taxed in Essex. Colchester had eight of them – including Ermingard and Hammus Flemyng – as well as a John Duch, two John Gaunts and two William Gaunts (from Ghent), Alice and Robert Haus, John van Myre and Reginald van Trude.

Other Flemings were found in nine Essex villages and towns. Three of the Flemings were recorded as *textor*, textile worker. Norfolk had eight Flemings (including three websters, a cordwainer and a tailor), five Bretons, two Brabons and a Brabant, two Douchmans in King's Lynn who were labourers, and seven named Fraunceys, Fraunce, Fraunk or Frensch. Only a handful of Flemings or Dutchmen were recorded elsewhere in England.

It is clear from all this that many of the French families that had settled in various parts of England by the late fourteenth century had no connection with the men who had fought at Hastings but were much later arrivals. How they chose their ultimate destinations – sometimes in villages and hamlets far distant from their native land – is a puzzle that can rarely be solved. On the edge of the Pennine Moors in southwest Yorkshire, Illions Farm stands at 950 feet above sea level. It is named after a medieval tenant whose surname was derived from a Breton personal name. In 1359 Robert Illian and his wife, Alice, became tenants, but it is likely that the farm acquired its name from an ancestor of his, for a deed from the beginning of the fourteenth century refers to land thereabouts that was held by John Ylian.[49]

These immigrants from across the English Channel must have stood out amongst their neighbours, but they formed only a small portion of the population. In the poll tax returns of 1377–81, Leicestershire had only about 40 householders with surnames derived from France amongst the thousands of its inhabitants. It is known, however, that some Continental immigrants assumed English surnames, such as Johnson or Skinner and other craft names.

A research project based at the Universities of York and Sheffield has identified about 65,000 foreigners in England between 1330 and 1550. From 1440 onwards, a series of specific taxes, known as 'alien subsidies', were levied on first-generation immigrants. In the first year of this tax, 14,500 'aliens' were recorded. They formed about 1 per cent of the English population, which is roughly the same percentage as in the 1901 national census. Many of these newcomers were scattered thinly across all the English counties, often as the only foreigners in a particular local community. In London, however, immigrants from the Continent of Europe formed about 6 per cent of the population. Many 'aliens' were servants or farm labourers, but others included skilled craftsmen such as goldsmiths and weavers.[50]

Long after the trauma of the Norman Conquest, the population of England was still largely descended from families that had been there for hundreds or thousands of years. The Englishmen who were recorded in Domesday Book as the holders of land before the Conquest did not possess hereditary surnames but were known simply by a personal name. The process by which surnames spread gradually down the social scale from the middle years of the thirteenth century onwards was a long-drawn-out one. It started later in northern parts of England, and it took a century or so longer to complete than in the South and the Midlands. The poll tax returns for Lancashire in 1379, for instance, show that many men were known simply as the son of someone. By the early fifteenth century, however, it was rare for an English person not to have a surname. It seems surprising now that medieval surnames were more varied and numerous than they are today. The Black Death and other pestilences reduced the national population by more than a third, and in later times many other surnames that had a single-family origin disappeared through the failure of male lines.[51]

The interpretation of these names presents many a trap for the unwary, for they often changed form over the centuries, but they are our chief source of information about where present-day families lived back in the Middle Ages. Time and time again, distinctive surnames that appear to have a single-family origin are still largely confined to the 'countries' where they originated several centuries earlier. Amongst my classmates at school in the 1950s, those named Armitage, Barraclough, Boyes, Coldwell, Haigh, Hepworth, Hirst, Jagger, Marsden, Maude, Micklethwaite, Priestley, Race, Senior, Sykes and others joined me in having surnames that originated in our part of the West Riding of Yorkshire. This experience is paralleled in many other parts of England.

CHAPTER THREE

England's historic towns and cities

Throughout England, the layout and the street names of the central parts of our historic towns and cities still provide visible clues to a medieval past. York has its Micklegate and its Bootham Bar; Shrewsbury has a Welsh Bridge and an English Bridge; and St Albans has its Kingsbury and Holywell Hill. Even Birmingham, Leeds, Liverpool, Manchester, and most of the other great Victorian cities that we regard as products of the Industrial Revolution, were medieval market towns in origin. The present pattern of streets in central Sheffield, for example, was created around a market place that was in existence by 1296 and probably long before. These streets were widened in the late nineteenth century and the remaining timber-framed buildings were demolished, but High Street, Far Gate, Market Place, Snig Hill, Barker's Pool and the Wicker remain familiar names to this day.[1] Medieval towns were small by modern standards, but they have left a permanent imprint on the English landscape.

The names of many English cities and towns, such as Manchester and Winchester, Chester and Chesterfield, or Doncaster and Lancaster, are taken from their Roman predecessors, but archaeologists have found little evidence of urban continuity after the collapse of Roman rule in the early fifth century. Indeed, most Roman towns had declined long before the end of the Empire. However, many sites were eventually re-occupied and some became urban centres again.

Under Anglo-Saxon rule in the seventh and eighth centuries, a few sea or river ports with productive hinterlands prospered through trade with Europe to such an extent that they grew in an unplanned way into new towns. The Anglo-Saxons knew them as *wics* and they resembled trading settlements on the other side of the North Sea. The major English ones were London (*Ludenwic*, commemorated by the name Aldwych), Ipswich (*Gipeswic*), Southampton (*Hamwic*) and York (*Eoforwic*). Much has been learned about them in recent decades through developer-funded excavations. *Ludenwic* grew quickly on the riverside just beyond the walls of the former Roman city, which was abandoned until the Viking raids forced people back inside. This trading centre prospered from about 730 to 770, and in 785 Westminster Abbey was founded alongside it. *Ludenwic* had several churches and its streets were well maintained.[2]

At the confluence of the river Ouse and the Fosse, Roman *Eboracum* was succeeded by the nearby Anglian *Eoforwic* and Viking *Jorvik*. York's present street pattern was created in the tenth century under Viking rule, with names such as Stonegate and Petergate that contain the Scandinavian element *gata*. The boundaries of the properties that stretched back from these ninth- and tenth-century streets have changed little since then. The walls of three adjacent timber houses that were recovered by excavation in the waterlogged soils of Coppergate consisted of several courses of horizontal plank cladding, supported on the inside by squared uprights. The excavators found amber and glass jewellery, combs made from antlers and a variety of objects carved from bone, and brooches, dress pins, fragments of clothing and hundreds of pairs of leather shoes. The densely packed streets of *Jorvik* were full of traders and craftsmen, who lived in conditions that appear rather squalid now. By 1066 York was the second-largest city in England.[3]

In the late 870s Alfred, King of Wessex, developed a network of burhs, or fortified planned settlements, as a co-ordinated system of defence that provided secure places for local government. Thirty-three of these towns were recorded in a slightly later document, the *Burghal Hidage*. No place in Wessex was more than 20 miles away from one of Alfred's burhs.[4] His enterprise was a major undertaking, for it has been calculated that at Wallingford (Oxfordshire, formerly Berkshire) 120,000 man hours would have been needed to construct the ramparts that protected a garrison of 2,400 soldiers at a strategic crossing of the Thames; parts of the ramparts survive to this day. Burhs such as Wallingford, which had a grid pattern of streets, were obviously intended to become commercial and administrative centres in more stable times.[5] At Wareham (Dorset) the massive ramparts and the street pattern of Alfred's burh still define the town.

During the tenth century, Winchester became a thriving city as the political and ecclesiastical capital of Wessex. The site had been an important Roman centre, known as *Venta Belgarum*, but the High Street, which ran between two gateways that were still in use, was the only Roman street that was incorporated into the regular grid pattern of the original burh. By about 900, a rectilinear pattern of cobbled streets had been created.[6] London, Chichester, Exeter and Bath are other examples of former Roman towns that were given new street layouts and defences at this time. Alfred built *Lundenburh* with a new grid of streets inside the safety of the Roman walls and allowed defenceless *Ludenwic* to decay, but much of London's development inside the walls and along the Thames waterfront occurred much later, in the late tenth and eleventh centuries. Other towns, including

Lincoln and Norwich, grew in a less organized way without a regular street plan, sometimes by the coalescing of previous small settlements.

Many English towns can trace their origins back to well before the Norman Conquest. After 1066, they grew in size and other towns were created. Throughout Europe, the commercial opportunities offered by the rise of population and increased agricultural and craft production encouraged kings, abbots and lords to promote the growth of towns by founding markets and fairs and by allowing townsmen to hold their properties by rent only, without any of the work obligations that were customary in the countryside. Over 130 new towns were created in England between the Conquest and the early fourteenth century.[7] Most of these were laid out around a market place, sometimes with a regular grid of streets, or perhaps grafted onto an existing village, leaving the parish church isolated from the new centre of commercial activity. At Bawtry, a thoroughfare town and river port on the Yorkshire-Nottinghamshire border, the church stands on the banks of the river Idle, out of sight from the huge rectangular market place and regular street pattern of the town that was founded about 1200. At Market Harborough, on the Leicestershire-Northamptonshire border, a town was planted on a virgin site with a new church at the heart of the market place but without a churchyard, for it long remained a chapel-of-ease within the parish of Great Bowden. Clues such as these, which have survived over the centuries, reveal how new towns were added to existing small settlements in the English countryside.

The most-successful towns became independent boroughs under the rule of a mayor and corporation. Royal charters were granted readily if burgesses were prepared to pay for the privilege, particularly during the reigns of Richard I and John. For example, in 1194 the burgesses of Doncaster obtained a town charter that guaranteed their privileges and customs and which served them well until 1467, when Edward IV incorporated the borough, with a ruling body consisting of a mayor, 12 aldermen and 24 common councilmen.[8] Many more towns remained 'seigneurial boroughs', whose burgesses were allowed some control over their affairs, perhaps through a guild, but who nevertheless still attended the manor court of their powerful lord. Sheffield and Chesterfield provide clear examples. In the country at large, most of the burgesses were Englishmen who had migrated from the neighbouring countryside, but towns including Norwich, Nottingham, Southampton and Wallingford developed 'French boroughs', while St Albans still has its French Row and Doncaster has its Frenchgate.

The market places of these new Norman towns were laid out in square, rectangular, or triangular shapes. In very many cases, for example at Newark or Ripon, the original plan has been well preserved even though most of the surrounding buildings are post-medieval. Property boundaries are remarkably tenacious. Elsewhere, it is common to find that the market place was encroached upon when the stalls that were used just once a week were replaced by permanent buildings. Such encroachments characteristically have no gardens, and narrow, twisting alleyways separate the buildings. The abbey end of the triangular market place at St Albans provides an example.

In Norman new towns, the properties of the wealthiest tradesmen, known to historians as burgage plots, were laid out from each side of the market place and its adjoining streets. Shops and inns had narrow frontages on to the prime trading positions, with private accommodation for the family on an upper storey that extended to the rear. Some of these medieval property divisions can still be observed in English towns today. Both the principal roads that converged on the market place and some of the narrow alleyways in the centre of town were often devoted to specialist market activities that are commemorated in street names such as Goose Hill, Horse Fair, Sheep Street and Swine Market. Pontefract, for example, acquired a second borough in the middle of the thirteenth century, known as West Cheap, whose original market place – now much encroached upon – is commemorated by the street names Market Place, Wool Market, Shoe Market Street, Corn Market, Beast Fair, Horse Fair, Roper Gate, Salter Row, and Middle Row, all of which speak of former trading activities.[9]

On the Shropshire-Herefordshire border, Ludlow is a classic example of a Norman town plantation alongside a mighty castle. It replaced the earlier hamlet of Dinham, which took its name from a great Bronze Age burial mound, the *Ludan Hlaw*, which was levelled in 1199 for the building of St Laurence's church. The castle was erected from about 1085, probably by Walter de Laci, from Lassy in Calvados, the Conqueror's trusted follower who was granted large estates in the Welsh Marches. The cliff on which the castle stands falls steeply to the river Teme on the west and the river Corve on the north. The town was founded alongside the castle, within the manor and parish of Stanton Lacy, and was built in several stages. The wide High Street, which extends eastwards from the castle gates, served as the market place, whose space has been much encroached upon at the eastern end by shops, with the narrow Market Street behind them. Old Street does not conform to the regular grid plan that is based on Mill Street and Bow Street and so probably pre-dates the town as the north-south route across the Teme some 200 yards to the east of the later crossing at Ludford Bridge. To the west of Mill Street, the original plan was altered by the extension of the outer bailey of the castle in the closing years of the twelfth century. The burgesses built their parish church in the northwestern corner of the town, once they had prospered through the cloth trade. The town walls were started in 1233 and were much improved between 1280 and 1317. Ludlow continued to expand and was outgrown in Shropshire only by the county town of Shrewsbury.[10]

Norwich provides an alternative example of how a successful old town that had expanded rapidly in the late Anglo-Saxon period was promoted to even greater heights by the Normans. By the eve of the Norman Conquest, Norwich had become a populous, sprawling place. For 20 years or more after the Conquest, the town suffered from severe disruption, and 295 empty properties were recorded in Domesday Book. In the early 1070s no less than 98 properties were destroyed to make way for a formidable royal castle, whose stone donjon was added in the twelfth century. Yet by 1075 a major, planned extension known as the New or French Borough was started down the slope immediately west of the castle, and by 1086 at least 125 French burgesses were trading in and around the large market place, which remains the commercial heart of the city to this day. Domesday Book also recorded a remarkable 46 churches in Norwich. In 1096 work began on a new cathedral for East Anglia and a priory for 60 Benedictine monks, on the edge of the river meadows, a quarter-of-a-mile away from the castle. Many houses and streets and at least two parish churches were demolished in order to create a precinct for the cathedral priory. Later, a bishop's palace was added on the south side of the cathedral. Royal and ecclesiastical patronage enabled Norwich to grow so large in this fertile and populous part of the kingdom that it became England's leading provincial city.[11]

Further south in Suffolk, Bury St Edmunds had been founded as a burh after the Danish invasions. Bury had only 310 inhabitants in 1066, but 20 years later a new town was flourishing. Domesday Book records:

[H]ere are 30 priests, deacons and clerks together, 28 nuns and poor people who daily pray for the king and for all Christian people; 75 bakers, ale-brewers, tailors, washerwomen, shoe-makers, robe-makers, cooks, porters and agents . . . Besides whom are thirteen reeves over the lands of the abbey who have a house in the town, and under them five bordars. Now 34 knights, French and English, with 22 bordars under them. Now altogether there are 342 houses on the demesne of the land of the abbey, which was all under the plough in the time of King Edward.

Abbot Baldwin (1065–98) was responsible for the great rebuilding of the abbey and the foundation of a new town, which was laid out on a grid pattern of streets, immediately to the west of the monumental gate-tower at the entrance to the abbey grounds. Churchgate Street ran due west from the line of the presbytery and the nave of his great new church, and five streets were laid out in parallel lines from north to south. At the abbey gates, Angel Hill became a market place and the site of a great medieval fair. The Great or Butter Market at the northwest corner of the new town was soon encroached upon by Moyses Hall, whose first floor provided domestic accommodation above a vaulted undercroft that was used for commercial and other functions. The pre-Conquest town to the south, above the meadows alongside the river Lark, was partly destroyed by the new abbey, which became one of the six greatest Benedictine foundations in England. Most of its buildings were demolished upon the dissolution of the monasteries in Henry VIII's reign.[12]

Yet some other old burhs failed to flourish under the Normans. The most spectacular instance of decline is provided by Thetford, an Anglo-Scandinavian diocesan centre and mint town, once well defined by its ramparts, whose cloth, metalwork and pottery industries supported a population of over 4,000 people at the time of the Norman Conquest. Thetford soon had one of the largest motte-and-bailey castles in England, an abbey, and 12 parish churches, but by 1086 the number of burgesses had fallen by nearly a quarter and 224 properties lay empty. Ten years later, Herbert de Losinga (the Bishop of Thetford) moved his see to Norwich, and when King's Lynn began to flourish further down the river Ouse, it took away most of Thetford's trade and the town declined into a modest market centre.[13]

Only a few houses from the Norman era survive in English towns. In the twelfth century, merchants and moneyers built stone houses in London and the leading provincial centres. Two of the best survivors were erected on and just below Steep Hill, Lincoln, in about 1170, when the city was at the height of its medieval prosperity, ranking just below York and Norwich. Solidly built of local Oolitic Limestone to prevent fire and deter violence, such houses provided working and storage space in the shops on the ground

FIGURE 5 *The twelfth-century Jew's House on Steep Hill, Lincoln, is one of the oldest surviving town houses in England.*

floor and living accommodation above. Lincoln once had many other such houses in the lower parts of the town.[14]

William the Conqueror invited the first Jewish immigrants to live in England's cities. York's Jews numbered about 40 households in Coney Street, and their burial ground lay beyond the northern city wall at Jewbury. They lived peacefully until the night of 16 March 1190, when the propaganda of the First Crusade aroused such violent anti-Semitic rioting that they were forced to seek refuge inside York Castle. The mob, urged on by neighbouring lords who owed huge debts to the Jewish money-lenders, set the castle on fire and were intent on murder, so when all was lost, the Jewish fathers cut the throats of their wives and children and were themselves then killed by their rabbi. At dawn, the few remaining Jews pleaded for mercy in return for Christian baptism, but although they had been given a promise of safety, they were all killed. In calmer times a few years later, other Jews settled in York. By 1218, England had ten urban Jewish communities under royal protection. They prospered until 1290, when King Edward I expelled them all.[15]

During the fourteenth and fifteenth centuries, more formal and elaborate structures of town government emerged, together with a rich urban culture of ceremonies and pageants, most notably the Corpus Christi mystery plays of York and Coventry. The larger towns became corporations; the very largest were counties corporate, with their mayors answerable directly to the king. A corporate bureaucracy ensured the security of a town's records, for urban authorities were well aware of their importance for maintaining rights.

The changing fortunes of medieval towns

In 1334 Bristol, York, Newcastle-upon-Tyne, Great Yarmouth, Lincoln, Norwich, Shrewsbury, Oxford, Salisbury and Boston were England's leading provincial cities and towns.[16] The most thriving places were either ports or centres of the woollen cloth trade. Some of them prospered as never before. In the 1230s Canterbury had at least 200 small lock-up shops, about six or seven feet wide, that were open for small businesses of all kinds, many of them sited on the fringes of the cathedral for the pilgrim trade. In the first half of the fourteenth century, Winchester's tradesmen formed specialist groups all the way along the High Street, starting near the West Gate with fishmongers and saddlers facing the tailors and skinners, then with goldsmiths and spicers, butchers and drapers, and ending with cutlers and dyers, all clamouring for business in a way that would seem very foreign today.[17] Meanwhile, Oxford and Cambridge grew as university towns in the continental manner, taking in students from abroad as well as from many parts of England. Merton became Oxford's first college in 1264. Peterhouse, the earliest college in Cambridge, was founded 20 years later.[18]

The fortunes of boroughs depended increasingly on the wool trade. London, Boston, Hull, Yarmouth and Southampton sent the bulk of English wool to Continental merchants. Beverley men gathered the wool shorn on the Wolds for export to Italy and Flanders, while the traders of Salisbury and Coventry prospered from weaving. Shrewsbury was the market place for Welsh cloth, while Leicester was a wool town with a weekday market, a Saturday market, a hay market and a horse fair.

The most famous annual fair was that held at St Ives (Huntingdonshire; now Cambridgeshire), where the monks of Ramsey Abbey laid out a great triangular market place and fairground whose outline is preserved in the street plan today. Continental and English merchants brought wool, cloth, wine and all sorts of other goods up the Great Ouse from King's Lynn or along the old Ermine Street and the road from London. Their memory is preserved in the names of French Row, Ypres Row, Lincoln Row, Beverley Row and Leicester Row, together with Barkers' Row, Canvas Row, Skinners' Row and Spicers' Row. Then, during the fifteenth century, the three-week September fair at Stourbridge near Cambridge became pre-eminent.

The major ports were amongst England's wealthiest medieval towns, though their fortunes were uneven. Southampton was the leading port on the south coast, exporting wool and grain and importing wine from France and Spain, silks and dyes from Italy, timber from the Baltic, haberdashery and household goods from the Low Countries, and a whole range of other items, including oil, iron, salt, linen and canvas. Even some Derbyshire lead was brought for export in wains that were drawn by oxen many miles overland. The south coast had numerous small ports, but only Plymouth rivalled Southampton.[19] The Cinque Ports of Kent and Sussex, founded by royal charter in 1155 and granted freedom from import duties, became more important after the loss of Normandy in 1204, but they were frequently troubled by French pirates and by war with France.

The North Sea ports prospered because they connected the richest parts of England with the wealthy Low Countries and the Baltic Sea, and because of the fishing. Ipswich soon recovered from Norman devastation. The twelfth and thirteenth centuries saw rapid growth and the creation of suburbs beyond the ramparts that were reconstructed in 1203. The natural harbour at the head of the Orwell estuary provided safe shelter for large numbers of ships and boats. Markets were held daily and the town's sacred buildings included three friaries, two priories, three hospitals, seventeen parish churches and three chapels.[20] Great Yarmouth's fortunes came from herrings and salt and from its river and road connections with bustling Norwich. A long, thin island of sand and shingle that was gradually created by the sea and strong on-shore winds blocked the northern channel of the estuary and deflected the river Yare southwards for eight miles. Yarmouth was already a small trading community with 70 burgesses at the time of the Norman Conquest; now the sheltered shore allowed fishermen to beach their boats, spread their nets and deal with catches when the herring shoaled in the autumn. In the late thirteenth century the growing town was enclosed within walls to the east of the river in England's most unusual town plan, whereby the long streets that curved gently from the church of St Nicholas (the patron saint of fishermen) and the market place in the north were linked by about 150 narrow alleys or 'rows'.[21]

But what the sea provided it could also take away. Dunwich, on the Suffolk coast, was perhaps England's wealthiest port after London in the middle of the twelfth century; two centuries later, most of it was destroyed. In its heyday, Dunwich stood on a hill about 40 feet above the sea. Within its earthen ramparts and gates, it contained eight or nine parish churches and several religious houses, including friaries, a Templars' church and a maison dieu. Markets were held every day of the week. On 14 January 1328, the sea choked the harbour with shingle and forced the river mouth to the north. By 1350 it was reported that the sea had destroyed more than 400 houses and some parish churches, shops and windmills. Dunwich long continued as a smaller settlement and the last of its churches and the site of the western gate did not slide down onto the beach until the twentieth century. The village that remains above the crumbling cliff is the successor to the western suburbs of the medieval town.[22]

Salt making was a major industry around the Wash in late Saxon times, when Lynn grew as a port at the estuary of the Great Ouse. The right to gather the tolls of the Saturday market and annual fairs was granted by Bishop Herbert de Losinga to the monks of Norwich soon after 1100. Bishop's Lynn, as it became known until the name was gradually replaced by King's Lynn, grew in the twelfth century, around the large, sub-rectangular Tuesday market place within the 'New Land' to the north and by the dumping of soil to extend the quays westwards. Ramparts and four timber towers were erected along the line of the natural bank of the estuarine lake that had given Lynn its Celtic name. By the fourteenth century, King's Lynn was the third-ranking port in England, serving a huge hinterland linked by waterways.[23]

To the north of the Wash, Boston too became one of England's greatest ports. 'Botolph's Town' took its name from its parish church. The Norman borough was planted in the parish of Skirbeck on the banks of the river Witham, with a ditch marking its other three sides. A large, triangular market place, later much encroached upon, stretched outwards from the church. By 1206 the burgesses were paying more duties than any other port but London. Wool was its principal export, but it traded in many other goods and its annual fair was internationally famous. It was connected to Lincoln by the river Witham and linked to the Trent by the Foss Dyke and so took away the trade of Torksey, once a flourishing town and inland port for wool and lead but now only a hamlet with just one of its parish churches and the ruins of the former priory remaining from its golden age. From Lynn and Boston, ships plied a coastal trade as far north as Berwick and Scotland or sailed across the North Sea to the Low Countries and Scandinavia and eventually to the Baltic Sea and Iceland. The sailors brought back herring from Scotland, cod from Bergen, timber from the Baltic and fur from the Arctic Circle.[24]

The small town that had been founded at the confluence of the rivers Hull and Humber during the third quarter of the twelfth century by the Cistercian monks of Meaux Abbey was known as Wyke, but when King Edward I bought the manor in 1293 'to increase the fitness of the port for ships and traffic' he changed its name to Kingston-upon-Hull. The quay was enlarged, new approach roads from Beverley and York were constructed, more markets and fairs were held, a mint was established, and 50 new burgage plots were laid out to the west of Holy Trinity church. In 1299 the townsmen were granted a borough charter with freedom from tolls throughout the kingdom, and from 1304 they had the right to return two members of Parliament. In 1321 and 1327 the burgesses obtained licences to build massive town walls and towers, England's first public work undertaken in brick, and in 1331 they were granted complete independence from the Crown. Holy Trinity church was gradually rebuilt on a much grander scale in brick, and by the time its tower was completed in the fifteenth century it was the largest church by area in the country. Hull's success caused the decline of neighbouring small boroughs along the lower reaches of the Ouse and the Humber: Drax, Airmyn, Brough, Hedon and Patrington were unable to compete.[25]

The strangest North Sea port of all was at Ravenser Odd on a headland at the mouth of the Humber. Around 1235, sand and stones that were swept down the coast by the North Sea and the wind were deposited at the tip of the Spurn peninsula to create an accessible sandbank. Fishermen began to dry their nets there and the timbers of a wrecked ship were used to build a hut where meat and drink were sold to passing seafarers. Soon, the Count of Aumale founded a borough on the headland, which by the 1260s had attracted over 100 burgesses, trading mostly in herring and other fish. The chronicler of Meaux Abbey described it as 'distant from the mainland a mile or more. For access it had a sandy road no broader than an arrow's flight yet wonderfully maintained by the tides and the ebb and flow of the Humber'. But in a great storm the sea breached the causeway and Ravenser Odd became an island. Even so, the borough continued to thrive and to return members of Parliament until the terrible years between 1334 and 1346 when about 200 houses, amounting to two-thirds of those in the town, were submerged under the sea. Its demise was much more rapid than at Dunwich. The chronicler wrote:

> All men daily removing their possessions, the town was swiftly swallowed up and irreparably destroyed by the merciless floods and tempests. This was an exceedingly famous borough devoted to merchandise and very much occupied with fishing; having more ships and burgesses than any on this coast.[26]

Scarborough too, nestling below its castle and St Mary's church, depended on the fishing trade. It achieved borough status in about 1163 and was enlarged by the creation of Newborough at its southern end. In 1253 the famous Scarborough fair was first held on the shore; it lasted an exceptionally long time, for 45 days in August and September.[27] But by far the most important borough and port in the North East was Newcastle, which had now outgrown both Durham and Gateshead to become the leading town in the four northern counties. The bridge across the Tyne carried the Great North Road, a vital artery for moving soldiers and military supplies to the war zone further north. Newcastle's merchants enjoyed a legal monopoly on the export of northern wool, the coal trade was already well established both along the coast and across the North Sea, and a considerable tonnage of lead and iron was exported.[28]

The northwestern coast had nothing comparable. By 1300, Chester was a flourishing town with 270 shops and a port on the river Dee connected to the Irish Sea, but it did not have much trade beyond. Liverpool began life as a planned town in 1207 under King John's direction, with burgesses, a Saturday market and an annual fair, but as yet it was of little importance. It occupied a virgin site between the river Mersey and the liver pool, a natural harbour into which two streams drained, whose name was derived from the sluggish nature of its water, perhaps clotted with seaweed. Seven streets were laid out in a simple pattern, but Liverpool long remained a small, isolated community.[29]

Some of the new planned towns failed to fulfil expectations. A classic case is New Winchelsea (Sussex), where the original grid plan can be studied on the ground. Floods had swept Old Winchelsea into the sea after the great storms of 1244 and 1287, so when King Edward I acquired the manor he laid out a new town on higher ground. Thirty-nine quarters, varying in size from one to three acres, were designated for houses, but 27 of them are now overgrown with grass. Prominent positions were reserved for a market place, two churches and a friary, but only the parish church of St Thomas survives amidst a large churchyard. The sea retreated, and the estuary became silted. By 1575 the town had fewer than 60 inhabited houses.[30]

The successful boroughs sustained their population growth through immigration, mostly from the surrounding countryside. Immigrants had opportunities to rise to the top positions in their adopted towns. The legend of Dick Whittington, Lord Mayor of London, was based on fact and inspired others to follow him. Having made his fortune in the capital city, a merchant often retired to live in splendour in his native place. A notable example is William Grevel of Chipping Camden, whose memorial brass in the parish church records his death in 1401 and describes him as a 'citizen of London and flower of the wool merchants of all England'. He built the finest house in the High Street and gave generously towards rebuilding and beautifying the parish church. Wealthy men such as Grevel dominated their boroughs to such an extent that when towns were assessed for tax they paid a large proportion of what was owed. None of these men founded great urban dynasties, for few merchant families remained in trade for more than two or three generations, but they were often linked through a web of marriages and by their leadership of guilds and fraternities to most of the leading neighbouring families.

The houses of the wealthiest inhabitants of a town were not set apart in special quarters but were commonly surrounded by the cottages and hovels of the poor. Labourers and their families lived in fireless lodgings, often outside the town walls; for baking their bread, they had to rely on the common oven. Craftsmen tended to live and work in particular quarters according to their trades, which are sometimes still commemorated in street names. Their cottages and workshops hardly ever survive from this early period; the oldest row with a secure date is that in Goodramgate, York, erected late in 1315 as a series of unheated cottages consisting of a ground-floor living room and workplace and an upper chamber and store. Humble dwellings such as these were crowded together in filthy streets; the splendour of medieval cathedrals should not blind us to the fact that they were set amidst squalor. Thirteenth-century Canterbury was exceptional in having a populous suburb along Wincheap, the Ashford road beyond the West Gate, even though the town had plenty of open spaces within its walls.

The dramatic collapse of the English population from the high level that had been achieved before the Black Death naturally affected urban economies. The chill wind of recession was felt throughout western Europe, as smaller populations meant less demand for the products of urban merchants and craftsmen. Some of England's most famous provincial towns withered during the late fifteenth and early sixteenth centuries and suffered badly during a decade of unprecedented economic hardship in the 1520s, when trade was poor and King Henry VIII's tax demands were at their most extravagant.

The desolation that overwhelmed many of England's leading cities, such as Canterbury, Gloucester, Lincoln, Shrewsbury and Winchester, was nowhere more evident than at Coventry. A dramatic crisis between 1518 and 1525 brought its textile industry to its knees and forced its leading merchants to refuse public office because they could not meet the costs.[31] Norwich was the leading provincial city, but even before the fire that destroyed 718 houses in the early sixteenth century its citizens were complaining about the 'many houses, habitations, and dwellings' that were uninhabited and going to ruin.[32] Some once-prosperous towns, such as Tickhill in South Yorkshire, were affected so badly that they lost their urban status, while many smaller places had to abandon their weekly markets and annual fairs.[33]

In 1400 York had ranked as England's first provincial city, with a population of more than 12,000, but by the 1520s it had fallen to sixth position and had fewer than 8,000 inhabitants. The decline had begun in the 1420s when the Merchant Adventurers no longer made large profits from foreign trade and former customers began to prefer cloth made in the West Riding countryside rather than in the city. Within a generation, York was in the depths of recession. In 1487 the corporation declared that fewer than half the number of 'good men' who had been citizens in the past were now living within the city walls or the suburbs, and their records noted reduced incomes from house rents and a sharp drop in the number of new freemen. Yet York remained the secular and ecclesiastical capital of northern England, the seat of the archbishop, the residence of the high sheriff, and the place where the body that became known as the King's Council in Northern Parts met, and it was the only place outside London to have a royal mint. Though York was small by European standards, it was famous for its buildings, which ranged from the Minster and St Mary's Abbey to the numerous parish churches and chapels, hospitals and colleges.[34]

Even Bristol, the second-largest seaport in the land and a separate county since 1373, had 800 households 'desolate vacant and decayed' in 1518. It had flourished mightily in the middle decades of the fifteenth century as the secure harbour from which to export the cloths made in its large hinterland and through which Bordeaux wine and products from as far away as the Mediterranean and Iceland were imported. In later years, Bristol's leading merchants sponsored John Cabot's voyages of discovery to the New World. A fine bridge over the river Avon contained houses and shops on each side, and numerous religious buildings, the halls and chapels of the craft guilds, and timber-framed merchants' houses dominated the townscape. Bristol had 18 parish churches, 4 friaries, a priory and an Augustinian monastery that was converted into a cathedral in the 1540s. But the most splendid building of all was the church of St Mary Redcliffe, arguably the most impressive in the land, a cruciform structure vaulted throughout and finished with an elegant spire, much of it paid for by William Canynges, the wealthiest of all the late-medieval merchants and ship-owners of Bristol.[35]

The cloth industry remained vital to the prosperity of numerous English towns, yet the disruption of the export of wool during the Hundred Years War with France had encouraged the development of weaving as a rural industry in pastoral parts of the South West, East Anglia and the West Riding to such an extent that towns such as Coventry and Salisbury lost much of their trade. One York mayor thought that the West Riding clothiers had proved too competitive for the merchants and manufacturers of his city because they had the advantage of water-powered fulling mills and a workforce of spinners, carders and weavers who were able to keep a few animals on their smallholdings and who had little expense in maintaining themselves; unlike the people of York, whose provisions were dear and hard to come by. By the end of the fifteenth century, the export of wool to foreign merchants had declined to a mere trickle and the great days of the once-flourishing ports of Boston and King's Lynn were over. In their place arose a new breed of merchant who dealt with finished cloth, which was exported through London, Bristol, Exeter, Hull, Poole and Southampton.

In Suffolk, the market town of Lavenham was one of the most important industrial and manufacturing centres in England.[36] Although the cloth industry was already well established there in the early fourteenth century, the success of Lavenham was not based on the local wool. Suffolk had few natural advantages and its wool was thought to be inferior to that of most other counties. As Thomas Fuller observed in the seventeenth century, counties like Leicestershire, Lincolnshire, Northamptonshire and Cambridgeshire 'had most of wool, had least of clothing'.[37] Human initiative, particularly in the form of encouragement from the powerful de Veres, Earls of Oxford and lords of the principal manor of Lavenham, seems to have been all-important in the local cloth industry's development in its formative years. By the 1460s, Suffolk was at the forefront of the English cloth trade, and by the first half of the sixteenth century Lavenham was one of the richest manufacturing centres in England, with a flourishing business dominated by its leading families: Spryng, Braunche, Grome, Jacob and Sexteyn. This new wealth allowed the rebuilding of Lavenham parish church in splendid style from about 1485 to the 1520s. The coats of arms and merchants' marks of the leading families were displayed for all to see, but hundreds of other local people contributed according to their means. The wealth of the late-medieval town is also evident in its remarkable collection of high-quality, timber-framed buildings, including two guildhalls and numerous open halls that have since been subdivided and provided with rooms above a ceiling. An outstanding example on the edge of the market place is Little Hall, dated by the tree rings in a gable to 1390, with a fine crown-post roof. Lavenham was not short of space and so the houses were laid out parallel with the streets, rather than at right angles to them.

Lavenham's clothiers used credit to conduct their business of making and selling cloth. They dealt with the merchants of Blackwell Hall, London, and many of their products ended up in Flanders and Holland. The industry was a domestic one, with men, women and children working mainly in their own homes as employees of the clothiers. During the 1520s, at least 58 per cent of the workforce in Lavenham were involved in the cloth industry, a higher proportion in a single trade than in any other town in England at that time. Another third of the working population of Lavenham in 1522 were employed at the usual retail trades, crafts and services of Tudor market towns: tailors, bakers, butchers, millers, barbers, smiths, chandlers, tanners, shoemakers, scriveners, and so on. In 1524 Lavenham was the fourteenth-wealthiest town in England, with many prosperous families, yet in the following year the church bells were rung to 'rouse the district' in a mass protest against another heavy tax at a time of declining trade. The tower of Lavenham church was never topped with pinnacles; that at East Bergholt was raised only a few feet off the ground and remains a ruin to this day.

In 1334, 16 of England's 25 leading provincial towns lay in the eastern half of the country. Two hundred years later, the balance was substantially the same, though some towns had moved up or down the order. By

FIGURE 6 *Lavenham retains much of its character from its hey-day as a prosperous late-medieval clothing town.*

continental standards, English towns were small. Beyond London, only three towns – Norwich, Bristol and Newcastle-upon-Tyne – had over 10,000 inhabitants, and fewer than a dozen others had between 5,000 and 10,000.[38] When he visited Newcastle in about 1540, John Leland commented that the strength and magnificence of the walling of the town far passed all the walls of the cities of England and of most of the towns of Europe.[39] This flourishing port on the Tyne exported wool, cloth, hides and sheepskins from the uplands to the west.

In the late Middle Ages, England's overseas trade was relatively unimportant in the economy as a whole: the internal market was probably at least ten times as large, possibly twice as much as that. Provincial towns had an impressive range of trades and crafts, with large numbers of men employed in the three basic groups – clothing, food and drink, and building. Northampton and Leicester, Midland towns with about 3,000 people each in the 1520s, had 63 and 60 different trades respectively. Coventry, which was twice as large, had 90, while York, Bristol and Norwich each had about 100.[40] The market place remained the hub of towns both large and small. Tudor England had some 760 markets, the majority of them serving a neighbourhood of only a few miles, for society remained intensely local.[41]

Yet most towns were known for a particular speciality. Brine was boiled to produce salt on a large scale at Droitwich in Worcestershire, and at Northwich, Middlewich and Nantwich in Cheshire, from where carriers followed well-established salt ways or salter gates to the market towns of central and northern England. Sheffield was already famous for its cheap cutlery, though it had provincial rivals such as Thaxted and Salisbury to contend with, and it could not compete at the quality end of the market with the cutlers of London.

Each trade was entered either through learning from a father who was a qualified master or by serving an apprenticeship, after which a man could set up on his own or work as a journeyman. The hours of work, regulated by the statute of 1495 and 1515, decreed that between 15 March and 15 September the wage-earner should arrive before five o'clock in the morning and continue his toil until seven or eight o'clock in the evening. Out of this time, he was allowed half an hour for his breakfast, and an hour and a half for his dinner and afternoon sleep. During the rest of the year, he was expected to work from dawn till dusk. In reality, working practices varied from place to place, though the hours at work were always long; in 1496, for example, the master-cappers of Coventry fixed a 12-hour day from six o'clock in the morning. Of course, the pace of work was slow, with frequent pauses for talk; underemployment was common; and the number of official holidays was large by modern standards. Work was not an unremitting grind.[42]

The inhabitants of England's medieval towns formed only about 10 per cent of the national population. Before the Industrial Revolution, most English towns remained small by Continental standards. As yet, they were not divorced from the surrounding countryside, and their fields and meadows could usually be seen from the market place.

Early modern towns

In the second half of Elizabeth's reign, some old-established towns, like Stamford and Winchester, continued to decay, but others began to prosper again. The port of Bristol benefited from the cloth trade of its hinterland, and by the 1580s York merchants and tradesmen too were prospering from the general revival of trade throughout western Europe. Young immigrants from the Yorkshire Dales, the Vale of York and the northwestern counties came in search of work there as tradesmen, craftsmen, shopkeepers and labourers, and York's markets flourished once again. Baltic iron, pitch, tar, flax, boards, wainscotting, salt, grain, oil, wine, sea fish and eels were brought up the river Ouse to be distributed far and wide, and the boats returned ladened with lead from the Yorkshire Dales.[43] At the same time, inland ports such as Stockton, Bawtry and Doncaster were revitalized, and Hull flourished once more as an international port.

The leading provincial towns were active in internal trade and in retailing and handicrafts. Urban industries were generally more broadly based than before, though a few towns that had previously been of little importance flourished by concentrating on one or two industries. Some West Riding towns acquired a decidedly industrial character during Elizabeth's reign. Broad cloths were finished by expert dressers, croppers and dyers in Leeds, the principal market for wool was at Wakefield, but the wonder of the age was Halifax. William Camden thought:

> There is nothing so admirable in this town as the industry of the inhabitants, who notwithstanding unprofitable soil, not fit to live in, have so flourished by the cloth trade (which within these last seventy years they fell to), that they are both very rich, and have gained a great reputation for it above their neighbours.[44]

Further south, Sheffield became the leading provincial centre for the manufacture of cutlery. In 1608 a courtier wrote to the Earl of Shrewsbury about his forthcoming visit to Sheffield and joked that he expected to be 'half choked with town smoke'. In 1624 a Cutlers' Company replaced the manor court as the body that regulated the trade throughout 'the country called Hallamshire', and by the middle of the seventeenth century well over half the workforce of the large parish of Sheffield was directly involved in the manufacture of knives and scissors, and some of the surrounding communities were specializing in such products as scythes, sickles, forks or nails. Hallamshire provides a classic example of how the nature of the work created a distinctive local society. Its cutlers had the inestimable advantage of water power for grinding; by 1660, metalworkers were the tenants of two out of every three of the 49 water wheels on Sheffield's streams. In 1662 Thomas Fuller observed that most of the common knives of country people were made in Sheffield and that it was a matter of wonder 'how a knife may be sold for one penny'. Sheffield was a cutlery town long before it became Steel City.[45]

The first reliable urban plans and views that were made in the sixteenth and seventeenth centuries reveal that most of the larger English towns were still enclosed within their medieval walls. The main use of the walls now was to keep out beggars, toll evaders and those suspected of carrying plague, rather than for military purposes, though in 1569 the York walls prevented rebels led by the Northern Earls from entering the city. Elizabeth's government, convinced of their usefulness for defence, rebuilt the elaborate walls of Berwick-on-Tweed and Portsmouth. Fine examples of timber-framed Elizabethan town houses can still be found in many English towns, for example, Ireland's mansion (c.1575) and Owen's mansion (1592) in Shrewsbury. A series of disastrous fires in diverse small towns, such as Oswestry (1564, 1567), Portsmouth (1576), Nantwich (1583), Darlington (1585) and Stratford (1594 and 1595), encouraged some local authorities to ban thatch as a roofing material, for example in Norwich (1570), Bristol (1574) and Cambridge (1619), but wood usually remained the preferred building material for houses well into the seventeenth century.[46]

A typical county town such as Derby housed just 2,000–2,500 people, but most of the 500 or 600 market towns of Elizabethan England were only half that size or less. Such places were craft and retail centres that depended on the agriculture of the surrounding countryside, and they were urban in character only on market days and at the annual fairs. They were well endowed with gardens, and their open fields, meadows and pastures could be seen from the market place. England remained an under-populated, rural country, with less than 10 per cent of its population living in towns.

In the 1660s the leading provincial towns in terms of the size of their population were Norwich, York, Bristol, Newcastle, Exeter, Ipswich, Great Yarmouth, Oxford, Cambridge, Canterbury, Worcester, Deptford, Shrewsbury, Salisbury, Colchester, Greenwich, Hull, Coventry, Chester and Plymouth.[47] The eighteenth century was a time of civic pride when new public buildings such as theatres, concert halls and assembly rooms were built, and rows of Georgian houses with symmetrical frontages were arranged in squares and approached by paved footpaths and streets lit with oil lamps. This new taste in polite architecture came with increased wealth and the growth of leisure and learning. The classical style was adopted throughout the land, but places retained their distinctive identities through their use of a variety of local building materials.[48] Bath and Stamford owe a great deal of their character to the use of good-quality local limestone, while other towns, such as Ashbourne, are characterized by the use of local, hand-made bricks. Further east, the drainage of the Fens turned Wisbech into a prosperous market town and port. The brick Georgian architecture along The North Brink, on the bank of the river Nene, reflects the wealth of the eighteenth-century merchants.

Oxford and Cambridge remained the only English university towns, catering mostly for those who wished to enter the Anglican ministry. Although the number of students declined, this was an era of noble new buildings. At Oxford, Wren designed the Sheldonian Theatre and Christ Church's Tom Tower, and at Cambridge the Library for Trinity College. The eighteenth century saw the erection of some of Oxford's finest buildings, including the Radcliffe Camera, designed by James Gibbs, and major classical structures at The Queen's College, Magdalen College, All Souls College, and Christ Church. Both Oxford and Cambridge have numerous elegant buildings from the Georgian era.

The fashion for a new type of town, the spa, which offered health cures based on the supposed healing properties of sulphur and chalybeate springs, spread from the Low Countries and Germany to Bath, Epsom, Wells, Tunbridge Wells and the northern resorts of Buxton, Matlock Bath, Harrogate and Scarborough. Sea bathing was an added attraction at Scarborough, which was the first place in England where it became popular.

The inhabitants of the spa towns doubled during the season, when well-to-do families, their servants, and dependent traders, physicians, and the like came to take the waters. Most of the entertainments on offer were fashioned on those of London, and it is no coincidence that Epsom and Tunbridge Wells were reasonably close to the capital. People flocked there for a long weekend to partake of a holiday camp atmosphere. Bath remained a rather dowdy town until the beginning of the eighteenth century, when it began to be transformed into the most fashionable of the spas.[49]

On her various tours in the 1690s, Celia Fiennes found thriving towns to admire, declaring Nottingham 'the neatest town I have seen, built of stone and delicate large and long Streetes much like London and the houses lofty and well built, the Market place is very broad'. Ipswich was 'a very clean town' with twelve churches and streets of a good size, 'well pitch'd with small stones'; the Market Place at Leicester was 'a large space very handsome with a good Market Cross and Town Hall'; and Northampton was 'a large town well built, the streetes as large as most in London except Holborn and the Strand, the houses well built of brick and stone'.[50]

Meanwhile, the old market towns of Manchester, Birmingham, Leeds and Sheffield were emerging as specialized industrial centres. By the middle of the seventeenth century, Manchester's trade was said to be:

> not inferior to that of many cities in the kingdom, chiefly consisting in woollen friezes, fustians, sack-cloths, mingled stuffs, caps, inkles, tapes, points, etc, whereby not only the better sort of men are employed but also the very children by their own labour can maintain themselves.[51]

Raw cotton was imported at first into London from the Levant, then during the second quarter of the seventeenth century it was brought from the East and West Indies. By the early eighteenth century, American and West Indian cotton came through Bristol, Lancaster and Liverpool. Defoe noted that the Bristol merchants 'not only have the greatest trade, but they trade with a more entire independency upon London, than any other town in Britain'. The shopkeepers had 'so great an inland trade that they maintain carriers just as the London tradesmen do, from all the principal countries and towns from Southampton in the south, even to the banks of the Trent north'. Defoe regarded the merchants of Bristol as, 'Whatsoever exportations they make to any part of the world, they are able to bring the full returns back to their own port, and can dispose of it there.'

Defoe thought that Liverpool was 'one of the wonders of Britain' with 'an opulent, flourishing and increasing trade'. Other than London, no town in England could equal Liverpool for the splendour of its streets and buildings. Newcastle-upon-Tyne was also 'a spacious, extended, infinitely populous place' with 'a noble, large and deep river', which allowed 'ships of any reasonable burthen' to 'come safely up to the very town'.[52] Metalworking districts such as Newcastle enjoyed a boom period from the late seventeenth century onwards. By 1700, Birmingham had about 7,000 inhabitants, while the population of the central urban township of Sheffield rose from 2,207 in 1616 to 10,121 in 1736.[53] Some other industrial towns and villages also grew, but it was not until after 1700 that the pace quickened.

The royal dockyard towns developed in an equally dramatic way. During the sixteenth century, the main ones had been at Deptford and Woolwich on the river Thames. These continued to expand, but by 1640 Chatham had become the leading government dockyard with a range of dry-docks, forts and other works at the mouth of the river Medway. Portsmouth, too, developed during the wars with Holland and France later in the seventeenth century, and smaller dockyard towns grew at Falmouth, Plymouth, Sheerness and Harwich. The population of all these places rose and fell in times of war and peace, though Deptford had a fairly constant population of 4,000–5,000 by the 1660s, and Chatham grew to over 5,000 by 1700, a five-fold increase during the course of the seventeenth century. They had much in common with the new industrial towns of the North and the Midlands.[54]

After the Great Fire of London, the City was rebuilt very quickly. John Ogilby's survey of 1676 depicts a crowded scene, but the old layout of the streets had been improved and strict building regulations were enforced. A new, larger Royal Exchange had been opened, most of the livery companies had rebuilt their halls, and work was soon to begin on the new cathedral. A map of 1682 shows Westminster as a western suburb, with narrow alleys, yards and courts clustered around the Abbey and Houses of Parliament, but with many fine houses encroaching upon the surrounding fields. Whitehall, too, was becoming more residential. The St James's Square development started in the 1670s, and the open fields between Piccadilly and modern Oxford Street became criss-crossed with streets. But when a map of London and its suburbs was drawn in 1717, the western expansion had not got as far as Chelsea and Kensington. By the time that John Rocque's map of London was published in 1746, however, the West End included newly laid-out squares – Berkeley, Hanover, Grosvenor – with grid patterns of streets and imposing town houses for the landed aristocracy, courtiers and successful city financiers. London grew so rapidly that by the middle of the eighteenth century it had become the largest city in Europe. No other English town came anywhere near it in size and importance. By 1700 the inhabitants of the City and its burgeoning suburbs numbered about 490,000; by 1750 they totalled about 675,000.[55]

London had become a centre of conspicuous consumption and the capital of high fashion. Many of its citizens had money to spend, for one in four of them were middle class, compared with only about one in twenty of the inhabitants of the leading provincial towns. London's merchants, wholesalers and financiers were far richer than their counterparts in the provinces, and the City's shopkeepers traded on a completely different scale. The services offered by professionals, especially in the law and medicine, grew significantly, and the middle classes joined the members of the Court and the aristocrats and gentlemen who came to town for the season as patrons of musicians, painters and writers.

During the eighteenth century, London's suburbs spread far beyond the City walls. Wapping, for example, became a major centre for the victualling and supplying of the thousands of ships that arrived in the Thames from many parts of the world. The wharfs and quays along the river catered for the new colonial trades such as sugar refining, through which some merchants acquired great wealth. Many migrant labourers and seamen were housed along the mile-long Wapping Wall, east of Tower Hill, yet wealthy and middling merchants lived in the same suburb. London had not yet become a socially segregated city, with great extremes of wealth and poverty dividing the West and East Ends. Nevertheless, the capital city had a reputation for criminal activity and for the harsh treatment that was handed out for relatively minor offences. At the infamous gallows at Tyburn, 1,242 men and women were hanged on 243 'hanging days' between 1703 and 1772, with an average of three or four public hanging days a year, but with sometimes up to eight.[56] Everything in London was on a much larger scale than in the other cities and towns of provincial England.

CHAPTER FOUR

Organizing the countryside:

Villages, hamlets and farmsteads

The origins of villages

The old belief that present-day English villages date back to the time of the earliest Anglo-Saxon settlers has long been discredited. Archaeological evidence has shown that most of the original settlers lived in scattered farmsteads or hamlets, much like the natives did, and that villages were unknown in their homelands. Only a few early settlements that were large enough to be thought of as small villages, and which were ultimately abandoned, have been discovered by excavation.

At West Stow, in the Lark Valley on the heathlands of northwest Suffolk, a group of buildings has been reconstructed on excavated sites, using tools and techniques that would have been familiar to the original inhabitants. The trees were split with wedges and shaped into planks and beams with an axe. Charred timbers that were found in the excavations reveal that wide oak planks were used as walls and floorboards, and thatched roofs were supported by ash and hazel frames. The original settlement there had three groups of houses that supported a total population of about 60. Each group may have housed an extended family, with a communal, rectangular hall as their meeting place. The site seems to have been occupied from the early fifth century until about 650, so many buildings were replaced over time and new ones were added. In all, 69 houses, seven halls and seven other structures have been identified from their post-holes in the sandy soil. We cannot be certain that the people who lived there were Anglo-Saxon settlers rather than native British people, but this small farming community seems to have fared well and to have traded with the wider world in wool, cloth and hides.

The present village of West Stow stands a mile to the east by the parish church, but its foundation date is not known.[1]

Ongoing excavations and surveys led by Dominic Powlesland at West Heslerton, where the Yorkshire Wolds descend into the Vale of Pickering, have produced a great deal of evidence for a larger settlement, which was occupied continuously from about 380 CE to about 850, when the site was abandoned. It is estimated that about 75 people lived there at any one time, within ten houses that were centred on one of the halls. The post-holes of over 150 timber-framed buildings, each with a rectangular ground plan rather than a native roundhouse, have been discovered, together with numerous, sunken structures that served as granaries and outbuildings. No grand buildings have been found, so perhaps this was a village of ordinary farmers each of whom lived in a house that was up to 30 feet long by 15 feet broad. The contemporary cemetery just beyond the village has been excavated completely; like many other early Anglo-Saxon burial grounds, the skeletons show no evidence of violent death in warfare.[2]

The inhabitants of West Heslerton appear to have been generally healthy, though the average lifespan was not much more than 40 years. It came as a surprise when scientific analysis revealed that some of the bodies that were accompanied by swords were female, and that others adorned with beads and brooches were sometimes male. But who were the ancestors of these people? The new technique of stable isotope analysis, which determines where people spent their early years by an examination of their teeth enamel, does not support the idea that settlements such as this consisted largely of marauding warriors and settlers from across the North Sea. Most of the skeletons that have been examined were of people who had grown up locally or who had migrated from the west; only a very few came from the Continent.

English villages as we know them were created in a long drawn-out process that extended from the mid-Anglo-Saxon period to well after the Norman Conquest. The huge expansion of developer-funded rescue excavation during the past three decades has produced such an abundance of raw primary evidence that the accumulation of data ran far ahead of analysis until John Blair trawled through the mass of journal articles and unpublished reports. The results of his work have cast a whole new light on the origins of villages. First, he has clarified the regional contrasts in building culture by showing that between about 650 and 850 the 'ordinary' settlements were concentrated almost exclusively in a zone of eastern England comprising Lincolnshire and Norfolk – essentially the river-catchment basin of the Wash – together with parts of east Yorkshire. The contrast between the material culture of this area and the rest of England is very apparent. This finding challenges the prevailing view that a 'Central Province' of classic Midland nucleated villages and open-fields had developed by this time, though the possibility remains that, between say 1000 and 1200, the one morphed into the other.[3]

John Blair's second conclusion is that quite astonishingly large areas of grid-planning can be recognized within the zone that he has identified between c.650 and 850, and that the interpretation of the layout of fields, farms and settlements in all later periods will need to take account of it. Newly identified cases such as Stotfold (Bedfordshire) represent a settlement pattern that was neither fully nucleated nor fully dispersed, but which comprised extensive, low-density but structured groups of farmsteads spaced out at intervals of between 100 and 150 metres, using a standard module of four by four perches. Although these settlements were planned, they were very different from the later row-plan villages that represent a new phase of planning between c.1050 and 1200.

The strikingly regular plans of villages that were founded either just before or after the Norman Conquest are still evident on the ground today. The most common scheme was to create two parallel rows of farmhouses facing each other across the village street or green, with plots of equal size stretching behind each row as far as a back lane, which led to the communal arable fields and to the common pastures beyond, but many variants were designed to suit local conditions. In no case do we have documents that inform us precisely when a new village was created. The regularity of their plans suggests enforcement by major landowners or by local lords of the manor.[4]

Many other villages seem to have been formed not by deliberate planning but by the gradual merging together of small clusters of scattered farms. The major research programmes at Wharram Percy on the Yorkshire Wolds and at Raunds and Whittlewood in Northamptonshire have been influential in promoting this view.[5] The dispersed settlements of the early Anglo-Saxons were established within a framework of large units, known to historians as 'multiple estates' or 'folk territories', some of which were perhaps already ancient when the invaders arrived. From the tenth century onwards, these estates began to be broken into numerous small, independent manors, many of whose lords gave their names to the settlements that they controlled from their manor houses. These lords were normally resident and they made sure that their peasants paid full dues and worked the prescribed number of days ploughing, sowing, weeding and harvesting the demesne lands and paying duty to have their corn ground at the manorial mill.

As Mick Aston and Chris Gerrard remarked, 'There is nothing unalterable about the English countryside' and there are 'periods when human activity is more intensive and others when it seems barely perceptible.' Their intensive archaeological investigation of the 'ladder-like' plan of the village of Shapwick pointed to a tenth-century origin. A date between 947 and 957 seems most likely on historical grounds because it was in that decade that Glastonbury Abbey was re-founded under Abbot Dunstan. The whole of the core of the modern village was in use and occupied in the late Saxon period and no part of the village seems to have been occupied before the others.[6]

By far the largest numbers of Anglo-Saxon settlement names that date from after Bede's history, which was completed in 731, are those that end in *-ton* or *-ley*. A *-tun* was a farmstead that often grew into a village surrounded by its arable fields, whereas a *-leah* was a clearing in a wood, or a wood pasture, including grassy spots that had been denuded of many of their trees and shrubs well before the arrival of the Anglo-Saxons, perhaps by grazing animals rather than by deliberate felling. The first element of these names was often the personal name of the man who in later times would be known as the lord of the manor. Some of these village names changed when a Viking lord acquired the manor. In the Danelaw, the names of the larger settlements ended in *-by* and those of the smaller ones in *-thorpe*, while clearings in the landscape were known by the Old Norse word *-thwaite*. This evidence has to be treated with caution, however, for we now realize that our present place-names do not always go back to the foundation of settlements. Some places were settled long before they acquired the name by which we know them. Archaeologists and historians now emphasize continuity and gradual evolution over long periods of time rather than rapid change brought about by invaders with a different culture from the Continent.

Although villages are regarded as an essential part of the rural English scene, in some regions they are far outnumbered by hamlets and isolated farmsteads. Villages are found particularly in a 'Central Province' running down from Northumberland to Dorset, where farmers grew cereals in communal open fields that were divided into strips.[7] The old view was that the open-field village was the superior form of settlement and that other systems were not fully developed, but it is now accepted that hamlets and scattered farmsteads were well adapted to pastoral farming and that open-field villages were a late development on arable land, especially the heavy clay soils of the Midlands and neighbouring limestone belts.

The practicalities of the open-field system were spelt out long ago.[8] The large open fields were divided into long strips so that a plough-team of oxen did not have to be turned too often; the narrow width of the strips was determined by the amount of land that could be ploughed in a day's work; and the inverted and elongated 'S' shape of the strips allowed the ox-plough teams to turn when they reached the headland. The characteristic ridge-and-furrow patterns of this type of landscape helped to drain the land. The landscape had a rather bare appearance, for it contained neither fences nor hedges; the only markers were the stones or staves at the ends of the strips. A peasant with a 'yardland' of 30 acres had to travel to at least 60 (and more likely 100) strips that were dispersed over the fields, some of them more than a mile from his home, so that everyone had his share of good and bad land. Co-operation was necessary because a team of eight oxen was needed on the heaviest soils. This resulted in the strict rotation of crops in two of the three open fields, while the other one was left fallow, both to recuperate and to provide common grazing under the regulations that were agreed at the manor court. The two or three large open fields that were characteristic of villages in the central belt of England were typically divided into furlongs for cropping purposes, with the individual strips of each farmer scattered within them. Woodland and common pasture were in short supply. In some parishes by 1300 more than nine-tenths of the land lay in the communal arable fields.

The belief that open-field systems developed from simpler forms has become widely accepted. So has the idea of regional diversity. In 1983 Mary Harvey demonstrated the marked regularity of the open fields of Holderness in east Yorkshire, whose long, parallel 'lands' were often over 1,000 yards long, and in some townships over a mile long. These 'lands' were arranged in just two fields, which acted as the cropping units. The fields were sub-divided into a few large furlongs of identical structure. Each furlong had the same number of lands and each contained a similar proportion of broad and narrow lands, which lay in the same relative position to each other. She concluded that a powerful lord or lords had planned the system.[9] David Hall's extensive fieldwork and documentary research in Northamptonshire has shown that there, too, long lands were an early feature of field systems that by the twelfth century had developed into classic Midland open fields. He believes that they were of eighth- or ninth-century origin and that they were laid out in a deliberate act of planning. In some townships, the boundaries of the original furlongs can still be recognized.[10]

Sometimes the strips were allotted in the strict manner known as 'sun-division', so that each peasant got a fair share of good and poor soils facing south or north. Their existence adds to the evidence that the laying out of open fields was a planned operation, but we do not know who was responsible. Did strong lordship produce these common fields? Unfortunately, documentary evidence is sparse (and often non-existent) for the period when open-field systems began. Open-field systems were still evolving in the Norman period, but we have little information about them until the later Middle Ages.

Tom Williamson has argued that the concentration of open fields in the 'Central Province' of England could be explained only by environmental factors and practical farming decisions. Subtle differences in soils and micro-climates explained why they developed on the heavy clay soils of Midland counties such as Leicestershire and Northamptonshire but not in the adjacent and well-populated counties of East Anglia and the South East. The short period that was available for ploughing the heavy, water-retentive soils that characterize the Midlands meant that plough-teams had to be assembled quickly, so it helped to have farms in close proximity, rather than scattered across the landscape. Co-operation was also necessary on soils overlying limestone, where water came only from springs. Practical considerations such as this seem a more likely explanation for the development of open-field villages than the previous emphasis on cultural factors and population growth.[11]

The supposed superiority of the nucleated village surrounded by its extensive open fields is readily dismissed when we turn to Kent and East

Anglia, the most prosperous and populous parts of medieval England. Here, farmers who made their own decisions, with few communal regulations, grew corn on a commercial scale in a mixture of irregular open fields and closes.

Meanwhile, even in the corn-growing lands of the central belt, some parishes were farmed on different systems from that of their neighbours. A study of the twelve parishes of the royal Forest of Whittlewood on the borders of Northamptonshire and Buckinghamshire, led by Richard Jones and Mark Page, has shown that the Crown retained core blocks of pasture and woodland throughout the Middle Ages, and that peasant farmers lived in scattered farmsteads as well as villages and hamlets. This district had a great deal more woodland and waste than did neighbouring areas, and some of its agricultural land lay outside the open fields, in closes that were farmed individually with an equal emphasis on cereals and livestock.[12]

No documents survive to prove whether or not the re-planning of a village coincided with the rearranging of the surrounding arable fields into a communal open-field system, but late Anglo-Saxon charters sometimes reveal that open-field systems already stretched as far as the boundaries of a township or parish, and archaeological surveys have shown that associated ridge-and-furrow patterns overlie, and therefore post-date, spreads of earlier Anglo-Saxon pottery. In Whittlewood, the laying-out of open fields in the tenth century was a quite separate process from the re-planning of settlements, which for the most part occurred in the centuries after the Norman Conquest.

Many of the villages of County Durham and the Vales of York, Mowbray and Pickering still have a regular appearance that denote their planned origins in the decades following the Conqueror's infamous 'Harrying of the North'. At Appleton-le-Moors, near Pickering, where the manorial lord was the Abbot of St Mary's, York, the houses face each other across a street with only narrow grass verges in front of them. The strict regularity of its village plan is evident also in the crofts that extend to the two back lanes, which run parallel to the main street and form a boundary between the village and its fields. Some of the crofts have merged into larger units over the centuries, but the original pattern can still be seen. Elsewhere, the curious position of a parish church beyond the regular plan of a village may suggest that the original settlement stood alongside it.[13] In Derbyshire, for example, St Giles's church at Great Longstone stands on a knoll above the houses that are depicted on a map of 1617 in a regular pattern on both sides of the village green.[14]

After the Norman Conquest the documentary evidence for settlements becomes much fuller. Unique in Europe in its time, Domesday Book is the earliest systematic survey of England. Most English villages are named in its pages and in very many cases the Domesday Book entry is the first documentary source that we have for a particular place. It is clear that England was already an old country before the Normans arrived. Most of the land had been farmed for hundreds, if not thousands, of years, and many of the estate and field boundaries were already ancient. It is also evident that England was a land of great diversity, and that the richest and most-populated counties were Norfolk, Suffolk and Kent, the eastern counties that benefited from trade with the Continent. The amount of land that was cultivated at the time of the Norman Conquest or the acreage set aside as pasture, meadow or woodland was not much different from now. Yet the national population is estimated to have been no more than two-and-a-quarter million.

In the thirteenth and fourteenth centuries, documentary records at both the national and the local level became much fuller. Detailed tax lists survive from 1225 onwards, and those of the lay subsidies of the 1320s and 1330s and the poll taxes of 1377–81 are particularly informative. The earliest manorial accounts date from 1208, and manor court records start in the 1230s and become widespread later in the century. From the 1270s onwards, we can find information about ordinary people from thousands of charters and deeds and hundreds of surveys, tax lists, court rolls and bishops' registers as national and local administration moved from an oral to a written culture. England is exceptional in having such detailed local records from this early period.

Hamlets and farmsteads

Most medieval people did not live in nucleated villages surrounded by open fields. At the same time as this system was becoming established in the corn-growing lands of the Midlands, very different patterns of land use were developed in the rest of England, especially where the emphasis was more on livestock than on crops, and most families lived in isolated farms and hamlets rather than in villages.

In recent years, historians and archaeologists have transformed our understanding of the ancient landscape of the South West. When the great pioneer historian of the English landscape, William Hoskins, wrote about his native county of Devon, villages were thought to be 'early', and the scattered settlements that are so characteristic of the South West were regarded as 'late'. This assumption was largely based on the testimony of Domesday Book, but we now know that this is an incomplete record of the population, for the numerous free tenants of Devon and Cornwall were not usually listed. Hoskins assumed that their farms were created in the twelfth and thirteenth centuries, when the national population was rising, but the evidence of their names, many of which were derived from Old English personal names, suggests that they were much earlier. A change of fashion in favour of French personal names was well established by 1150, and probably much earlier amongst freemen.

Harold Fox's documentary research demonstrated continuity of settlement in the South West from well before the Norman Conquest. One of his examples was the Devon manor of Ashwater, whose Domesday Book entry noted 40 villeins and 12 bordars, with six slaves attached to the demesne. A manorial survey of 1346 recorded 38 privileged, though unfree, tenants and 13 serfs, with six cottages at the churchtown, near the demesne. The comparable numbers suggest that the settlement pattern had been established there in the pre-Conquest period. The many important changes in the rural landscapes of the South West that were made in the twelfth and thirteenth centuries were brought about by the colonization of the flanks of the high moorlands, in localities such as Cholwich, which Hoskins described in detail. The origins of the hamlet of Dunnabridge on the edge of Dartmoor can be dated to 1306, when five men started to pay rent for 19⅕ acres each, which they had taken in from 'the waste of the king', and which they promised to lime in the following year; the strip pattern of their new arable fields survived until the seventeenth century.[15]

The dispersed settlements and sprawling hamlets that characterize the South West were farmed under a mixture of open and enclosed field systems that were clearly established by the tenth or eleventh centuries, when they are mentioned in charter boundary clauses. Peter Herring, who has led the archaeological work on the rural Cornish landscape, notes that radiocarbon dating has started to reveal features of the wider picture, including lower-status settlements, which suggest a continuation of the late prehistoric/Romano-British tradition of enclosed settlements into the sixth century. But then we enter a dark period with a break in evidence before documentary sources begin. Herring observes that the fields that are derived from prehistoric antecedents tend to be on and around the West Penwith, Lizard and Bodmin Moor uplands, leaving well over half of Cornwall with an enclosed landscape that was formed in the medieval period.[16]

The old myth that the landscape of the South West was created by independently minded Celts has been demolished. Fox showed from documentary evidence that subdivided or strip fields were widespread in medieval Cornwall and Devon, but they were very different in form from the classic two- or three-field systems of Midland England. The southwestern settlements were generally nucleated hamlets rather than villages, the communal fields were small, and they were farmed on a convertible husbandry system of arable and grass rather than regular rotations of cereals. Labour services on the manor were less important than in Midland England, money payments probably more so. The recognition of the importance of resource sharing and co-operation between the member households of hamlets, generated from below rather than imposed from above, has been crucial to an understanding of the development of Cornish landscape and society. Vestiges of former communal fields are not easy to recognize on the ground, except in a few isolated instances, for enclosure occurred much earlier than in other parts of England. Most of these fields disappeared in the thirteenth and fourteenth centuries, and few were left by the sixteenth century.

FIGURE 7 *Long Tom Cross, St Cleer, Cornwall.*

Much remains unclear or controversial. Stephen Rippon's work on the Somerset Levels and elsewhere has led him to argue that the transformation of the southwestern landscape began as early as 680–830 within a framework of greater territorial stability. Archaeological and paleobotanical evidence suggests that this was a period of innovation, after which very little change occurred in the pollen record until the post-medieval period. He concludes that English villages and open fields emerged over a long period, with marked regional variation.[17]

As the open-field villages of Midland England grew in size to accommodate the rising population in the centuries after the Norman Conquest, so the hamlets and farmsteads spread further on to the wastes. This clearing of new land on the moorland edges brought fresh concerns. The inhabitants of neighbouring townships became increasingly fractious over where the boundaries of their commons lay and the precise nature of their rights where wastes were inter-commoned. A medieval boundary marker known as Long Tom Cross, on the edge of Bodmin Moor in the parish of St Cleer, is typical of the tall, granite stones, some inscribed with a cross, that were erected in the South West. Cornwall has about 700 surviving medieval stone crosses and Devon about 300.[18]

Another landscape that is very different from that of the clay vales of the Midlands is found in the large parishes that straddled the Pennines. At 8,116 acres, Thurlstone was the largest of the eight townships of Penistone parish, and no fewer than 6,522 of these acres were classified as commons and wastes before their enclosure in 1812–16. Thurlstone combined the Old Danish personal name *Thurulf*, with the Anglo-Saxon suffix *-tun*, for the Vikings had taken over an existing settlement and named it after their local lord. The regular plan of the village, with the crofts and tofts of the farmhouses in Town Gate stretching back to communal boundary lines, can still be traced on the ground. Judging by other examples, it was probably laid out after the Norman Conquest. Two small, communal townfields, divided into strips on the best arable land, lay immediately west and east of the village. They survived until 1696–9, when the 26 farmers who owned strips agreed to enclose them. The narrow, curving pattern of the former strips is preserved by many of the walls in the former West Field.[19]

As the population expanded in the twelfth and thirteenth centuries, new land was assarted from the wastes beyond these townfields, with the willing co-operation of the lord of the manor who received new rents. Here, as in much of the West Riding, these assarts can be recognized by the minor place-name *royd*, a local pronunciation of the more widespread Old English *rod*, meaning a woodland or moorland-edge clearing. Three of the farms that stand immediately beyond Thurlstone's West Field bear the name Royd. This dialect word has a distinct regional identity, bounded by the River Wharfe in the north and Hallamshire in the south, though it spread across the Pennines into east Lancashire. George Redmonds has identified 40 *royds* in the township of Almondbury, a few miles north of Thurlstone. Almost half of them had a personal name as the first element. Some were Old English or Old Norse in character, but many more were Middle English names dating from about 1175 to 1350. *Royd* was not used for new clearances after the Black Death, so it is a good indicator of the date range.[20]

The Old Norse term for a township was *bierlow*. A few miles from Thurlstone, within the huge lordship of Hallamshire, the soke of Bradfield was divided into four of these units. It was common practice throughout the lordship for farmers to hold some of their land by freehold and the rest by copyhold. Copyhold tenures were sometimes recorded as either 'hastler' or 'mattock' land. The tenants of 'hastler' land – a term that was seemingly derived from the Latin word for 'spear' – were the occupiers of the ancient farms and the ones from whom the various officers such as the constable were chosen. By contrast, mattock land took its name from the tool that was used for grubbing up small assarts or intakes in the twelfth, thirteenth and early fourteenth centuries.

The typical Hallamshire farmer was a smallholder who had common rights of grazing and turbary on the local moors and who often worked at a second occupation to improve his standard of living. Of the 253 married couples or single persons who paid the poll tax in 1379 in the soke of Bradfield, 236 paid the basic rate of 4d., thirteen paid 6d., and four paid 12d. Likewise, the lay subsidy returns of 1545–6 show that the district had a high proportion of householders who paid tax on small amounts of land.

Here again, the hamlet rather than the township or bierlow was often the unit that mattered when decisions about farming practices had to be made. Although these hamlets are poorly recorded, memories of their boundaries survived into Victorian times, long after their townfields and commons had gone, for the first edition of the six-inch Ordnance Survey maps often mark them. The South Pennine hamlets were ancient institutions. Domesday Book named small estates within the soke of Bradfield at Onesacre, Worrall, Holdworth and Ughill, all of which were regarded as hamlets in later centuries. It seems likely that the townfields of hamlets such as these were associated with the older farmsteads and that new farms were created within the outlying parts of hamlet territories in the years leading up to the disasters of the early fourteenth century. Wigtwizzle was 'Wicga's fork', a place-name that was derived from an Old English personal name that was attached to the confluence of two streams. Only a small cluster of households had doles in its townfields, but the other farms that were scattered within the hamlet shared with them an extensive moorland common that in 1741 was 'near four miles in length and more than two in breadth and contains 1960 acres of land'. The boundaries of this common are still marked by deep ditches that appear to have been dug out by communal labour in the late thirteenth century.[21]

Other parts of England beyond the central arable belt were organized in a similar manner. The parishes in the wood pasture counties on the Welsh Borders were divided into several townships and hamlets that each had their own small 'townfields' for the communal growing of cereals, numerous closes of all sorts of shapes and sizes, and extensive woods and commons. The parish of Myddle in north Shropshire, for example, covered nearly 7,000 acres and contained eleven townships, at least six of which had their own communal field, or in the case of the central village of Myddle two open fields that covered no more than 100 acres each. A nearby parish that was organized in a similar manner acquired the name of Ruyton-XI-Towns. The enclosure of almost all of Shropshire's townfields occurred early and by the agreement of the local farmers.[22]

Scattered settlements in straggling parishes were also usual in many parts of eastern and southeastern England. In Kent, the contrasting countrysides varied from the Foothills, the Downs, Holmesdale and the Chartlands to the dense woodlands of the Weald and the Romney marshes, each with their distinctive character and economy.[23] Essex has numerous greens, often known as 'tyes' or 'ends', that eventually attracted settlements around them. Peter Warner has shown that on the East Suffolk claylands the word 'moor' is more frequently encountered in early documents than 'common' or 'green', revealing perhaps the early character of the flat landscape, but that later settlements grew up on the edges of the greens that formed the boundaries of the older units.[24]

Hamlets are found within every English region, even in the heartlands of the Midland open-field villages. Far from being a somehow inferior type of settlement, as was once assumed, they were often more suited to communal farming than were large villages. Their versatility, adaptability, resilience and tenacity enabled most of them to survive the late medieval economic and demographic depressions, though many suffered and a proportion succumbed.[25] They ensured that England was a country with complex and different rural economies.

The broad division between the central province of open-field villages and the rest of England marked by hamlets and scattered farmsteads is not a firm one, for much variety can be observed at the local level. In the eastern part of the ancient parish of Sheffield, for instance, the township of Attercliffe consisted of two planned villages, surrounded by their open fields and commons with hardly a tree in sight, yet immediately on the other side of the River Don the more rugged terrain of Brightside bierlow had no village, and instead of open fields the land was divided into individual closes of all sorts of shapes and size, numerous managed woods, and a deer park.[26]

Forests, chases, deer parks and woods

Large parts of the English countryside, including some that had already been used for hunting before the Conquest, were turned into forests and chases by the Norman kings. The word 'forest' was used not in the popular sense of a dense wood but as a legal term that referred to an area that was under forest law (with its own courts and officials), in which deer and other game could be killed only by the consent of the king. At least 143 forests were in existence in England by 1215, when Magna Carta forbade the creation of new ones.[27]

Forests and chases produced very different types of countryside from that of the central corn-growing belt, though even there the forests of Bernwood,

Rockingham and Salcey provided extensive tracts of woodland and wood pasture. The whole of the county of Essex was placed under forest law, and its differences with neighbouring Suffolk were profound. Domesday Book shows that 41 per cent of the recorded inhabitants of Suffolk were freemen, whereas in Essex the proportion was as low as 7 per cent. An Essex parish tended to coincide with a single manor and to take the name of its Norman lord, whereas a Suffolk parish had up to four manorial lords. This division, which is immediately apparent upon crossing the river Stour, is evident in place-names. Essex has many settlements named after a Norman lord, whereas Suffolk villages often take their names from the dedication of the parish church. Thus, Essex has its Woodham Ferrers, Woodham Mortimer and Woodham Walter, whereas Suffolk has its Creeting St Mary, Creeting All Saints, Creeting St Olave and Creeting St Peter.[28]

Forests varied in character and size. They were only partly wooded and they often included moors, heaths or fens. The New Forest, which was created in Hampshire shortly after the Norman Conquest, is the only one that is still ruled through its court and officers. The much smaller forest at Hatfield in Essex preserves the medieval character of its landscape, with deer, cattle, coppice woods, pollards, scrub, timber trees, grassland, fens and a seventeenth-century lodge and rabbit warren. As hunting was only an occasional pastime, parts of forests were set aside for cultivation or for grazing livestock other than deer, either by being let out to rent by the lord or by the local farmers' use of common rights. Forests often contained villages as well as hamlets, farmsteads and cottages within their boundaries. The private equivalent of a royal forest was a chase that a lord was authorized to create by royal charter. These chases were much larger than deer parks, but their boundaries were undefined by ditches, banks and palings.

Jack Langton and Graham Jones have produced maps to show the extent of forests and chases up and down the land.[29] For instance, they covered many parts of the Pennines. Within Hallamshire, the Norman lords of Sheffield Castle had an enormous deer park of 2,461 acres, and 10,767 acres of moorland and woodland over which to hunt from a lodge on a prominent position high above the Rivelin Valley. This hunting district was divided between Rivelin Chase, Loxley Firth or Chase, and Hawkesworth Firth.[30] 'Frith', or 'firth', was an alternative term for a chase that has produced place-names such as Holmfirth and Chapel-en-le-Frith.

In northwest Derbyshire, The Forest of the Peak covered about 180 square miles. Some parts may have been used before the Norman Conquest, for much of it was rough moorland that had belonged to the royal manors of Hope and Longdendale. The forest was divided into three wards and was administered from Peak Castle, the residence of the forest bailiff, high above the Norman new town of Castleton. Four verderers held inquests into forest trespass; they presided over the swainmote courts, presented cases at forest eyres, and were responsible for looking after the deer. Below them were twelve regarderers, who enquired into offences; the woodwards, who managed the woods; the agisters, who collected rents for feeding cattle or pigs; and the rangers, who were responsible for the observance of forest law in the remote parts. About 1225, the officers built their own chapel at Chapel-en-le-Frith.

The name of the hunting lodge is commemorated by Chamber Farm, which stands on a knoll just north of the present village of Peak Forest. Yet hunting was only an occasional activity. Much of the forest was farmed in the same manner as in other Pennine districts. Grants of land were made to religious houses in the twelfth and thirteenth centuries. Other parts were divided into townships and hamlets. The wastes were constantly encroached upon, both by the foresters and by local peasants. An enquiry in 1251 concluded that 131 people had built new houses without licence in the forest since the previous enquiry in 1216, and that 127 new houses had been built with a licence. By then, the Peak Forest, especially in the limestone district in the south, had villages surrounded by open fields. In the thirteenth and early fourteenth centuries, it even had small market towns at Castleton, Tideswell, Chapel-en-le-Frith, Glossop and Charlesworth. Large numbers of cattle, sheep and horses grazed the upland pastures. A survey of the Forest of the Peak in 1516 recorded about 980 cattle, 4,000 sheep and 320 horses, to the detriment of the 360 deer that were in so poor a condition that they were unlikely to survive the winter.[31]

The greatest changes to the rural landscape in the early modern period were brought about by sales of Crown estates when the early Stuart kings tried to rule without the need to raise money through Parliament and so were forced to raise money by selling some of their possessions. Some Crown forests were 'disafforested' before the Civil War and the rest were enclosed during the late seventeenth century. At the same time, ambitious drainage schemes in fenland districts began in the late 1620s, when Charles I commissioned a Dutch and Flemish company organized by Cornelius Vermuyden to drain Hatfield Chase in South Yorkshire. In the 1630s a more spectacular scheme of Vermuyden's reclaimed 190,000 acres of the Bedford Level (named after the fourth Earl of Bedford) between Cambridge, Peterborough and Wisbech. What is now known as the 'Old Bedford' river, 70 feet wide and 21 miles long, was completed in 1631. The project was continued after the Civil War by the cutting of the 'New Bedford' river and other massive drains. Large blocks of reclaimed land were allotted to the 'adventurers' who had put their money into this scheme, but here, as at Hatfield Chase and in the Isle of Axholme further north, local smallholders who had managed to earn a sufficient living before drainage were now faced with the loss of valuable common rights. They reacted violently.[32]

In 1673 the Duchy of Lancaster overrode the opposition of the poorest inhabitants and began to enclose the extensive commons and wastes of The Forest of the Peak. These were divided between the freeholders and the Duchy, whose officers leased their share to farmers of large sheep flocks. The commons of the manor of Hope and other parts of the High Peak were enclosed in 1675, an agreement to divide the Castleton commons was reached by 1691, but the enclosure of common pastures near Chapel-en-le-Frith was not completed until 1714, when the freeholders were allowed to enjoy their 973-acre portion. Many of the field walls in this part of Derbyshire date from this time.[33]

In the Middle Ages the private deer park was a sought-after status symbol for manorial lords. At least 1,900 deer parks were created in England, especially in the Midlands and the South, though they were not all in existence at the same time. The national distribution of parks corresponds closely with areas where woodland was recorded in Domesday Book. The 'hays' that sometimes appear in that record may have been the first, but most deer parks were created during the twelfth and thirteenth centuries, when many royal charters to empark were issued upon payment of a fee. In the North, a charter of free warren, which allowed a general right to hunt, was regarded as authority to enclose a park, but many well-documented parks survive in the landscape for which no royal licence exists. Some deer parks were converted to other uses during the fifteenth and sixteenth centuries, but the fashion was revived briefly during the reign of Charles II.

The main types of deer that were kept were the native red and roe deer, and the fallow deer that were probably introduced by the Normans. They

FIGURE 8 *The ditch and bank of the medieval deer park at Bradgate, Leicestershire, with the ruins of the Tudor brick house in the background.*

required a varied environment that included woods and open grassland. Parks were not just status symbols for occasional hunting, however, for they were also a valuable source of timber and coppiced wood and of pasture for domestic animals. The management of a deer park was the responsibility of a pallister. Parks were enclosed by deep ditches and a high earthen bank, topped by an oak palisade, or a fence or a stone wall. The favoured shape of a park was circular, for this reduced the amount of fencing, but local conditions often dictated other shapes. Many of these medieval deer parks have left their imprint on the English countryside.[34]

The outline of Holmesfield Park in north Derbyshire is almost as clear now as it was in the thirteenth century, though in medieval times the ditch would have been deeper and the bank higher. In 1252 John Deincourt, whose family had held the manor since the Norman Conquest, obtained a royal charter of free warren. In 1343 his descendant, William Deincourt, brought to court several men who had not only broken into his estate and had driven away 20 oxen, 30 cows and 200 sheep, fished his stews, and carried away his fish, but had also hunted in his park, carried away deer, and assaulted his men and servants. The deer park remained in use until Elizabethan times, when it was converted into a coppice that is still known as Holmesfield Park Wood. The presence of bluebells, wood melick, yellow archangel and wood anemone supports the suggestion that the wood is centuries old. The general consensus amongst botanists is that no one species is a reliable indicator of antiquity but that combinations of certain plants provide firm evidence.[35]

England's deciduous woods now look very different from their appearance in previous centuries. Since the early twentieth century, many of them have not been managed, so there is a tendency to regard them as the 'natural' parts of the countryside. But woodland management was practised from prehistoric times onwards. By the time of the Norman Conquest, only 15 per cent of England remained covered by woods, a much lower proportion than in other Western European countries, and much the same as at the present time. By then, many English townships had no woodland at all. The surviving woods were carefully managed as economic assets, mostly as coppice or springwoods, that is, trees that were felled just above ground level to allow the regeneration of young shoots. Woods and common pastures were increasingly valuable resources. Hedges were also a valuable source of timber and fuel from early times.

In his pioneering books,[36] Oliver Rackham showed that, historically, woods provided fuel and energy more than timber. Although some trees were grown to their full height for carpenters, the regular and most important product was underwood, which was felled in a rotation cycle every few years. Bundles of 'cordwood' provided fuel for the charcoal iron industry and for smelting lead, and the bark was stripped for the tanners. The rest of the underwood was used to make pit props, fences, hurdles, poles, gates, ladders, handles, furniture, logs, faggots, and so on, and the twigs and odd bits were used for kindling fires. Holly was grown in special 'haggs' as winter fodder for sheep and deer.

Most woods belonged to manorial lords, but copyholders often had grazing rights for their cattle and pigs, once the young shoots had become established. A surrounding ditch and bank, usually topped by a hedge, fence or wall, prevented encroachments and wandering livestock. In many cases, woods have thus preserved their shape and size over the centuries. Banks and ditches also marked the internal divisions of woods, for different parts followed separate felling cycles. This ancient tradition of woodland management declined in the nineteenth century, in face of competition from foreign imports, and it was largely abandoned after the First World War.

Deserted medieval villages

The population disasters of the fourteenth century brought about the decay of settlements throughout the land, and in numerous cases their total or near-total desertion. Yet until the 1940s when William Hoskins and Maurice Beresford began to combine their explorations of the countryside with documentary research, few scholars accepted the visual evidence for desertion in the form of earthworks such as an isolated church, often abandoned and in ruins, or house platforms and holloways amid the ridge-and-furrow patterns of former arable fields. A few scraps of literary evidence had also been ignored. For instance, an Elizabethan observer of a former Somerset village, which had been turned into pasture during the fifteenth and sixteenth centuries by the Bamfylde family, had noted: 'Hardington, the which village is wholly enclosed and made pasture; and so no house left but his owne, and he pulleth downe the churche, and it is scares knowne where the parsonage house stode.'[37]

Although a deserted site had often provoked comment, it was not until the publication of Beresford's *The Lost Villages of England* (1954) that the national nature of this phenomenon was widely recognized. Meanwhile, Beresford and John Hurst, with teams of volunteers, had begun to excavate the deserted village of Wharram Percy on the Yorkshire Wolds in a now celebrated, long-term project that remains the centre point of all discussions about 'deserted medieval villages', starting with attempts to date and explain the reasons for desertion, but then broadening to take in the origins and development of such places. It has become clear that villages expanded, contracted, moved about and completely altered their layouts over the centuries. It has also become apparent that the choice of the term 'deserted medieval villages' was an unfortunate one that we seem to be stuck with, for it took no account of widespread shrinkage rather than total desertion; it failed to recognize that desertions occurred over very long periods of time, sometimes long after the medieval period; and it ignored the less obvious desertion or shrinkage of hamlets and farmsteads.[38]

Some of these classification problems were highlighted by the excavation of the deserted village or hamlet of Hound Tor, on marginal land at a height of about 1,000 feet above sea level on the southeastern edge of Dartmoor. Hound Tor was recorded as a separate manor in Domesday Book, with a population of two villeins, four bordars and two serfs. It lay within the parish of Manaton and so had no church of its own. The archaeologists uncovered four thirteenth-century longhouses, four other smaller houses and three barns with corn driers, and a separate farmstead beyond the main group. The corn driers and evidence of terraces suggest that the farmers cultivated their own arable fields, even in this unpromising environment.[39]

When were such places deserted? The early explanations stressed that the main cause was depopulation in order to make way for sheep pastures. Criticisms of enclosures by ruthless lords of the manor began in the last two decades of the fifteenth century. The central government began to take the problem of desertion seriously, and in 1517 Cardinal Wolsey set up a national enquiry into how many houses had been demolished, how much land had been converted from arable to pasture, and how many deer parks had been enclosed since Michaelmas 1488.

It eventually became clear, however, that the desertion of Wharram Percy was a long drawn-out process that did not occur in the same way or at the same pace across the village. What the few late medieval records seem to show is a substantial decline in the number of holdings (perhaps as much as 50 per cent) between the late thirteenth century and the mid-fifteenth century. Further farmsteads were 'thrown down' at the end of that century, but others continued to be tenanted until around 1527, when the open fields were abolished and laid down to grass. A case can be made from the documentary sources for a number of buildings in the township continuing in occupation into the mid-sixteenth century, though these were probably cottages for smallholders and shepherds rather than farmhouses. By the 1570s, Wharram Percy seems to have become an infield-outfield farm, though the bulk of its territory was undivided pasture, where flocks of sheep were pastured and managed on a long-term basis.[40]

Most townships in the neighbouring district, on the northern Wolds and in the Vale of Pickering, continued to support villages that were farmed on open-field systems for another century or two after the pastoral conversion of Wharram. Susan Neave has identified the later seventeenth and early eighteenth centuries as a period in which many long-established Wolds villages experienced significant shrinkage, and some of them near total depopulation. It is now clear from her research that, for the East Riding at least, the classification of deserted and shrunken villages as distinct phenomena, with distinct chronologies and causes, is misplaced. Other studies, such as those by Stuart Wrathmell in Northumberland and elsewhere, have shown that desertions were caused when farms were reorganized in the seventeenth and eighteenth centuries.[41] Even in Leicestershire, at the heart of the Midland open-field system, the desertion of the classic site of Great

Stretton was a gradual process. Four households were recorded there in the hearth tax returns of 1664.[42] It is well known that in the eighteenth century great landowners sometimes cleared villages to create landscaped parks around their houses and re-sited them out of view. One of the most famous examples is that of Milton Abbas in Dorset, which Viscount Milton demolished in the 1770s and 1780s and then replaced with a new model village half a mile away. Many a great house owes its privacy and uninterrupted view to the decay or removal of a village at this time or later on.

Although most deserted villages are found in the classic central area of nucleated villages surrounded by their open fields, smaller shrunken and deserted settlements occur in all parts of England. They were abandoned at various times and in different circumstances. Devastating plagues and ruthless conversions from arable to pasture are only part of the story. The rights of copyhold tenants in one manor were sometimes strong enough for peasant farmers to defend their customs loudly and successfully, while in a neighbouring manor lordly power prevailed. Andy Wood quotes a Northamptonshire clergyman, who in 1625 was told by an 'ancient credible man' who as a young man lived in 'a neighbouring decayed inclosed towne before it was inclosed, at which time he thinkes there were two hundred persons more in it than now there are'. Twenty of the 36 or 37 farming families 'did constantly keep as good houses and hospitality as he who after ruined himself and the towne'.[43]

Enclosure

The late Middle Ages was a time when many families, ruthless or not, grasped their opportunities to better themselves. The acquisition of a lease of the lord's demesne lands or of a monastic grange was a sure way of making a profit and of rising in society. Such families found themselves in a good position to buy some of the lands that came on the market upon the dissolution of the monasteries. They were amongst the earliest advocates of enclosure.

The actions of ruthless landlords in overstocking the commons and making private enclosures caused bitter disputes, for smallholders and cottagers were dependent upon their grazing rights in order to make ends meet. The gentry families that grew rich under the early Tudors pursued their own selfish advantage unscrupulously, but they sometimes met with fierce resistance.

The most hostile reactions to enclosure came in the corn-growing districts of England, where commons were much smaller and the farming was organized communally in large open fields. There, the benefits of enclosure were restricted to the richer farmers, who were tempted by the rising prices for meat to convert arable land into pasture. This could sometimes be achieved by converting strips into temporary grass leys, but the freedom to farm as one pleased in enclosed fields without the restrictions of communal decisions led many farmers to prefer enclosure. A powerful landowner could force his weaker neighbours to agree, and sometimes he was able to drive them off the land. The outlines of former blocks of strips into which open fields were divided are often preserved in the landscape by hedges planted upon enclosure by the agreement of the farmers in later centuries. Elsewhere, the old plough patterns of ridge-and-furrow have survived in fields that have long been put down to grass.

The writers who believed in the benefits of enclosure argued that it would lead to increased yields and higher rents for the landowners. On the Yorkshire Wolds in the early seventeenth century, Henry Best thought that, although the initial costs such as fencing were high, enclosed lands were worth three times as much as those that were farmed in open fields.[44] Enclosure was particularly attractive to landowners when livestock prices were high and they could expect a quick return. In Leicestershire, Northamptonshire and north Buckinghamshire, some communal fields were converted to grass, for 'pasturage was more profitable than tillage', as one commentator wrote. In Leicestershire, about half the total area of the county was enclosed between 1607 and 1730, far more than in the Tudor period and rather more than that which was enclosed later by Act of Parliament. In many cases, a township was enclosed in stages.[45] It took nearly 200 years to enclose all the 700 acres of the small parish of Great Stretton.

In the populous open-field parishes of the Midland counties, the private benefits of any act of enclosure were bound to hurt someone else, and when blocks of strips were withdrawn from the communal husbandry of the open fields and the wastes were enclosed piecemeal, the agricultural routine of the whole township was disrupted. Resistance to enclosure was seen at its strongest in the Midland Revolt of 1607. Yet, although powerful landowners could impose their wishes upon weaker neighbours and could even turn them out, many a rural parish was not dominated by a single squire or by a small group of prosperous yeomen. In his classic study of the open-field Leicestershire parish of Wigston Magna, William Hoskins showed that 50 or 60 farming families were tenants of two great absentee lords, but another 20 or so peasants owned about 37 per cent of the land between them.[46] The social structure and the field systems of rural parishes were sometimes markedly different from one parish to another. Throughout England, the great majority of farms were run by peasant families who kept a small number of livestock and grew a variety of crops and who hoped to produce small surpluses for the nearest market in good years.

In different farming systems beyond the central corn-growing belt, the arable 'townfields' that were set amongst wood pastures or on the edge of moors or fens were often enclosed by the agreement of the farmers by the middle of the sixteenth century. By the sixteenth century, the open fields of the counties of Cornwall, Devon, Somerset, Worcestershire, Herefordshire,

Shropshire, Kent, Essex, Suffolk and Hertfordshire had either been completely or largely enclosed.

The assarting of the wastes that had stopped during the crises of the fourteenth century began again in Elizabeth I's reign as population levels recovered. Manors that had large commons and wastes continued to allow such clearances right up to the time of parliamentary enclosure, for they brought in extra rent to the lord and enough waste survived for communal grazing. Such piecemeal activities did not provoke hostility because nobody's interests were harmed. This was particularly so in those pastoral parts of England that had plenty of moorland, woodland or marshland, but where little land was farmed in open fields. Small and medium-sized holdings long remained characteristic of many parts of the English countryside, especially in pastoral areas, where farmsteads and hamlets were more usual than nucleated villages surrounded by their open fields and where many of the farmers had a by-employment to supplement their incomes.

Enclosure was often undertaken amicably by agreement, with none of the evil social consequences that were so evident in Leicestershire and Warwickshire and adjacent counties. The process was often started by the exchange or purchase of strips to form a separate holding. In cases where all the land in a township came under the ownership of a single individual or a small group of farmers, enclosure by agreement came readily. Hedges or walls were simply planted around blocks of strips by following their curved boundaries. Numerous examples of such walls survive in the limestone part of the Peak District, where they form a sharp contrast with the rectangular fields of parliamentary enclosure in the eighteenth and nineteenth centuries, the last stage of a long drawn-out process that was used only where complete agreement could not be reached. About 30 per cent of parishes on the Midland clays were transformed by parliamentary enclosure. In Northamptonshire, the proportion rose to 50 per cent.[47] Within a single generation, the medieval landscape of bare open fields was replaced by a more geometrical pattern of small, square or rectangular fields enclosed by hawthorn hedges.

It is clear that, long before parliamentary enclosure in the eighteenth and nineteenth centuries, the varied nature of the English landscape had a profound influence on the ways that settlements developed and farming was organized.

CHAPTER FIVE

Earning a living in the countryside

Farming the land

The old view of medieval peasant families was that their lives were hard and increasingly miserable as the national population grew and resources became scarce. They were thought to have been self-sufficient and to have produced just enough to keep themselves alive; they had onerous duties to perform for their manorial lords; and they were bound to the manor and could not move without the lord's permission. This gloomy view no longer prevails. Historians and archaeologists have shown that, although life could indeed be short and harsh, especially in the crisis years of the early fourteenth century, restrictions imposed by lords of the manor varied considerably from one part of England to another, and enterprising and resourceful peasant families could prosper by producing a surplus for sale in their local market towns. Although in theory peasants might have been tied to their manor and forced to stay put, in reality they moved around within the 'country' with which they were familiar.[1]

Although the term 'peasant' remains a useful one, it masks the differences in living conditions between the lowly tenants of a few acres and those who eventually rose to the status of yeomen. Domesday Book recorded numerous serfs, the slaves who worked as ploughmen, herdsmen or dairymaids, but by about 1100 serfdom had been more or less abolished. Nevertheless, the descendants of former slaves were the ones who worked the smallest farms and who bore the heaviest burden of services to their manorial lords.

The tenant farmers, who were known as villeins, formed about 40 per cent of the rural population in Domesday Book. Those who lived in an open-field village generally farmed a 'yardland' of 30 acres, or a 'half-yardland', and they had rights to cut hay in the meadows and to graze livestock on the common pastures. Villeins had to work a customary number of days on the lord's demesne land, but their holdings usually yielded a surplus for the market above their own requirements. Half the land on a farm was generally devoted to a variety of crops, the rest for keeping livestock. Although the national population was small by today's standards, farmers needed large acreages of land to produce sufficient food, for their crop yields were low by modern standards, whatever the nature of the soils. Wheat and rye (sometimes mixed as maslin) were sown in the autumn, and oats, barley and peas were the spring corns. The poor quality of the seed, inadequate drainage on the heavy clays, the lightness of the ploughs, a shortage of manure, and the laborious task of getting rid of weeds were burdens that the medieval peasant had to bear.

Above them in the social scale were farmers who held at least some of their land by freehold. Below them were the bordars and cottagers, with smallholdings of three to five acres, who formed another 30 per cent of the rural population. As bordars did not have enough land to provide food for themselves and their families, they also worked for hire by their lords and their better-off neighbours. They were found especially in woodland and pastoral districts, where they could keep a few cows, pigs and sheep and work at by-employments such as weaving, cutting wood, digging turf, and mining.

By the end of the thirteenth century, estates in many parts of England were recording lower levels of productivity and some of the new clearances from the edges of woods, fens or moors were losing their fertility. A peasant family's dues and customs varied from one place to another, but grinding corn at the lord's mill for a fixed payment was a general rule. Some 6,000 water-powered corn mills were recorded in Domesday Book, often on sites that remained in use well into the twentieth century, whereas the first reference to a windmill in England is not found until 1185, when a post mill was recorded at Weedley, near South Cave, on the edge of the Yorkshire Wolds.[2]

Pastoral farms were no more productive than arable ones, for livestock were far smaller than now and they yielded less milk and meat, while disease was a constant threat. A cow gave 120–150 gallons of milk a year, which is only one-sixth of present-day yields. In Yorkshire, the average dairy cow at Bolton Priory produced just 72 pounds of butter and cheese annually, and a herd of 25 cows at Harewood gave birth to an average of just 17 calves a year in the 1260s and 1270s.[3]

Medieval hay meadows were valued at three or four times the level of surrounding arable lands, for they provided essential winter fodder. Most manors had some common meadowland, which was divided into doles or 'wongs' like the strips of the arable fields and sometimes reallocated to different tenants on a rotation basis every year. The large meadows that were found in broad valleys such as those alongside the Trent, Dove and Derwent were managed so that in springtime water could be channelled into them to stimulate the early growth of grass for sheep to graze, then again later in the season to promote the growth of the grass that was to be cut as hay. Water was brought along a system of dykes from rivers and springs or was run off the neighbouring arable fields, bringing nutritious silts and manures. A thin film of water was all that was needed to raise the temperature to the necessary level, but it was not allowed to stagnate. In the North and the East Midlands such meadows were known as *ings*, from the Old Norse word *eng*.[4]

In the thirteenth century, lay and ecclesiastical lords employed stewards to manage their estates directly, rather than lease their lands to tenants, as they did later, for the need to feed the growing population and the demand for wool from the clothiers of Flanders and Italy kept profits high. In arable districts, a lord of the manor's holdings were usually spread amongst the open fields of the village community, though sometimes a block of strips was enclosed into a 'flatt' or 'furlong'. In pastoral areas, huge estates could be devoted to specialist activities. The forests on either side of the border between Lancashire and Yorkshire provided space for vaccaries or booths, where butter and cheese were produced and young cattle were reared until they were taken to fatten on the lusher pastures in the valleys. The breeding of horses for riding or as pack animals was another speciality that appealed to large landowners; in 1332, for example, the Earl of Lancaster's stud in Duffield Frith in Derbyshire contained 113 mares and 112 other horses.[5]

By the last decades of the thirteenth century, the increase in the size of the national population forced 40 per cent of manorial tenants, amounting to between 1.5 million and 2.5 million people, to struggle with less than five acres of land to farm. Famine and disease caused by an unprecedented series of harvest failures and livestock disasters between 1315 and 1322 brought population growth to an abrupt end. The poor summer of 1314 was followed in the next two years by heavy, persistent rain that ruined both the hay and the corn harvests; the harvest failed again in 1321. During these dreadful years, flocks and herds were devastated by sheep murrain and cattle plague. In 1316 a chronicler at Lanercost Priory in Cumberland recorded: '[S]uch a mortality of men in England and Scotland through famine and pestilence as had not been heard of in our time. In some of the northern parts of England, the quarter of wheat sold for 40 shillings.' This was eight times the previous average national price. In the winter of 1319–20:

> the plague and murrain of cattle which had lasted through the two preceding years in the southern districts, broke out in the northern district among oxen and cows, which after a short sickness generally died; and few animals of that kind were left, so that men had to plough that year with horses.

Some of the townships and parishes that were weakened during the crisis years of 1315–22 were left vulnerable to the devastation that lay ahead. As the climate worsened, the North Sea destroyed the protective banks along the coast. In the East Riding of Yorkshire Hoton and Hyth townships were lost to the sea, and 33 acres of grassland at Orwythfleet and a 90-acre grange at Tharlesthorpe disappeared into the Humber estuary. Gales and tidal waves swept the material that was eroded from the coast and the banks of the Humber on to the ever-changing sandy headland of Spurn Point. Eventually, the parish churches of Hollym, Skeffling and Withernsea had to be rebuilt on safer sites much further inland.[6]

Then came the Black Death, which weakened many rural communities so severely that the old methods of communal agriculture were abandoned and thousands of settlements shrank or eventually became deserted. Fewer people meant less demand for cereals, so lords converted the open fields of their manors into pastures for cattle or sheep. The lucky survivors of the Black Death must have been traumatized by their experiences but, in material terms, many were able to benefit from the new situation in which they found themselves. Manor court rolls show that new tenants filled the vacant holdings on much more favourable terms than before. Lords had to be flexible and make concessions, otherwise their peasants went to live elsewhere. In the late fourteenth and early fifteenth centuries, many traditional feudal dues were no longer demanded. Families that had previously scratched a living from unsuitable soils at the edges of woods, moors, fens or marshes now seized the opportunity to improve their standard of living on more productive and larger farms. The wealthier and shrewder peasants bought extra property and founded dynasties of yeomen. They were constrained only by the higher wages they had to pay their labourers and by the lower rents that they could charge their sub-tenants. The world was turned upside down as lords were forced to compete for the services of labourers, as demand outran supply. High wages were paid to the harvesters of the crops in August and September 1349, when prices for grain, cheese and meat were exceptionally low. Disputes and hard bargaining were commonplace throughout England, and frequent attempts to regulate wages by enforcing the Statute of Labourers (1351) ended in failure. A long-term and dramatic shift in the balance of power between lords and tenants was underway.[7]

In the late medieval period, farming practices were adapted to the great variety of soils and landscapes across England. In some districts, particularly on the Midlands and Norfolk clays, the lack of tenants and labourers encouraged landowners to convert arable land into pasture. When the national population began to rise again in the sixteenth century, the growing demand for bread made it profitable to plough the pastures anew in order to grow cereals. Farmers found that their arable lands recovered their fertility when they were left under grass for a few years, so strips or even whole furlongs within the open fields were allowed a period of rest as grass leys, whilst remaining within the common-field system of farming. The switch to grazing was on such a scale that, in England as a whole, sheep were far more numerous than were human beings.[8]

Industries in the medieval countryside

In some parts of the English countryside, particularly in the pastoral districts, medieval farmers were able to supplement their incomes by working at textile or woodland crafts, hewing millstones in small quarries, or mining coal, lead, tin or iron. These activities helped to keep many a family above the poverty line. The districts of England that had plenty of woods and common pastures were the ones that offered most opportunities for craftsmen. Whereas at the time of Domesday Book the majority of English woods were in the form of wood pastures, by the late thirteenth century most of them were carefully managed for their coppiced underwood as much as for their timber.[9]

Medieval industries were generally small in scale and seasonal in nature, but the mining and smelting of minerals was sometimes organized on a large scale. In the later medieval period, the lead industry in the Mendips, the Peak District and the northern Pennines provided rich families with opportunities to lease mineral dues and to invest in smelting facilities on windy bole-hills. By the late fifteenth century, smelters, or brenners as they were known, were the dominant figures in the industry. In Derbyshire, the Vernons of Haddon Hall owned mines either by themselves or in partnership with other gentry smelters. They bought large quantities of ore directly from the miners, and they obtained other supplies from their collection of tithes and from rights known as lot and cope.[10]

The Derbyshire lead industry recovered its former vitality between 1480 and 1540. During those 60 years, output in the Wirksworth lead field increased six-fold. Most of the free miners who had customary rights to mine lead wherever they found it in the King's Field worked in gangs of two or three and employed a labourer to carry ore up the shaft and to clean it at the surface. Their freedom was largely illusory, however, for most of them were in debt to the smelters and merchants. Mines were normally worked as small opencast quarries that followed the lie of the lead rakes along the surface of the land. After the miners had moved further along a rake, poor scavengers known as 'cavers' dug over their rubbish tips in the hope of finding scraps of ore.[11]

The 400 or so miners who worked in the Peak District in the 1540s were usually part-time farmers who ceased mining at lambing and harvest times and when the mines were flooded in the winter months. Their farms were small but they had common rights of pasture and some were able to prosper in a modest way as the heads of well-established yeomen families. By the end of Henry VIII's reign, the Derbyshire lead industry was in decline through the lack of improved technology. The smelters were dependent upon the vagaries of the weather, and the miners could not reach the high-quality ores that lay below the water table. The lead industry could go no further until successful drainage technology was installed in the sixteenth and seventeenth centuries.

In Devon and Cornwall, the spoil heaps and engine houses of the deep tin mines of the nineteenth century have obliterated most of the evidence of earlier activities, though some ancient workings can still be seen on the fringes of Dartmoor and Bodmin Moor. In the early thirteenth century, an estimated million pounds of tin were smelted each year. The traditional method was to dig out the tin-bearing gravel in a stream with a shovel and a wheelbarrow and to put it on a sloping trough known as a tye, so that the lighter gravel could be removed by the flow of water. The remaining deposit was then sorted, and the most-promising material was shovelled into a small trough, or 'gounce'. Backfilling with soil and rocks from the next section enabled the digging to progress in stages. This ancient method was used well into the twentieth century, long after deep mining in neighbouring districts had come and gone. Water power was used for smelting by the end of the Middle Ages, much earlier than in other industries, otherwise the old methods long prevailed. The field remains of the tin industry make up the majority of Dartmoor's archaeological evidence from the period 1150–1700.[12]

In other parts of England, the coalfields where seams outcropped near the surface had been mined on a small scale from at least Roman times, but documentary evidence is rarely found before the thirteenth century.[13] Some medieval bell pits for the mining of either coal or ironstone survive in the landscape, but they are difficult to distinguish from later pits of this type, for the technique was used until well into the nineteenth century. The bell shape was produced by the digging of a vertical shaft to the seam, which was then worked in all directions until fear of roof collapse lead to the abandonment of the pit and the digging of a new shaft alongside. Rows of bell pits sometimes survive as dramatic features in the landscape. They were formed when miners threw their spoil around the heads of the shafts. Otherwise, the coal was extracted in drift mines.

Some early evidence for the mining and forging of iron comes from the great Cistercian estates. The iron ore that was dug by the miners was washed and crushed, then smelted into wrought iron by the bloomery process, which used charcoal as fuel to achieve temperatures of 1,100–1,300 °C. Water-powered bloomeries were in use in England from the fourteenth century onwards, and they remained important in some regions until the middle of the seventeenth century. This method was capable of producing 20–30 tons of pig iron on each site in a year. Impurities in the iron were removed by repeated hammering that resulted in the medieval waste tips that are often commemorated by the name Cinder Hills. Smiths wrought the blooms of iron into finished articles in their forges, using a coal-fired hearth and bellows, anvil and hammers, chisels, files and tongs. Their methods did not change much over the centuries.[14]

After the first English blast furnace was built in 1496 at Newbridge, in Ashdown Forest, and skilled French ironworkers were attracted from Lorraine, the charcoal iron industry developed rapidly along the rivers and streams of the Weald of Kent and Sussex.[15] At first, production was geared to supplying the Crown with arms, but soon a general trade began to grow rapidly. Some of the old bloomeries were turned into finery forges to convert pig iron into bars for the smiths of London and the South East. But the industry did not spread to the Midlands and the North until the second half of the sixteenth century.

The greatest medieval industry, both in the towns and the countryside, was the manufacture of cloth. The trade brought prosperity to East Anglia, the Cotswolds and neighbouring parts of Somerset and Wiltshire, and to the West Riding of Yorkshire, where fulling mills were installed in the river valleys alongside the corn mills. The first English reference to a fulling mill comes from 1185, in a survey of the Knights Templar lands at Temple Newsam in Yorkshire. The earlier practice had been to scour, thicken and felt cloth by 'walking' or trampling fullers' earth into newly woven pieces by foot, and so for a long time afterwards fulling mills were known in the North as 'walk mills'. Walker became a North Country surname, whereas Fuller was preferred in the East, and Tooker in the South West.[16]

Christopher Dyer has revealed the world of John Heritage, a wool man whose business flourished in the late medieval 'country' that was centred on Moreton in Marsh during the first two decades of the sixteenth century. Moreton lay on the frontier between the lowlands of Warwickshire and the Vale of Evesham on the one hand, and the high ground of the Cotswolds on the other, but the two landscapes were bound together by many links and contacts, not least by the wool traders who were constantly on the move from the villages to the market towns, buying wool for London-based merchants who exported fleeces to Calais for the clothmakers of Flanders. After the Black Death, the local lords withdrew from the direct management of agriculture. Peasants enjoyed more freedom and many of them gained land as farming shifted from arable to pasture. Some of the largest grazing fields, known as leasows, occupied the sites of abandoned villages. The 'country' where Heritage bought his wool included 29 abandoned sites, forming one of the most concentrated pockets of deserted settlements in England. Yet Dyer estimates that the leasows and large enclosed pastures accounted for no more than 5 per cent of the productive land in Heritage's 'country'. As demesnes and glebes cannot have accounted for more than 20 per cent, at least 75 per cent must have been held and cultivated by numerous peasants who kept sheep, in flocks of 60–100, on the common pastures and fallow fields. They must have sold to traders like Heritage at least as much wool as the large-scale sheepmasters. This rural society was in a constant state of tension, for those who wished to pursue mixed farming felt threatened by acquisitive graziers who coveted their land.[17]

The manufacture of cheap woollen cloth had long been a modest trade in the Halifax-Bradford district, but by the late fifteenth and sixteenth centuries the Upper Calder Valley had become the largest producer of kerseys in the whole of England, with a flourishing export trade to Blackwell Hall, London, and many parts of west Europe. The population of the extensive parish of Halifax grew from about 1,000 people in 1439 to around 8,500 in 1548, and 70 per cent of these parishioners lived in the countryside. The preamble to the famous 'Halifax Act' of 1555, which allowed exemption from the government's ban on middlemen, argued that the inhabitants of the parish 'being planted in the great waste and moors, where the fertility of ground is not apt to bring forth any corn nor good grass, but in rare places ... by exceeding and great industry' lived entirely by cloth making. The majority of the inhabitants being unable:

> to keep a horse to carry wool, nor yet to buy much wool at once, had ever used only to repair to the town of Halifax ... and there to buy from the wool driver some a stone, some two, and some three or four, according to their ability, and to carry the same to their houses some three, four, five or six miles off, upon their heads and backs, and so to make and convert the same either into yarn or cloth, and to sell the same and so to buy more wool.

This domestic industry was a family affair in which the children did the carding, the women the spinning, and the men the weaving.[18]

The blessing of natural resources does not fully explain why the Calder Valley became pre-eminent in the cloth business, for most of the wool was imported and the industry did not flourish in every district that had plentiful supplies of fuel and water. The combination of farming a smallholding and making a piece of cloth each week in the farmsteads, hamlets and villages on the hillsides above the Pennine valleys was successful in districts that had light manorial burdens and which were free of the restrictions imposed by urban guilds.

Salt was a precious commodity that was used to preserve food, not just to add flavour. Numerous minor place-names allow us to identify the routes along which salt was brought from the Cheshire 'wiches' – Northwich, Middlewich and Nantwich – and from Droitwich further south to the market towns of central and northern England. They include Salters' Lane, Salter Hill, Salter Ford, Saltersbrook, and field names such as Salter Close and Salter Field, which suggest overnight grazing stops. Chesterfield still has its Saltergate, an ancient route that led to the original market place by the church before the present one was laid out in the mid-twelfth century.[19]

Other rural industries were on a much smaller scale and they have left only scattered pieces of evidence. Some villages with suitable clays were distinguished by the inclusion of Potter or Crocker in their names.[20] An account book of 1466 reveals that eight millstone hewers worked in a Peak District quarry near Hathersage under a supervisor during the summer months and that some of the finished millstones were taken as far as Loughborough, about 45 miles away.[21] The specialist craft of carving alabaster monuments, images of saints and altar pieces gained an international reputation in the late Middle Ages. Alabaster was a form of gypsum that was quarried in the Trent Valley. In the early fifteenth century, Thomas Prentys and Robert Sutton of Chellaston in south Derbyshire were the acknowledged masters of this craft.[22] Fishing, too, was a part-time occupation that was combined with farming, and by the end of the fifteenth century specialist fishing villages were developing along the south Devon coast and elsewhere, such as at Robin Hood's Bay and Staithes in north Yorkshire.[23]

The medieval transport system for the conveyance of farm produce and industrial goods was more efficient than what we were once led to believe. From the twelfth and thirteenth centuries onwards, sturdy medieval bridges were built of stone rather than timber. The considerable expense of erecting and maintaining bridges that were wide enough to take wheeled vehicles could only be justified by a regular flow of traffic. Many English bridges retain medieval work, which formerly allowed the passage of just one vehicle at a time, though they have usually been widened to at least twice their original width. These bridges across the major rivers are much older than the surviving packhorse bridges that were mostly built between 1650 and 1750.[24]

Meanwhile, the greater development of the eastern counties, orientated towards France, the Low Countries and Scandinavia, compared with the rest of England, meant that the river systems that were centred on the

FIGURE 9 *An abandoned millstone in the Peak District.*

Thames, Wash and Humber were dominant. Major improvements of waterways and the digging of canals occurred in the Fens, with the most-substantial works along the course of the river Nene. Many villages on the edges of the fenlands were minor ports. One of the most notable of these was Reach (Cambridgeshire), where topographical evidence for a hythe and a huge village green alongside the port and the three-mile canal that was linked to the River Cam is still immediately recognizable. The canal was first constructed by the Romans and re-cut in the Middle Ages; it continued in use until the coming of the railways.[25]

Farming in the early modern era

As the national population returned to its pre-Black Death level in the late sixteenth century, improved farming practices provided enough food for everyone in all but the worst years of harvest failure. Farming became a bit more specialized as yeomen and husbandmen sought to offer products that paid best at the market place. The sixteenth and seventeenth centuries saw improvements in the quality of livestock when herds of cattle and flocks of sheep were reared on improved pastures that were fertilized regularly and ploughed and sown with clovers, while richer meadows supplied better winter feeding and some of the strips in the arable fields were converted into grass leys on either a temporary or permanent basis.[26]

Agreements to restrict the number of animals that could graze the commons were made in manor courts throughout the land, and in many cases parts of the commons were enclosed by the agreement of all who had traditional grazing rights. In districts more suited to grazing than growing crops, the communal arable fields had virtually disappeared by the end of Elizabeth's reign, except in lower altitudes, and much of the best meadow and pasture land had been divided into small closes. But even lowland regions that had once favoured cereals now turned to livestock. Henry Best of Elmswell on the Yorkshire Wolds believed that enclosed lands were worth three times as much as the strips in open fields. If agreement could be reached, enclosure was an attractive option for enterprising farmers when livestock prices were high and a quick return seemed likely. So was engrossing, the amalgamation of two or more farms into one, a practice that was particularly evident in the open-field villages. But in many places enclosure of the commons led to bitter conflict between those who benefited and those who were deprived of their common rights.[27]

Meadows were valued highly in manorial surveys. In the seventeenth century, more sophisticated systems of 'floating' were installed, using weirs, hatches, channels and drains to keep the water moving over them, in order to encourage early and lush growth. The most-elaborate schemes were developed in Dorset and other parts of Wessex, and in the Golden Valley of Herefordshire, but river valleys in the Midlands, such as those of the Trent and the Dove that offered good grazing for dairy cattle, were soon improved in a similar manner as farmers began to specialize in the production of cheese.[28]

Food that could be bought in the markets of London and the towns of southern and eastern England became more varied with the development of market gardening on a commercial basis by Protestant refugees from the Low Countries. Dutch gardeners on the outskirts of towns grew cabbages, cauliflowers, turnips, carrots, parsnips, radishes, artichokes, onions and other produce for summer salads. Most gardens were small, for they required intensive spadework and frequent manuring. During the dearth years of the 1590s, attitudes to what many people had considered inferior food changed abruptly, for the poor had to eat vegetables in order to survive.[29]

Home was the normal place of work, both in the towns and the countryside, and the family was the unit of production. The great majority of the population consisted of what William Harrison in his *Description of England* (1577) called the 'fourth and last sort of people ... the day labourers, poor husbandmen ... copy-holders, and all artificers as tailors, shoemakers, carpenters, brickmakers, masons, etc.' The division between rich and poor in the countryside became sharper in the Elizabethan era as renewed population growth and the rapid rise in the price of foodstuffs benefited the larger farmers and worsened the purchasing position of the growing numbers of farm labourers.

Throughout the English countryside, life was lived at an intensely local level, with much variety of experience even between adjacent parishes. For example, Wigston Magna was the most populous parish in Leicestershire, but by 1622 the neighbouring community of Foston, which was said to have some of the finest sheep pastures in the county, consisted only of the squire, the parson and three or four labouring families. Margaret Spufford showed that in the parish of Chippenham on the Cambridgeshire chalk lands farms were amalgamated until the characteristic medieval holding, ranging in size from 15 to 45 acres, disappeared. By the mid-seventeenth century, local society there was becoming more polarized between the owners of farms with over 50 acres and the growing numbers of cottagers. A similar trend can be discerned on the western clay plateau at Orwell. At Willingham, on the fen edge, however, where stock farming and dairying were the mainstays, the number of poor families increased considerably, but smallholders continued to flourish well into the eighteenth century.[30]

Increased trade led to the establishment of new markets and fairs or to the obtaining of charters to confirm prescriptive rights. Across England, the market system had become so effective by the late seventeenth century that farmers were able to concentrate upon what they could do best, and certain agricultural regions began to specialize in their products. The dairying industry, for example, became an increasingly important sector of the agricultural economy. The production of butter was a particular feature of the northern Vale of York and south Durham, where the surviving vernacular houses at the river ports of Stockton and Yarm demonstrate the wealth that could be generated. At the same time, the Cheshire cheese trade expanded rapidly. Long before the introduction of clovers and improved grasses, the natural quality of the herbage in the meadows and pastures of the Cheshire Plain and the local availability of salt enabled farmers with only small or medium-sized herds to produce cheese which factors exported down the River Dee and along the coast to London and the naval ports, or by horse and wheeled vehicles to midland market towns and fairs. Between 1660 and 1740, five out of every six inventories accompanying the wills of Cheshire farmers recorded cheese and sometimes rooms described as 'cheese chambers'. North Shropshire, the Dove Valley (separating Staffordshire from Derbyshire), Gloucestershire, Warwickshire, Leicestershire and Suffolk also prospered in a similar way, but Cheddar cheeses fetched the highest prices for they were thought the best. By 1750 all the cheese-producing areas that were of national importance in Victorian times were already sending their produce to London.[31]

Stock farmers, too, benefited from a sustained demand for meat. The droving trade was at its peak between the seventeenth century and the railway era. Cattle were driven from the Highlands of Scotland and the Welsh hills to the lowland pastures of midland, southern and eastern England, along traditional routes, grazing at the roadside and in rented pastures. Other droving routes covered much shorter distances to link the various fairs and market towns. This extensive trade in cattle meant that most herds were a motley collection, for careful breeding had not yet taken hold. Regional types that could nevertheless be recognized included the black longhorns of Yorkshire, Derbyshire, Lancashire and Staffordshire, the pied cattle of the Lincolnshire fens and marshes, and the red cattle of Somerset and Gloucestershire, but many other local breeds were also kept. Outbreaks of rinderpest caused recurring problems.[32]

Cereal growers fared less well, for grain prices fell steadily between 1660 and 1750, and the many corn growers who were also sheep farmers found that low wool prices persisted for most of the seventeenth century. One response was to try new crops on suitable soils. Turnips began to be valued not only as a garden vegetable but as a field crop for cattle, sheep and poultry. From the late seventeenth century onwards they were often grown in open fields, on light soils but not on heavy clays, and by the 1720s and 1730s they were well established in the Norfolk four-course crop rotation: wheat, clover, oats or barley, turnips or seeds. Their cultivation cleaned the land and they were much valued as fodder for sheep folded on the arable. Meanwhile, potatoes had been introduced from America into Ireland and by the middle of the seventeenth century into western Lancashire and Cumbria. The peaty soils of the reclaimed Lancashire mosslands and the mild climate proved ideal for their cultivation. Small plots of potatoes were soon a common sight in fields as well as in gardens, and by 1680 a specialized potato market had been established at Wigan. Some other westerly areas, notably Cornwall, adopted the crop early, but most of the rest of England had to wait another hundred years before the potato was welcomed as a staple part of the working-class diet.[33]

Some parts of rural England, such as the chalk downlands of the South, remained predominantly agricultural under the close control of great estates and manors. Few people dwelt on the South Downs, which the Revd Gilbert White described as 'that chain of majestic mountains', for the tenant farmers and landless labourers lived alongside the streams in the chalkland valleys. The arable land continued to be farmed in open fields and the farming system was that of 'sheep and corn husbandry'. This was a very different 'country' from those districts where rural crafts provided a welcome extra source of income.[34]

The coastal marshlands provided another type of distinctive landscape, one that was dissected by drainage dykes and bounded by high sea walls or embankments. Here were boundless prospects of flat pasture, without trees or hedges. In Romney Marsh and the Marshland near the Wash, settlement was intensive and large areas of land were under the plough, for the marsh soils were naturally rich and fertile. But elsewhere, many marshlands were used exclusively for pasture, and the settlement pattern was a scatter of isolated farms.[35]

The growth of rural industries

England was industrially backward in the early sixteenth century compared with its European neighbours, but from about 1540 new crafts were gradually established and others were placed on a commercially significant basis for the first time. They included the mining of copper and the making of glass and paper; gunfounding and the manufacture of gunpowder; the weaving of silk, cotton and linen; and the creation of a range of New Draperies to rival the traditional textiles. Consumer products such as soap or stockings, pins and needles, and pots and pans transformed the lives of people throughout the land. Joan Thirsk showed how the 'Commonwealth men' at the centre of Elizabeth I's government made England far less dependent upon foreign imports by introducing new crafts into places that had little or no previous experience of them. Their many 'projects' included the making of pins in the Yorkshire villages of Sherburn-in-Elmet and Aberford, and the manufacture of needles in such scattered places as Redditch (Worcestershire), Long Crendon (Buckinghamshire) and Hathersage (Derbyshire). Elsewhere, established industries were developed by new techniques and ideas that were often brought in from abroad. In 1567, for example, a monopoly organization known as the Company of Mines Royal imported German workers into the Coniston area of Westmorland to find and mine copper. After the Company lost its monopoly in 1689, the industry expanded considerably.[36]

One of the most successful of these government projects was launched in 1611 when alum works were opened on the cliffs of the North Sea at Mulgrave, Asholme and Sandsend. Soon, alum was sold to English dyers and tanners and exported to the continent of Europe, the East Indies, and the New World.[37] The most successful of all these projects, however, was the enlargement of the textile industry by craftsmen from France and the Low Countries who introduced the skills of making lighter-weight cloths with different combinations of long wool, silk, and linen yarn, or new products such as tufted taffeties, wrought velvets and braunched satins. By the early seventeenth century the manufacture of some of these New Draperies had spread from Norwich throughout Norfolk, Suffolk and Essex and to other parts of England.[38]

The textile industry remained the biggest employer outside agriculture. Its various branches responded quickly to changing fashions. The growing national population provided ready markets for the cheap products of the West Riding, such as the narrow kerseys of Halifax parish, the broad cloths that were made further east, and the Penistones and Keighley whites from the periphery of the textile district, all of which were sold in Blackwell Hall in the City of London by the beginning of Elizabeth's reign. In the Pennine foothills, most families aimed to produce one piece of cloth per week in combination with farming a smallholding. Fulling mills spread along the river valleys, but the clothiers' smallholdings and cottages were scattered on the hillsides.[39]

In the Yorkshire Dales, too, the crafts of making woollen and linen cloths provided extra income for cottagers and farmers. Eighty-six of the 207 probate inventories from Nidderdale appraised between 1551 and 1610 recorded wool, yarn, spinning wheels, looms, or tenters. Queen Elizabeth's government introduced the knitting of long stockings in and around Richmond, Barnard Castle, Askrigg and Doncaster. Each Dales family aimed to knit three dozen pairs a week, and by 1644 over 2,000 dozen pairs per annum were being shipped from Stockton-on-Tees. An enquiry held in Dentdale and Garsdale in 1634 was told that the farms were:

> so small in quantity that many of them are not above three or four acres apiece, and generally not above eight or nine acres so that they could not maintain their families were it not by their industry in knitting coarse stockings.[40]

Lacemaking was another Elizabethan project, which took root in the South Midlands and Devon. It survived as a handicraft ('pillow' lacemaking) for females until the Victorian period in Bedfordshire and adjacent counties.

During the seventeenth and eighteenth centuries, the English woollen industry was carried on in the same regions as it had been in the late Middle Ages; all counties had some weavers but East Anglia, the West Country and the West Riding were pre-eminent. Defoe was impressed by the 'very populous and large' market towns and villages of Norfolk, and especially by the 'ancient, large, rich, and populous' city of Norwich, where the weavers employed 'all the country round in spinning yarn for them'. He enthused too about the clothing towns of Somerset, Wiltshire, Dorset and Gloucestershire, and the numerous villages, hamlets and scattered houses where poor people earned a living spinning yarn for the weavers of 'fine medley, or mixed cloths, such as are usually worn in England by the better sort of people; and, also, exported in great quantities to Holland, Hamburgh, Sweden, Denmark, Spain, Italy, &c.' He was impressed by the houses of the wealthy clothiers of Bradford-upon-Avon and Devizes and particularly by the town of Frome, which had 'prodigiously increased within these last twenty or thirty years', with 'many new streets of houses'. The cloths that were made in Frome were mostly sold at Blackwell Hall, London.[41]

When Defoe passed through some of the West Riding's populous textile villages on his journey from Halifax to Leeds, he thought they presented 'a noble scene of industry and application'. In 1755, the Revd J. Ismay observed that in Mirfield about 400 of his parishioners were employed in carding, spinning and preparing wool for the looms, and that another 200 made broad cloth for Leeds market. He continued:

> The dwellings at or about Hopton Hall are increased in less than forty years from three to eleven, and the inhabitants from seventeen to eighty . . . There are forty pairs of looms for weaving of white broad cloth in the hamlet. [Not far away] about two years ago only three families lived on the north side of Lee Green, but now the number amounts to twenty-three and more new buildings are about to be erected.[42]

The West Riding had a unique combination of woollen and worsted industries in close proximity. Worsteds were made in the upper valleys of the Calder and Aire; kerseys and other narrow woollen cloths in the district stretching from Halifax to the villages south of Huddersfield; broad cloths in the neighbourhood of Leeds (the finishing and marketing centre); white or undyed cloths in the Calder Valley; and coloured cloths in the parish of Leeds and in the villages to the west and south. The West Riding's success was ascribed by contemporary opinion to the peculiar structure of its industry, which provided opportunities for men of enterprise and initiative. In East Anglia and the West Country, wealthy merchants and clothiers who employed large numbers of outworkers dominated the trade, but the characteristic West Riding enterprise was the independent family unit which produced one piece of cloth each week for the local market hall. Only a small amount of capital was needed for such a venture, which was often profitably combined with running a smallholding. The worsted industry, however, was organized on a capitalistic basis and, as the population rose, cottagers were employed on a piece-rate at a specialist task such as weaving, spinning or combing.

Meanwhile, the East Midlands hosiery trade was growing in both the towns and the surrounding countryside. The Revd William Lee of Calverton (Nottinghamshire) had invented the stocking frame back in the 1580s, but it was slow to take hold in his native district. By 1660, however, about 650 framework knitters were at work in farmsteads and cottages in Nottinghamshire, Leicestershire and south Derbyshire. The earliest knitters commonly had a single frame and a smallholding, but during the eighteenth century men with little or no land became the characteristic figures in the trade. Framework knitting became one of England's most spectacular growth industries. It provided employment for the growing population and supplied much of the capital, the techniques and the labour force for the revolution that Derbyshire helped to pioneer in the textile industry.[43] Silk-weaving continued in its strongholds in Spitalfields, Canterbury and Coventry, but the silk-spinning, or 'throwing', mill that George Sorocold designed for Thomas Crotchett in 1702 on the river Derwent at Derby introduced a new centre of the trade. In 1718–22, Sorocold designed a much larger mill on an Italian model alongside it for Thomas Lombe. This mill produced yarn of a superior quality and was the prototype of the cotton mills that Arkwright and Strutt erected further up the Derwent Valley later in the century.[44]

As the national population grew, so did the demand for fuel in the form of coal or turf. In York it was said in 1597 that turves were 'now the greatest part of our fuel'. They were brought up the Ouse from Thorne and the other villages around Inclesmoor, as were coals from Newcastle.[45] The output of coal from many English mines was restricted because they were too landlocked to compete with the North East in national markets. Keith Wrightson has shown that from the second half of the sixteenth century onwards, the Northumberland and Durham coalfields were exploited on a massive scale, and on the south bank of the Tyne Whickham was transformed into one of England's earliest industrial communities. The coastal trade to London flourished mightily and coal was now used for household and industrial fires in places that had relied on wood before.[46]

Northumberland and County Durham continued to lead the way in the coal industry, as they had done since the Middle Ages when the coastal trade to London was established. By Elizabeth I's reign the precocious development of the coalfield on either side of the river Tyne was a national wonder. In 1700 about 43 per cent of British coal was mined in the North East, and by 1750 output there had doubled. Horse gins and Newcomen engines were installed to wind up the coal and to pump water from the deeper mines, while tramways known as 'Newcastle roads' allowed horses to move the coal along rails. Landowners owned or leased the mines and saw to the transport and sale of coal. On the other English coalfields, the scale of operations remained small by comparison, and miners were usually part-time farmers who did not form a separate group within their local communities.

Until the second half of the sixteenth century, glass for windows or tableware was generally imported from the Continent, for the products of the Weald or Staffordshire were of inferior quality. Immigrant glassworkers from Lorraine, who settled in the Weald, introduced new techniques that raised standards. In the second decade of the seventeenth century, when coal rapidly replaced wood as the fuel in the manufacturing process, the industry was re-sited in the coalfields by wealthy landowners who employed the descendants of the Lorrainers. Glass was used sparingly in most domestic buildings in the Middle Ages because of the cost, but it was used on a lavish scale in the Elizabethan prodigy houses that fitted as much glass into a wall as possible. 'Hardwick Hall, more glass than wall' remains a popular saying in Derbyshire.

By the late seventeenth and early eighteenth centuries, the glass industry was entirely fuelled by coal. The descendants of the Lorraine glassworkers left the woodlands of the Weald to start new businesses in the coalfields of the Midlands and the North. Furnaces became more complex, particularly in their flue systems, and the technology was increasingly sophisticated. High-quality sand and red lead were used in the manufacture of crystal glass; rape ashes provided a source of alkali for green bottles; bluepowder and manganese were used as the main colouring agents; and salt petre converted any iron into a less-colouring state, so as to avoid amber coloration in window glass. A cone erected at Catcliffe between Sheffield and Rotherham in the 1740s by William Fenny, as one of a pair, is the best surviving example in Europe; glass was made there until the early twentieth century.[47]

Coal was the vital fuel for the growing pottery industry and for tile works and limekilns. By 1660, north Staffordshire was emerging as the most important manufacturing district, with about 38 potteries (28 of them in Burslem); by 1715 the number had increased to about 67. Their most distinctive product was slipware, and the products of Thomas Toft, a Burslem potter, remain collectors' items. From the 1720s onwards, north Staffordshire potters began to experiment with imported clays and flints to make more-stylish wares. Their success in perfecting the manufacture of white, salt-glazed stoneware enhanced their national reputation.[48]

The iron industry expanded well beyond its Wealden base in response to increased demand for iron in building, agriculture, shipping, and the arms trade. The new charcoal blast furnaces, worked by water wheels, could cast up to 200 tons per annum to be re-worked at the forge into 130–150 tons of bar iron. By the mid-seventeenth century, improved furnaces were producing about 400 tons of pig iron per annum. Gentry partnerships invested in woods, furnaces and forges and in wire and slitting mills to supply wire drawers and nailmakers. The new technology arrived in the Midlands and the North in the 1560s and 1570s, though the main period of expansion in these regions began in the 1580s; by the 1630s the total iron production of the Weald had been overtaken by the rest of the country.[49]

The major technical development in the iron industry during the early eighteenth century was Abraham Darby's success from 1709 onwards in using coke as the fuel for the smelting and refining processes. In the 1750s, George Perry of Coalbrookdale reminisced that:

In the year 1700 the whole village consisted of only one furnace, five dwelling houses and a forge or two; about forty years ago the present Iron Foundry was established, and since that time its trade and buildings are so far increased that it contains at least 450 inhabitants and finds employment for more than 500 people.[50]

Practical difficulties prevented the widespread use of coke beyond Shropshire until the second half of the century, so the era of the charcoal blast furnace lasted until the mid-eighteenth century. Nevertheless, production grew in response to increased demand. Most of the pig iron that was smelted at the blast furnaces was converted in finery forges into wrought-iron bars for blacksmiths, nailers and other smiths. Three tilt hammers of a design first used in Germany were at work reducing bar iron and steel on Sheffield's rivers by 1740, fifteen by 1750.[51] The iron industry remained dominated by gentry partnerships, such as that controlled by the Spencers of Cannon Hall in South Yorkshire, whose bar iron went mostly to the local nailers. Nailmaking was essentially a rural craft that required little capital or technical knowledge and it was normally combined with farming until the rapid increase in population destroyed this old way of life. Large quantities of nails – outnumbered only by those from the Black Country – were sent by river and sea to Deptford, where merchants distributed them widely in England or packed them off across the Atlantic.[52]

The English iron industry was hampered by the inferior quality of its ores, but by the later seventeenth century Swedish iron from the Dannemora district was imported from Oregrund across the North Sea and up the navigable rivers to be converted into cementation steel. It was reported in 1677 that:

steel is made in several places as in Yorkshire, Gloucestershire, Sussex and the Wild of Kent and cetera. But the best is made around the Forrest of Dean, it breaks fiery with a somewhat coarse grain. But if it be well wrought and proves sound it makes good edge tools, files and punches. It will work well at the forge and takes a good heat.

The cementation steel furnace at Derwentcote (County Durham), restored by English Heritage in 1990, dates from the 1720s or 1730s, when northeastern England led the way in steel production and several furnaces were active in the Derwent Valley. Cementation furnaces were built of brick around two sandstone chests, which were shaped like coffins and heated by a coal fire, which was brought to a bright red heat (1,050–1,100 °C) and kept at that temperature for up to a week. The first cementation steel furnaces in South Yorkshire were erected by minor gentry and yeomen families in or near Rotherham and Sheffield, but the town of Sheffield, the eventual world leader in the industry, did not acquire its first steel furnace until about 1700. The industry took root and flourished there because the expanding cutlery industry provided a ready market for its products. Then in 1742, after many years of trial and error, Benjamin Huntsman achieved success in melting steel in crucibles that was more uniform and pure. His superior product gained world status for Sheffield, enabled Hallamshire to overtake London as the leading national centre of cutlery production, and stimulated the rapid growth of an edge-tool industry for which Sheffield soon had an international reputation.[53]

In Elizabeth's reign, the Derbyshire lead fields became the most productive in Europe. Huge investments were made in ventilating and draining the deeper mines and in building smelting mills in the river valleys. In the 1540s, Derbyshire's mines had yielded only 3,000 loads of lead; but by 1600, annual output had reached 34,000 loads; and by the 1640s, 120,000 loads. Smelters and merchants enjoyed massive profits, and many small settlements in the White Peak were turned into industrial villages as 'poor country folk' swelled the ranks of miners, cavers and hirelings from the early 1570s onwards. By 1581 the number of men who mined or sieved lead ore in the Peak District was estimated at about 2,000. On the eve of the Civil War, some 90 per cent of the male working population of Wirksworth, Cromford and Middleton were involved in lead mining.[54]

Dalesmen, too, could find work in lead mines, either as miner-farmers in small partnerships or as wage labourers in the new, deep mines, notably that which was sunk and drained at Greenhow by Sir Stephen Proctor of Fountains Hall. A new community was housed close to the mine at about 1,250–1,300 feet above sea level. The lead industry of the Peak District, the north Pennines and the Mendips continued to flourish in the late seventeenth and the early eighteenth centuries, despite occasional slumps in demand and increasing technical difficulties as mines were sunk to deeper levels. Large-scale capital enterprises, dominated by the gentry families of north and west

FIGURE 10 *Three Elizabethan knives, found in the Thames' mud banks by Simon Moore. Their marks identify them as Hallamshire products.*

Derbyshire, increasingly took control of all aspects of the lead industry: mining, smelting, transporting and marketing. Nevertheless, large numbers of farmers, craftsmen and even some free miners held shares in large mines or became partners in drainage operations. Mining remained a heavy 'pick-and-shovel' job and, even in the deep mines, underground transport remained primitive. Daniel Defoe gave a vivid description of a Peak District lead miner who emerged, first with 'a hand, and then an arm, and quickly after a head, thrust up out of the very groove we were looking at':

> The man was a most uncouth spectacle; he was cloathed all in leather, has a cap of the same without brims, some tools in a little basket which he drew up with him, not one of the names of which we could understand but by the help of an interpreter. Nor indeed could we understand any of the man's discourse . . . He was as lean as a skeleton, pale as a dead corps, his hair and beard black, his flesh lank, and, as we thought, something of the colour of lead itself.

As mines were worked at deeper levels, substantial investment was needed to overcome ventilation and flooding problems. By 1700 more than 30 drainage soughs had been constructed in the Peak District, and by the late eighteenth century some of these were over a mile long. In 1717 Yatestoop Mine in Winster became the first Derbyshire mine to install a Newcomen-type engine to pump water through the soughs and to wind the ore to the surface; by 1730 the annual output of the Yatestoop mine equalled the total output of the whole Derbyshire lead field in 1580.[55]

The leather industry also flourished in these years, for hides were used for making garments and footwear, harness, horse collars, saddles, straps, bags and bottles, and in Hallamshire for bellows, grinders' belting and sheaths for knives. By the late 1620s West Riding tanners were importing about 4,000 hides a year from London as back-carriage on boats that sailed up the Humber and the navigable rivers. Tanneries had an obnoxious smell and attracted flies, so they were placed on the edges of towns and in remote parts of the countryside. Like glass furnaces and corn mills, they remained in the ownership of the same families down the generations.[56]

The coastal trade in bulky goods grew by two-thirds between 1660 and 1702 after numerous private Acts of Parliament had authorized private companies to improve the navigability of the major rivers. It has been calculated that by about 1730, long before the golden era of canals, about 1,160 miles of English rivers were navigable for light craft, though much of the river traffic was seasonal because of summer droughts. A Severn trow could carry about 40 tons of agricultural and industrial produce to and from the major inland ports at Gloucester, Worcester and Bewdley, and further up river at Shrewsbury. The overland and water transport systems were complementary rather than rivals. A horse could tow up to 30 tons on a navigable river, so it was cheaper to send heavy, loose materials, such as coal, clay, lime, sand, gravel, salt and grain, and bulky goods such as pigs of lead or bars of iron, by water wherever possible.[57]

By 1670 the proportion of the workforce that was engaged in farming had shrunk to no more than 60 per cent, and by 1750 to 46 per cent. The growth of rural industries increased the diversity of the various 'countries' of England. When the Revd F.E. Witts, the parson of Upper Slaughter in Gloucestershire, travelled to Bristol via Chipping Sodbury in 1833, he noted 'this old triste and deserted-looking place' in his diary and observed:

> Here the aspect of the country is uninteresting, pastured by ragged horses and donkeys and geese, and bordered by mean-looking cottages, half dilapidated and a general air of discomfort prevailed. The country is indeed more populous than our Cotswold hills; but the people have a less rural cast, being chiefly colliers or engaged in the hat and other manufactories. One tract of common over which we passed is called Coalpitheath, a ragged-looking spot, people and their dwellings being all out at elbows. As we drew nearer to Bristol the country improved.[58]

Likewise, in *Adam Bede*, George Eliot's character Dinah Morris remarked that Snowfield, some 20 miles away, was a typically bleak place:

> very different from this country ... They have a different sort of life, many of 'em, they work at different things – some in the mill, and many in the mines ... we've many more Methodists there than in this country.

The general picture that emerges throughout England from contemporary descriptions such as these is of diverse economies that were related to the peculiar circumstances in which people found themselves. For employment, local people had to turn to whatever jobs were available at the time, regardless of the wider situation. In that way, they stood noticeably apart from the experience of their neighbours.

CHAPTER SIX

The greatest buildings in the land

The purpose of castles

The buildings that survive from the Norman period are those of the rich and the powerful. The castles that are now a proud part of England's heritage were once the overbearing symbols of an army of occupation. The Normans consolidated their victory at Hastings by forcing the natives to construct earthen castles in the form of ringworks and motte-and-baileys. The *Anglo-Saxon Chronicle* observed of William: 'Castles he caused to be made, and poor men to be greatly oppressed', and of the anarchy of Stephen's reign:

> Every great man built him castles and held them against the king; and they filled the whole land with these castles. They sorely burdened the unhappy people of the country with forced labour on the castles; and when the castles were built, they filled them with devils and wicked men.[1]

In this poorly documented period it is impossible to establish a firm chronology for the erection of castles. Surviving earthworks suggest that about 1,000 sites in England and Wales date from between 1066 and 1200, though perhaps only 500–600 were occupied at any one time.[2] About 200 castles belonged to the monarch or barons, while the rest were owned by knights. Some parts of England were relatively unaffected, but in other districts, notably the Welsh Marches, castles were a common feature of the countryside. Meanwhile, the urban landscapes of leading medieval cities such as Durham, Lincoln or Norwich, where large areas were cleared of housing to accommodate the new castles, provide a forceful reminder of the impact of the Norman invasion.

Historians once studied castles purely from a military point of view, but since Charles Coulson's pioneering studies a new approach has gradually been adopted.[3] Archaeologists and landscape historians, while acknowledging the need for some military protection, now stress the primary importance of a castle's symbolic role. A crenellated building could have been an emblem of lordly status rather than a response to military insecurity. One of the dominant themes of castle architecture was nostalgia, rather than the desire to produce a defensive military structure. Castles were aesthetically pleasing to the military eye. They were more akin to later country houses than to fortresses. This academic consensus has not yet got through to the general public or to many promoters of the tourist industry.

The debate over the military role of the castle came to the fore in the 1990s, when the purpose of Bodiam Castle (Sussex) was reinterpreted. In 1385 Sir Edward Dalyngrigge, a Sussex landowner, royal administrator and veteran of the Hundred Years War, obtained a royal 'licence to crenellate' in order 'to make into a castle his manor house of Bodiam, near the sea, in the county of Sussex, for the defence of the adjacent country'. The wording seems specific, for at that time the south coast was suffering from French raids, but landscape historians have concluded that as Bodiam was nowhere near the sea, it was in an odd position to deter coastal raiding. The defensive provision of the building was shown to be highly suspect and impractical. The building was deliberately nostalgic in its construction.[4]

Soon afterwards, a number of medieval 'designed landscapes' were identified. Leeds Castle (Kent) was shown to be a fine example of the way in which the use of water and parkland could be combined to great visual effect. In 1279 the manor of Leeds had passed to King Edward I. At this date the castle was probably just a motte-and-bailey with an adjacent deer park, but during the 1280s it was substantially rebuilt and surrounded by a large ornamental lake. The main focus of building was the tower, which was raised on what was probably the site of the Norman motte. This was known as the 'Gloriette', a term that meant a suite of lordly accommodation within a park or garden. More ponds were constructed to the south, northwest and east to create a huge medieval water garden. It is clear that the eastern pond was designed to provide a pleasing view from the Gloriette.[5]

The idea that the primary role of castles was not defence was then taken back further in time. The mightiest of the late twelfth-century castles was that at Dover, which was begun on a fortified Iron Age and Roman site by William the Conqueror and rebuilt in the 1180s by King Henry II as the largest castle in England. Both the architectural and the documentary evidence support the interpretation that it was conceived as a showpiece monument that was intended to be displayed to visitors. English Heritage have recently recreated the original visual impact of the interior to stunning effect, by presenting the great tower as if Henry II and his court were in residence, receiving a great foreign visitor on pilgrimage to Canterbury. The bright colour schemes are based on contemporary objects, wall paintings and manuscripts. A document dated 1247 reveals that Dover Castle was indeed deliberately displayed in all its glory to such visitors. King Henry III ordered the constable of Dover that: 'When Gaucher de Chatillon shall come to Dover he shall take him into the castle and show the castle off to him in eloquent style, so that the magnificence of the castle shall be fully apparent to him.'[6]

Even the White Tower of London and Colchester Castle, the two earliest and sturdiest examples of Norman castles, dating from the 1070s, have been reinterpreted in this manner. Both were placed deliberately on the ruins of major Roman buildings. At Colchester, the stone keep, or donjon, was built on the site of a Roman temple dedicated to the emperor-god Claudius. The White Tower was placed within an earlier ringwork that occupied an angle of the Roman wall. As Robert Liddiard observes:

> The internal arrangements suggest that the White Tower was effectively a giant ceremonial building containing a series of reception rooms. Rather than being intended to frustrate an intruder, the entry to the building appears concerned with creating a grand approach.... The whole ensemble is reminiscent of entrances to Classical buildings.[7]

Although some castles were besieged during the various civil wars during the anarchy of Stephen's reign (1135–54), and northern castles such as Norham and Durham were regarded as 'bulwarks against the assaults' of the Scots in later centuries,[8] the majority of castle owners (especially those in lowland England) spent most of their time without fear of attack. Castles were built to dominate an area and to provide accommodation on a suitably grand scale for the monarch or a baron, rather than to act merely as a place of refuge. Their surrounding parks, warrens and fishponds speak of a relaxed lifestyle in an ornamental landscape setting.

Markets were usually established alongside the castles to supply food and goods to the people who lived and worked there, but the fortunes of these ventures were varied. In Yorkshire, for instance, the broad High Street that descends the hill below Skipton Castle was used for markets and fairs, and it remains the busiest part of the town to this day. But at Skipsea in the East Riding, the castle that was once the military and administrative centre of the Norman Honour of Holderness lies in ruins, and the borough is deserted.

The major cathedrals

The sheer amount and scale of building in the two centuries after the Norman Conquest was unprecedented. The formidable castles that were erected by the Norman kings and barons were matched and then surpassed by splendid cathedrals, abbeys and priories. In the generation after 1066 England's seventeen medieval cathedrals were either founded or rebuilt. By 1200 most of the 650 monasteries of England and Wales had been created or reconstructed, and throughout the land parish churches and chapels were erected or redesigned in the Norman style.[9] Grand stone buildings, more substantial than anything that had been constructed before, became a familiar sight in every county.

England's varied geology produced regional contrasts in the outward appearance of these buildings. It was usual for local materials to be used because of the high cost of transport, though good quality stones could be moved relatively cheaply down the major rivers or by sea. The most highly regarded building stones were brought from Caen in Normandy or from England's Oolitic Limestone belt.

The Normans were the greatest builders of their time, with cathedrals as far away as Sicily. Edward the Confessor's abbey at Westminster was the first to be erected in England in the Romanesque manner, or the Norman style as it became known much later. Every cathedral in the country was rebuilt in the 40 years after the Battle of Hastings, on a much larger scale than before, as churchmen from Normandy and elsewhere on the Continent were appointed to key posts. The first cathedral to be reconstructed in the new style was Canterbury, where Lanfranc had been appointed archbishop in 1070. At the same time, a major reconstruction of English dioceses was underway: Dorchester was moved to Lincoln; Elham to Thetford and then to Norwich; Sherborne to Old Sarum and later to Salisbury; Lichfield to Chester and then to Coventry; Wells to Bath; and Selsey to Chichester. The longest and most successful move was that to Lincoln, whose diocese stretched from the Humber to the Thames. The new bishop was Remigius, a monk from Fécamp in Normandy who had fought at the Battle of Hastings. At Lincoln, he needed a stronghold against the threat of Danish invasion, and it is thought that the high wall, immense arches and deep recesses that were later incorporated into the west front of the cathedral were originally part of a huge, fort-like headquarters for the bishop. The cathedral, the bishop's palace, and the castle were contained in a new enclosure, which had been created by demolishing 166 houses within the Roman walls on the limestone ridge.[10] They still provide a sharp visual contrast to the city that flourishes at the bottom of Steep Hill.

Meanwhile, another major project was underway at Winchester, where Walkelin, a former royal chaplain and canon of Rouen cathedral, had been appointed bishop in 1079. Winchester was the richest and most important see after Canterbury and York. The church that Walkelin built was twice as long as that at Canterbury, and it remains the longest cathedral in Europe. It was provided with a crypt, transepts with aisles, and a massive interior that was deliberately unpainted. This was Norman might at its most impressive. During the next decade, St Paul's, London, and York Minster were also rebuilt on a huge scale. Before the eleventh century was out, perhaps ten cathedrals were at some stage of complete rebuilding.

England's outstanding Norman cathedral is that which towers above the river Wear as it winds around a wooded precipice at Durham. It has been justly described as 'the incomparable masterpiece of Romanesque architecture not only in England but anywhere'.[11] The Norman interior is unusually complete. Begun in 1093, the whole of the church, except for the towers, was completed in only 40 years, and every part was vaulted. At the west end, a Galilee chapel, where the Venerable Bede was finally laid to rest, served uniquely as a Lady Chapel. The shrine of St Cuthbert, to whom the church is dedicated, stood in the cathedral's eastern apse.

The cultural unity of Christendom enabled the French Gothic style of architecture and its accompanying choral music in the form of polyphony instead of plainchant to sweep across Europe. The English kings, barons and leading clergymen all spoke French and had many contacts abroad. Wells cathedral, which was begun in the new style in the 1170s or 1180s, was the first medieval building in England in which the pointed arch was used throughout. Gothic buildings soared to unprecedented heights, with tall, pointed arches rising from slim columns and with walls supported by the counter-thrust of elegant buttresses. French Gothic was never accepted as a whole, as it was in Germany, but was modified to suit English building traditions. One of the outstanding and best-preserved examples of Early English Gothic is Salisbury Cathedral, built of Chilmark limestone and Purbeck marble between 1220 and 1266 in a precinct on the edge of a new town that was laid out to a grid pattern in the valley below the previous hill-top site of Old Sarum.[12]

In the thirteenth century, 'marbles' from the Isle of Purbeck (Dorset) were widely appreciated for their decorative qualities in cathedrals and parish churches. Until the seventeenth century, and sometimes beyond, large quantities were quarried near Corfe Castle or close to the sea; holloways can still be traced across the heath towards the south shore of Poole Harbour. The stones were exported far and wide by sea and navigable rivers such as the Witham from Lincoln to Boston.

The English Church was immensely wealthy in the Middle Ages. Though the country's Gothic cathedrals lacked the height, and often the stone-vaulted roofs, of France, they were noted for their length and their artistic decoration. Gothic architecture was seen less as a technical challenge than as a decorative system in which walls, vaults and glass could all be richly ornamented with highly polished Purbeck marble shafts, painted arches and vaults, and glorious stained-glass windows. Until the Reformation, English buildings had a colourful and costly appearance that is hard to grasp today; the west front of Wells cathedral, for example, was adorned with vividly painted statues.

England's great cathedrals were not built in a single campaign, but were added to over the centuries. What would now be regarded as vandalism in tearing down old buildings to start anew was commonplace in the Middle Ages. The new Decorated Gothic style was first used for Henry III's Westminster Abbey choir and nave, which were built between 1245 and 1269, and whose tracery was a source of inspiration for almost a hundred years. It soon spread throughout England. In the 1290s the chapter house of the collegiate church at Southwell (Nottinghamshire) was decorated with a wonderful collection of stone carvings that depicted nature in a lively and realistic manner in the form of leaves, fruit and flowers, together with representations of goats, hares, birds, fabulous creatures, and human heads as portraits or caricatures. York Minster has about 60 per cent of England's surviving medieval stained glass, but the new Gothic styles that were adopted elsewhere in Yorkshire were based more on that of Selby Abbey's seven-bay choir of 1280–1340, which has the entire range of Decorated tracery types, most famously in the east window.[13]

The octagonal lantern above the crossing at Ely Cathedral was one of the greatest achievements of medieval carpentry. Between 1322 and 1328, eight massive stone columns were erected to support the tall arches that span the crossing and provide the octagonal base for the central tower. Another 14 years were needed to construct the astonishing timber lantern that was designed by William Hurley. Eight vertical oak posts, each of them 63 feet high and weighing ten tons, were raised more than 100 feet in the air to be positioned on the stone base. A complex framework of timber struts and curved members with a compression ring at the top were needed to brace the posts and to support the timber vault above. The soaring lantern remains one of England's most inspiring sights.

The final form of medieval Gothic, the Perpendicular style, was a distinctive English contribution, unaffected by developments in French Gothic or by the Italian Renaissance. The earliest examples from the 1330s occur in large ecclesiastical buildings. St Stephen's chapel, Westminster, and the chapter house of Old St Paul's, where the mullions of large windows were extended downwards so as to make panelling on the wall spaces below part of a continuous design, have been demolished, but contemporary work survives in the South West, where former abbeys at Bristol and Gloucester achieved cathedral status in the sixteenth century. Naves were also built in the Perpendicular style at Canterbury (by Henry Yevele, the King's master builder) and at Winchester (by William Wynford).

During the fifteenth century the central towers of a number of English cathedrals, including Gloucester, Wells and Durham, were completed or heightened in Perpendicular Gothic style. After the great east window of the new choir of York Minster had been completed by the master glazier John Thornton in 1405–8, work began on the cathedral's central tower and then on the two towers at the west end. They were surpassed in beauty by Bell Harry, the central tower at Canterbury Cathedral, designed by John Westell and built between 1494 and 1497 with 480,000 red bricks faced with Caen limestone. Meanwhile, the west front of the great collegiate church at Beverley was completed about 1450.

Cathedrals were surrounded by many other buildings, starting with the bishop's palace and the houses of the dean, treasurer and other senior clergy and canons, all within a close that was physically separated from the rest of the city. At York, the Cathedral Close was surrounded by a 12-foot wall with four gates, under a royal licence of 1285.[14] The mayor and aldermen of the city had no powers or influence within this separate jurisdiction.

Monasteries and other religious institutions

The great abbeys that have lain in ruins since Henry VIII dissolved them and confiscated their properties were mostly founded or re-founded by the Norman kings and barons. It was a peculiarity of the English ecclesiastical system that eight of the medieval cathedrals – Canterbury, Carlisle, Durham, Ely, Norwich, Rochester, Winchester and Worcester – were united with monasteries, so that the bishop was also the titular abbot, though the effective head of the monastery was the prior. The remaining cathedrals – Chichester, Exeter, Hereford, Lichfield, Lincoln, London, Salisbury, Wells and York – were run by a bishop and secular canons, who were housed nearby.

The Benedictines formed the largest and wealthiest monastic order in medieval England.[15] Most of their important abbeys, notably those that were associated with cathedrals, were situated in towns. A Benedictine abbey had stood on the site of St Alban's martyrdom since 793, but the church was entirely rebuilt between 1077 and 1115 under the direction of Paul de Caen and Richard D'Aubeney, the first two Norman abbots. This was one of the earliest and most ambitious rebuilding projects, and when it was finished the abbey church was a third longer than the new Canterbury cathedral. The builders had to use flints, together with bricks from the ruined Roman city of Verulamium close by. The huge brick piers of the interior were plastered over and painted, but no carvings were possible and a timber roof had to suffice. From 1154 to 1396, St Albans was the premier abbey of England.

The Benedictines owned one of England's greatest and richest abbeys at Bury St Edmunds, and they used limestone from their quarries at Barnack to build an abbey at Peterborough (which became a cathedral in 1541). In the North, the Normans soon set about rebuilding some of the Benedictine abbeys that the Danes had destroyed and establishing new ones elsewhere. William the Conqueror led the way in Yorkshire by founding Selby Abbey, which became one of the richest monasteries north of the Trent. In the late 1070s Reinfrid, one of the Conqueror's knights who had been saddened by the sight of the ruined monasteries at Jarrow, Monkwearmouth, Whitby and York, took monastic vows and, together with Aldwin, the future prior of Durham, resolved to restore them. Then, in 1088 King William II founded St Mary's Abbey, York, on or close to what appears to have been the site of the former monastery of Galmanho. Other renowned Benedictine foundations include Abbotsbury, Crowland, Ramsey, Sherborne, Tavistock, Tewkesbury and Tynemouth. The abbey church at Tewkesbury remains one of the finest examples of Norman architecture in the country.

Much of the inspiration for the tenth-century monastic revival in Wessex had come from the Cluniacs, a reformed Benedictine order, which had been founded in Burgundy in 909. They placed great emphasis on liturgy within splendid buildings, with much more time than was usual devoted to the singing of the Office, and to psalms and prayers, ceremonies, intercessions, and masses. The first Cluniac house in England was Lewes Priory, which was endowed in 1077 by William de Warenne, one of the Conqueror's mightiest barons, and his wife, Gundrada, on the site of the Saxon church of St Pancras in the valley of the river Ouse below their castle at the centre of their great lordship in Sussex. However, most of the 36 Cluniac priories that were established in England were small and, apart from Much Wenlock, their ruins are insubstantial.[16]

In the early thirteenth century several orders of friars were founded to preach to urban audiences and maintain themselves by begging, for they did not accept gifts of property other than towards the building and maintenance of their churches and friaries. In 1221 the Dominicans (Black Friars) from Spain became the first preaching order to reach England. The Franciscans (Grey Friars), the Carmelites (White Friars), and the Augustinians (Austin Friars) soon followed them. The Grey Friars church in London once ranked second to Old St Paul's in size. The Crutched Friars and the Friars of the Sack also gained temporary footholds, but did not flourish. The main orders of friars were welcomed and were supported by members of the royal family, noblemen, bishops and burgesses. They were rarely perceived as a threat to the existing monasteries, but they did arouse the hostility of parish priests, who saw their main source of charitable funds diverted from their churches. The number of friars grew quickly, but by the early fourteenth century

FIGURE 11 *The ruins of the Cluniac priory at Much Wenlock, Shropshire, still dominate the town.*

enthusiasm had begun to wane. Friary ruins are insubstantial, for after the Dissolution their prime sites in the leading towns were vulnerable to redevelopment.[17]

Many of England's greatest abbeys were built in the remote countryside instead of in towns. They belonged to monastic orders that originated in France. The Cistercian order was founded at Cîteaux in Burgundy in 1098 in an attempt to return to the simplicity of the Benedictines, their white habits contrasting with the black of the original order. They were remarkably successful with 750 monasteries throughout west Europe by the late Middle Ages. The first to be established in England was that at Waverley, Surrey, in 1128, and by the end of the twelfth century over 100 houses had been founded in England and Wales. The Cistercians lived frugal, devotional and meditative lives and they refused endowments other than uncultivated land on remote sites that could be improved by the manual labour of large numbers of lay brothers, many of whom worked at outlying granges. Huge tracts of moorland were converted into sheep pastures to produce wool to sell to Italian merchants, and much ingenuity and energy was devoted to developing the iron and lead industries.

Cistercian abbeys were large communities in the medieval countryside, bigger and busier than most contemporary villages. In North Yorkshire in the mid-twelfth century, Rievaulx Abbey had 140 monks and over 500 lay brothers. Under the guidance of St Ailrid, the greatest abbot of his age, teacher, author, administrator and confidant of kings and barons, this became the most renowned Cistercian abbey in England. Its success inspired 13 Benedictine monks to leave St Mary's Abbey, York, for a life under the Cistercian rule in remote Skeldale, where Archbishop Thurstan had given them an uncultivated tract of land, watered by pure springs or fountains. Soon, Fountains Abbey was the richest and one of the most celebrated Cistercian monasteries in the land. Because of their remoteness, Fountains and Rievaulx escaped the worst destruction at the dissolution of the monasteries, and they remain the most complete Cistercian abbeys in England, as famous now as they were in the Middle Ages. Other notable English Cistercian abbeys with substantial ruins include Beaulieu, Buildwas, Byland, Furness, Jervaulx, Netley and Roche.[18]

The Cistercians played an important role in the adoption of French Gothic ideas when they began to replace the austere churches of their predecessors. At Rievaulx Abbey the contrast between the lavish east end of the church, which was rebuilt for the monks in the early thirteenth century, and the stern Norman architecture of the lay brothers' western part shows how far the Cistercians had moved from their original ideals. At Fountains Abbey, too, the Chapel of the Nine Altars, which was completed by 1247 at the east end of the church, is very different in style from the ruined Norman nave.

The sheepwalks of the Dales and the North York Moors provided the wool that was the mainstay of the economy of Yorkshire's wealthiest

Cistercian houses. Credit was raised from Florentine merchants for advance sales of wool for up to 20 years, but this made the abbeys financially vulnerable to outbreaks of scab, such as that which affected the Rievaulx flocks in 1280. By 1291 Fountains Abbey owed debts totalling £6,373.[19]

As the lands that had been granted by the faithful were scattered, the usual practice of the monks was to administer their estates from the granges that they built in the countryside. These granges housed a few lay brothers and farm servants and often had a chapel attached. The best-surviving buildings are the great estate barns, such as those at Great Coxwell in Oxfordshire, which belonged to Beaulieu Abbey, and at Bradford-upon-Avon in Wiltshire, a property of Shaftesbury Abbey.[20]

The canons of the Augustinian order chose to live to a regular, monastic rule, but with daily contact with the outside world. They originated in Italy and France in the mid-eleventh century, and their first English house was St Botolph's Priory, Colchester, which was founded in 1103. The Austin or Black Canons, as they were known in England, soon obtained the patronage of King Henry I. Their emphasis on poverty, celibacy and obedience attracted many other donors, so that by the middle of the fourteenth century they had over 200 houses in England, Scotland and Wales. Many of these were small, but some priories – Bolton-in-Wharfedale, Bridlington, Carlisle, Cirencester, Colchester, Guisborough, Haughmond, Kirkham, Lanercost, Lilleshall, Merton, St Frideswade's (Oxford), Thornton, Ulverscroft and Walsingham – became large and famous. The canons sometimes shared their churches with their lay neighbours. At Cirencester they built a separate parish church, in splendid style, at the abbey gates. Elsewhere, canons were seconded to be vicars of parish churches that were under the patronage of the priory. The order also founded hospitals, including St Bartholomew's and St Thomas's in London.[21]

Another order of regular canons, the Premonstratensian, was founded at Prémontré in northern France in 1120. They, too, were much involved with their local communities. Their first priory in England was at Newhouse in Lincolnshire, founded in 1143. By the end of the twelfth century, they had 31 abbeys and three nunneries scattered around England, mostly sited in remote places. Surviving ruins are best seen at Bayham Abbey on the border of Sussex and Kent. Whereas the Cistercians sought refuge in remote situations, the White Canons were actively involved with their local societies. The surnames recorded at Beauchief Abbey in north Derbyshire suggest that most of the abbots and canons came from the neighbourhood. The leading landowners within Scarsdale wapentake witnessed the most important charters, and numerous other local people made small gifts, such as vestments or a silver cup. In return they received the hospitality of the fraternity, attended services and had annual masses said for them after they died. The abbey's property comprised a 780-acre home estate, the tithes of five parishes, large stretches of countryside for grazing cattle and sheep, and water-powered corn and fulling mills. The canons served as vicars or chaplains in local churches and they founded at least one school.[22]

Meanwhile, the Gilbertine canons had formed the only monastic order that originated in England, when in 1131 Gilbert, parish priest at the village of Sempringham in Lincolnshire, built a small convent beside his church. By the time of his death 50 years later, the order had twelve monasteries, ten of them double houses for nuns and canons, but only Sempringham and Watton in the East Riding were modestly wealthy. The Gilbertines were celebrated for their high standards and their charity. The rural poor of Lincolnshire had good cause to appreciate the welfare that they provided.

After the Norman Conquest separate nunneries were generally favoured instead of the previous practice of creating double houses for monks and nuns. Nunneries were small, poorly endowed institutions, which catered especially for the widows and daughters of the richer families. They usually accommodated only 12 or fewer Benedictine or Cistercian nuns under a prioress. They date mostly from the twelfth or thirteenth centuries and their remains are generally unimpressive.[23]

The spread of monasticism had been remarkable; every part of England was affected, for the various orders received numerous bequests of land and often became the owners of the tithes of a parish. The monasteries were not only renowned for their spiritual life but for the scale of their farming and industrial activities in the countryside and their sponsorship of commercial activities in some of England's leading towns. Clergymen and nuns also ran the numerous medieval hospitals that were founded as charitable institutions.[24] Yorkshire had 90 or so of these, the largest being that of St Leonard's, York, a twelfth-century foundation that, in 1280, accommodated 229 sick people.

The military-religious orders that were created to protect pilgrims and to guard holy places after the first crusaders had captured Jerusalem in 1099 offered a different type of religious institution to benefactors. The Knights of the Hospital of St John of Jerusalem, who provided lodging and care for the sick, the poor and pilgrims, received substantial endowments of land, which they managed from their headquarters at St John's Priory, Clerkenwell, London, and from about 50 preceptories in various parts of England. The Knights Templar, formed in 1119 to protect pilgrims in the Holy Land, became known throughout Europe. Little remains of their 50 or so preceptories in the British Isles, though these are sometimes commemorated by place-names such as Temple Normanton in Derbyshire. Their headquarters was the Temple Church, Fleet Street, London, which retains some of its Norman architecture, and their best-known building is the much-restored Round Church in Cambridge, which was erected about 1130 on the model of the Holy Sepulchre in Jerusalem. The Hospitallers and Templars attracted numerous small donations from ordinary farming families, and their policy was to let their scattered lands to peasant farmers. Every parish had men of religion amongst its landlords.[25]

The most-remarkable surviving buildings that were erected by the Knights Templar are their two enormous timber-framed barns at Little Cressing (Essex). The Barley Barn is thought to be the earliest surviving barn in

England and probably in Europe. The removal of sapwood by the carpenters has destroyed the outmost tree rings, but it can nevertheless be dated by its tree-rings to after 1205 and probably by 1235. The barn was partly rebuilt at different times from the fifteenth and sixteenth centuries onwards. Today it is 118 feet long and 45 feet wide internally, with five equal bays and half bays at each end. The Wheat Barn is better preserved and dates from sometime between 1257 and 1280. Woodland was managed to produce fast-grown straight oak trees, and the timber was used when it was green, for then it was easier to work. Each of the barns would probably have been completed in a single building season between March and November. The barns were roofed at first with tiles that were slightly larger than those in use today; both have about 45,000 tiles with a total weight of 55 tons. It has been shown that the measurements used in the ground plans and elevations are multiples or simple fractions of a medieval unit known variously as the rod, pole or perch (16½ feet), set out by dividers, straight edges, cords and pegs. Each barn had about 1,200 joints.[26]

Like the great lay landowners, the cathedrals, abbeys, priories and religious orders had extensive estates, substantial capital and knowledgeable staff familiar with the latest ideas and technology. They managed huge acreages of arable land, meadows and pastures, woods and moors, and were instrumental in reclaiming wetlands, including the Fens, Romney Marsh, the Hull Valley marshes and the Somerset Levels. The best-preserved series of fishponds in England are those that were owned by the Knights Templar in the bottom of the valley below the Northamptonshire village of Harringworth. Fishponds were commercial concerns that included breeding 'stews', dams, sluices and various supply and overflow channels. The Fens and fenland rivers provided vast quantities of fish, partly for export to places further afield. Most surprising of all is the realization that the Norfolk Broads were created by the natural flooding of the huge turbaries that had been cut by their monastic owners to meet the commercial demand for peat. In other parts of England, monks were also pioneers in the application of new mining and smelting techniques in the iron and lead industries.[27]

The Crown's valuation of ecclesiastical property in 1536 revealed a large gap between a few rich monastic establishments and the rest; only 4 per cent of English monasteries had incomes of over £1,000 per annum, whereas nearly 80 per cent had to be content with less than £300 per year. Long before Henry VIII's reign, monasteries had struggled to attract new endowments and to recruit people who were prepared to take the vows. During the reign of Henry VIII, England had about 10,000 monks and 2,000 nuns, far fewer than 200 years previously. Much of the old fervour had gone and many monasteries and convents had insufficient numbers to run their estates efficiently; instead, it had become the normal practice to lease them to local gentry and yeomen. Conditions and standards varied widely from monastery to monastery, but they were never as lax as the propagandists for dissolution made out.

King Henry VIII did not start with the clear intention of destroying all the monasteries. His government began by dissolving those institutions (except the Gilbertines) that had fewer than a dozen monks or nuns and an annual endowment of under £200. In the first year, 374 were dissolved, 90 of them in Yorkshire and Lincolnshire. These suppressions added to fears and rumours that that parish churches, too, were about to be dissolved, church goods confiscated, and a tax imposed on baptisms. Thousands of people still resorted to monastic shrines in search of charity, medical help and spiritual support, and widespread resentment of the policies of a remote central government quickly turned into a spontaneous and popular rebellion known as the Pilgrimage of Grace, which began in Lincolnshire and the East Riding of Yorkshire and quickly spread to other parts of England. Its brutal suppression effectively deterred further protests against the dissolution of the monasteries and the progress of the English Reformation.[28]

The attack on the greater monasteries began at Bury St Edmunds early in 1538. In the five years between 1536 and 1540, all 650 monasteries in England and Wales were dissolved and their possessions confiscated by the Crown. The last monastery to fall was Waltham Abbey on 23 March 1540. Today, about a third of the former monasteries have no physical remains, and another third have only insubstantial ruins. The monks were provided with pensions that varied in value from monastery to monastery but which were assessed fairly and were paid over the succeeding years. In the aftermath of the Pilgrimage of Grace, the royal commissioners met with little opposition. King Henry VIII sold the estates that he had confiscated to noblemen, gentlemen, courtiers, lawyers and merchants in the biggest re-distribution of land since the Norman Conquest.

Once an abbot or prior had surrendered his monastery, it was plundered to prevent reoccupation of the site by the monks and to provide a quick profit for the Crown. Chattels and movables were auctioned on the site, lead roofs were stripped, building stone was carted away and livestock and crops were confiscated. On 26 November 1539, for instance, the abbot and 31 monks at Fountains were forced to leave the abbey, and their 1,976 horned cattle, 1,146 sheep, 86 horses, 79 swine and 221 quarters of grain were sold to Sir Richard Gresham. At Roche Abbey in South Yorkshire:

> All things of price [were] either spoiled, carped away, or defaced to the uttermost . . . it seemeth that every person bent himself to filch and spoil what he could . . . nothing was spared but the oxhouses and swinecoates and such other houses of office, that stood without the walls.[29]

The market was flooded with property at bargain prices.

A Court of Augmentations had been established at the beginning of the dissolution of the monasteries in March 1536 in order to deal with the newly acquired spoils; only about 2.5 per cent of the plunder was given away. Prominent purchasers included groups of London speculators who bought in order to resell at a profit; lawyers, government officials and merchants; and the commissioners who enforced the surrender of the monasteries. The great estates of the Cavendish, Russell and Thynne families began in this way, and many another man who did not scruple to grab his share of the spoils was able to increase his fortunes substantially. Local gentry families benefited most in the long run.

Some noble and gentry families who converted monasteries into residences retained part of the medieval structure. The monastic cloister of the Benedictine abbey at Audley End in Essex was preserved when Thomas Audley, former Speaker of the House of Commons and Lord Chancellor, built a great house on the site. When the courtier Sir William Sharington bought a medieval nunnery in Wiltshire, now known as Lacock Abbey, for £783, he spent another £1,333 on new buildings but left the old structure virtually intact. And when Sir John Byron, Sheriff of Nottinghamshire, converted the Augustinian priory at Newstead, the upper floor became the principal suite of domestic apartments while the lower floor was used for storage and service.

Palaces and great medieval houses

In more than a dozen Norman towns, the bishop was the wealthiest individual. Bishops built their palaces next to their cathedrals. Only a few castles, most of them royal residences, rivalled these buildings in scale and quality. Like the kings of England, bishops led peripatetic lives in order to administer the affairs of their realms and dioceses, and so several establishments were needed where they and their entourage might be accommodated in comfort and where guests might be entertained on a lavish scale. The medieval English bishops had more than 150 residences between them, though most of these were rural manor houses rather than palaces. It was said that Alexander, bishop of Lincoln from 1123 to 1148, never travelled 'without so vast a band of followers that all men marvelled', but in 1179 Pope Alexander III decreed that no bishop on a visitation should have a retinue of more than 40 or 50 men; this number was reduced later to 30.[30]

After the king, the bishops of Winchester were the richest and most powerful men in Norman England, and their palace was the grandest in the land. The bishop of Durham was also the secular prince of the palatinate of Durham, and so he was the wealthiest prelate after the bishops of Winchester and Canterbury. The motte-and-bailey castle that William the Conqueror had built at Durham in 1072 was handed over to the bishop as a bastion against the Scots and was soon replaced by a stone castle. In the first decades of the twelfth century Bishop Flambard cleared away all the houses that lay between the castle and the cathedral in order to create a processional way through a unique enclosure. He and his successor, Bishop Puiset, subsequently laid out the castle bailey as a courtyard containing halls and a chapel. Other great clerical magnates made their own innovations in different ways. Many bishops' palaces were improved out of recognition between the 1460s and the 1530s with the construction of splendid new gatehouses and ranges of lodgings.

The great houses that were built by Cardinal Thomas Wolsey, the Ipswich butcher's son who rose to be Archbishop of York and Lord Chancellor to King Henry VIII, demonstrate his ambition and the scale of the wealth that could be obtained from holding the great offices of church and state. Wolsey began Hampton Court as a private venture in 1514, but in 1525 he had to hand it over to King Henry, who in 1536 completed the Great Hall, with its wonderful hammer-beam roof. Wolsey had also begun building Whitehall Palace, but after his fall in 1529 Henry took it over and finished it. No monarch was more active in building than Henry VIII. By the end of his reign in 1547 the Crown owned about 60 houses of varying size, ranging from palaces that were designed to accommodate the whole Court to small hunting lodges and modest buildings that were fitted out for brief royal visits. They were once scattered all over the South East and, to a lesser extent, the Midlands and the South West, but the only palaces from this reign to survive are those of Hampton Court and St James.[31]

High-ranking clergymen and great lay lords promoted the use of brick as a prestigious building material, particularly in eastern England, where no stone of adequate quality was available, but sometimes further west, too, because of its rarity value. Brick was used for bishops' palaces such as Bishopthorpe on the outskirts of York; castles including Caister in Norfolk, Herstmonceux in Sussex, and Kirby Muxloe in Leicestershire; gate-towers such as Oxburgh Hall in Norfolk; great manor houses as fine as Gainsborough Old Hall in Lincolnshire; colleges as notable as Eton in Buckinghamshire; and town walls, starting with those at Hull and Beverley in the East Riding of Yorkshire. Although bricks were invariably made close to the building site, their variety of colours came not just from the nature of the local clays but from the firing process, for medieval brick-makers knew how to produce a black finish which could then be used to pick out patterns on a wall or up a tower.[32]

When Compton Wynyates in Warwickshire was completed by about 1520, it remained moated and had timber service buildings at the front, but it was built in fashionable brick. In Essex, about the same time, Henry, 1st Lord Marney, Keeper of the Privy Seal, rebuilt the parish church at Layer Marney in brick and erected an impressive brick tower or gatehouse with mullioned and transomed windows and crestings made of terracotta; while at Castle Hedingham, John de Vere, 13th Earl of Oxford, constructed new brick ranges and towers around the twelfth-century keep of the castle about the same time as he paid for a new brick upper storey to the nave, porch and tower of the local church, all emblazoned with his personal arms and insignia. Fantastic brick chimney stacks became popular in many parts of the South East, even in smaller houses.

After the Reformation, the Crown and the Church no longer took the lead in building great palaces. Queen Elizabeth's courtiers expected to do well from the profits of office and they led the way in building the great 'prodigy houses' that characterize her reign. Her chief minister, William Cecil, Lord Burghley, began to build Burghley Hall near Stamford in the 1550s as a modest classical building, but as his power grew, so did his new house, with turrets, bay windows, and a hall with a hammerbeam roof. A spectacular gatehouse greeted visitors from London just before the Great North Road entered Stamford.

The great houses of the leading families in late Elizabethan England can be regarded either as energetic and imaginative expressions of the age or as vulgar displays of newly found power and wealth. Tall chimneys, turrets and strapwork designs created dramatic skylines, and the striking grid patterns of glittering windows lit great chambers and long galleries. Old-fashioned architectural features gave newly rich and powerful families a comfortable though illusory sense of ancient authority. The Elizabethans also delighted in dainty devices. The great chamber that the German glass painter Barnard Dinninghof designed at Gilling Castle for Sir William Fairfax has a plaster frieze that depicts the coats of arms of almost all the Yorkshire gentry and the images of six musicians performing for the guests. The Triangular Lodge that Thomas Tresham erected on the edge of his Northamptonshire estate was composed in multiples of threes in honour of the Holy Trinity. Bess of Hardwick adorned her magnificent new house in Derbyshire with her initials (ES for Elizabeth, Countess of Shrewsbury), and in her great chamber real trees were incorporated within a vividly coloured plaster frieze that represented her as the goddess Diana presiding over a boar hunt in the forest. Much attention was also given to formal gardens, designed in symmetrical and knot patterns that could be viewed from mounds or raised terraces, and enclosed by a wall. Other features included towers, garden houses and bowling greens. At Haddon, within the same county, formal gardens climbed up the hillside in terraces leading from the new long gallery.[33]

The Jacobean gentry continued to build in the same style but they introduced new fashions in the details, and in those parts of the country where local building stone was not available they turned instead to brick. One of the finest brick buildings was Hatfield House, which Robert Cecil, Lord Burghley's second son, built between 1607 and his death in 1612. Robert Lyminge, the carpenter and part-designer of Hatfield House, was then chosen as the architect for Blickling Hall, the Norfolk country house of Sir Henry Hobart, Lord Chief Justice. In this way, the architectural styles of the Court and the City of London spread deep into the countryside.

A new type of superior accommodation was introduced into southern England by Royalist exiles returning from France and the Low Countries after the restoration of Charles II. The medieval concept of a great open hall separated from the service rooms by a screens passage was abandoned. The

FIGURE 12 *The Triangular Lodge at Rushton, Northamptonshire, was designed by Sir Thomas Tresham in 1593. The number three, symbolizing the Holy Trinity, is apparent everywhere.*

servants were no longer numerous and they had their meals in their own quarters near the kitchen and went about their chores via their own staircase, placed discreetly at the rear of the building. The fashion spread to the rest of the country when provincial nobles and gentlemen who lived in London during 'the season' copied the new designs at home. 'Restoration houses' such as Ragley Hall (Warwickshire) were compact in plan, comfortable and warm to live in, and visually satisfying in their symmetry. They were normally two storeys high, though often with attics and a basement. Gables were abandoned in favour of a double-pile house with a hipped roof and a central lead flat. Such houses were no longer vernacular in style but were given classical proportions and details. Minor gentry were usually content with a plain, symmetrical elevation, but the grander buildings had a flight of steps and a pediment adorned with the owner's coat of arms. The hall was now reduced to an imposing entrance room with a great parlour beyond and smaller rooms to the side; and in the upper storey the great chamber was replaced by the saloon as the most splendid room in the house.[34]

Huge landed estates were created in the late seventeenth and eighteenth centuries as noblemen enclosed, bought, exchanged, and above all acquired property through inheritance and marriage. The growing number of stewards, agents and attorneys offered services that enabled landowners to secure their estates and to choose legal schemes that transferred property intact. Great landowners were conscious of their standing in society and their family's past achievements and they took their duty to future generations seriously. Even a failure of male heirs and the necessity of indirect inheritance did not weaken this sense of obligation. The wealth with which to build a country mansion and surround it with formal gardens and, later, a landscaped park came from appointment to national office, with access to court sinecures. The price of land rose as noblemen from remoter parts of the realm bought estates nearer the capital city, and those who had made their fortunes in commerce consolidated their position in society in the accepted manner.[35] The style of a nobleman's house and the size of his estate demonstrated his political power and his standing in local society, and many eighteenth-century aristocrats tried to live like the senators and philosophers of the ancient world, surrounded by classical art, architecture and improving literature. The old settlements that interrupted their view were removed out of sight, though in some cases superior accommodation for the estate's tenants was provided in new model villages close by.

The great country houses that were erected in the first two decades after the 'Glorious Revolution' of 1688 were designed by architects who developed an English Baroque style of building based on past and contemporary buildings on the Continent. The noblemen who had played a prominent part in the 'Glorious Revolution' received their rewards. William Cavendish, the Earl of Devonshire, was elevated to a dukedom, and the Hampton Court team of architects, painters, sculptors, ironworkers and gardeners converted Chatsworth into what is now the nation's favourite country house.

Castle Howard, the most astonishing building of the new era, was the home of Charles Howard, third Earl of Carlisle, who on two occasions served as the First Lord of the Treasury, the office soon to be equated with that of Prime Minister. Visitors, who came along an avenue marked by mock fortifications and an obelisk, were left in no doubt that they were at the home of a great man long before they reached the state rooms or audience chambers. Castle Howard was Sir John Vanbrugh's first serious attempt at architecture, but the vast experience of Nicholas Hawksmoor, the second in command, helped him to create a remarkably successful building that set the style for the provincial palaces of the nation's leading figures. Vanbrugh and Hawksmoor went on to design Blenheim Palace for John Churchill, first Duke of Marlborough, as a gift from the nation for defeating the forces of Louis XIV of France in 1704 on the banks of the Danube.

The growing fashion for young noblemen to make a Grand Tour of the Continent brought them into contact with the achievements of the classical era and the villas and public buildings of Andrea Palladio of Vicenza and Venice. Palladio's *Four Books of Architecture* (1570, translated 1715) enabled them to reflect on what they had seen when they returned home. During the second quarter of the eighteenth century, the strict Palladianism of the Earl of Burlington's circle became the new orthodoxy amongst the ruling Whig aristocracy. The great Whig palaces, as they became known, were statements of power from the triumphant ruling class. Plain external dignity was matched with the opulence of the internal rooms, and strict symmetry prevailed throughout. Houghton Hall in Norfolk was built between 1722 and 1735 for Sir Robert Walpole, Britain's first Prime Minister. Servants, grooms and humble visitors entered the house through the rusticated ground floor of the main rectangular block, while the family and their guests used the steps to the staterooms on the first floor, Palladio's *piano nobile*. But the greatest Palladian house in Norfolk was Holkham Hall, built for Thomas Coke, Earl of Leicester, in yellow-grey brick and approached along a three-mile avenue through an enormous park.

Meanwhile, the country house with the longest front in England was built at Wentworth Woodhouse (South Yorkshire) for Sir Thomas Watson-Wentworth, the future Marquis of Rockingham. By 1750 the surrounding park had been extended to over nine miles in circumference, and by the close of the century the estate had grown in size to 17,200 acres. Hundreds of other symmetrical houses, big and small, were erected in more modest fashions up and down the country, surrounded by their gardens and parks. The fashionable national styles of the houses of the wealthiest families and the sheer size of these buildings and the grounds surrounding them made a sharp contrast with the vernacular traditions of their neighbourhoods. England had not seen anything like it before.

CHAPTER SEVEN

Parish churches and chapels

Up and down England, the oldest symbol of a local society is usually the parish church. The Anglo-Saxons and Vikings created many of our ancient parishes and the system was largely complete by the end of the Norman period. Alec Clifton-Taylor once observed that although English parish churches were built to the glory of God, they also reflect the sheer joy of creation, the pride and ambitions of rich patrons, and the healthy rivalry between neighbouring towns and villages. Time and time again, parish churches are the visual centrepiece, the dominant building of the place that they serve. About 11,000 of them are listed as being of special architectural or historic importance, and about 2,000 of these are Grade A. Only Italy and France can match the English achievement.[1]

The study of church buildings is an old interest, which was once thought to have been more or less completed, but it has come back into fashion with renewed vigour, thanks to archaeological excavations, corpuses of Anglo-Saxon and Romanesque sculptures, detailed accounts of medieval stained-glass windows, murals and grave slabs, and the publication of new, enlarged editions of the Pevsner guides and historical accounts such as Sir Stephen Glynne's church notes from the mid-nineteenth century.[2]

The earliest parish churches

The domestic buildings of the Anglo-Saxons, even the mightiest ones in the land, were timber framed and do not survive. By contrast, large numbers of churches that were built in stone and brick long before the Norman Conquest are still standing, at least in part. Some are on sites that were used for Christian worship during the later years of the Roman Empire. The place-name element *eccles*, which refers to a church served by a group of priests, is regarded as evidence of such survivals. An outstanding example is Ecclesfield (South Yorkshire), whose medieval parish covered the whole of the 71,526 acres of 'the country called Hallamshire', the most southwesterly of the Northumbrian shires.[3]

The present south chancel wall of St Martin's church, which stands outside the city wall at Canterbury, is built of Roman brick. It is thought to have been the south wall of the nave of the church that Bertha of Paris had rebuilt for her private use in 562 upon her marriage to Aethelbert, King of Kent and overlord of most of southern England. In 597 this royal church became the base for St Augustine's mission to those parts of Britain that were no longer Christian. The abbey that is dedicated to St Augustine and which stands between St Martin's and the eastern wall of the city became the burial place for bishops and kings. The early churches from Augustine's mission were laid out more or less in line from west to east, a usual practice of the early Anglo-Saxon church. Those in Canterbury comprised Sts Peter and Paul (founded in 597), St Pancras (c.600) and St Mary (c.620). One of the walls of the western porch of St Pancras's church, which stands almost to its original height, is made entirely of Roman bricks; the ground plan of the church is preserved intact except for the apse and the side-chapel.

These early Kent churches, and others including those at Lyminge, Reculver and Rochester, were laid out in the Roman manner by almost standard methods. They consisted of a rectangular nave with a square porch, or narthex, at the west end; a chancel with an apse at the east end, which was separated from the nave by a triple arcade carried by lofty columns; and two square chambers, or porticus, projecting from each side of the building at the junction of the nave and chancel. Another early southeastern church that was built to the same plan is St Peter at Bradwell-on-Sea (Essex), which is sited within a former 'Saxon Shore' fort of the Roman period.[4]

Many of the earliest churches were built on sites that were considered holy in pre-Christian times. In 597 Pope Gregory instructed Augustine's mission not to alienate the native population by the wholesale destruction of their religious buildings but rather to convert heathen temples to Christian use. A striking example of a pagan site that was converted in this way is seen at Rudston (Yorkshire), where a prehistoric monolith was capped with a cross and enclosed within the churchyard that was laid out alongside it. The village name comes from two Old English words: 'rood' (meaning 'cross') and 'stone'.[5] It is impossible to know just how many churches were erected on pagan sites. The eradication of pagan beliefs even amongst the leaders of the English was a slow process. To the Venerable Bede's disgust, King Raedwald of East Anglia had both a Christian and a pagan altar in the same temple.

Christianity made rapid progress once the larger Anglo-Saxon kingdoms emerged in the first half of the seventh century. Remarkably, some of the architectural features at the twin monastic sites of Monkwearmouth and Jarrow in Northumbria date back to the time when Bede lived there as a Benedictine monk in the early eighth century. The stonework of these northeastern churches gives them a very different appearance from the brick churches of Kent. A stained-glass window in St Paul's Church, Jarrow, which was made in 681, is the oldest surviving stained glass in Europe.[6]

County Durham also possesses England's finest small Anglo-Saxon church at Escomb, built within a circular churchyard on the banks of the river Wear. The tall, box-shaped nave and the smaller, square-ended chancel are intact. A great many of the stones of the building have characteristic Roman tooling, and a re-used Roman stone on the exterior of the north wall of the nave is inscribed VI LEG, now set upside down, signifying the sixth legion that had served in this district. Five small windows, splayed internally, were inserted high in the lofty walls, together with a circular sundial, the oldest in the country that is still in its original setting. The church is a truly remarkable survival from this early Christian period.[7]

The archaeological and architectural study of Anglo-Saxon churches made great advances with the publication of Harold and Joan Taylor's *Anglo-Saxon Architecture* (1965), and a series of important excavations and surveys. The great majority of Anglo-Saxon churches were simple two-cell structures that were rebuilt and enlarged in later centuries, but four outstanding early buildings still fulfil their ancient role in midland England: at Brixworth (Northamptonshire), Wing (Buckinghamshire), Deerhurst (Gloucestershire) and Repton (Derbyshire). They are of international importance and make an outstanding contribution to our heritage. David Parsons and Diana Sutherland have examined the church at Brixworth,

FIGURE 13 *Escomb, County Durham, has the most complete Anglo-Saxon church in England.*

stone by stone and brick by brick, and have concluded that the main body of the church was erected towards the end of the eighth century, probably by the order of King Offa of Mercia, and that the rest was remodelled before the end of the ninth. Much of the Anglo-Saxon work consists of reused material from earlier buildings, some of which were as far afield as Leicester, about 25 miles away.[8]

These early churches were known as 'minsters', a word that was derived from the Latin *monasterium*, for communities of priests served them. Some are commemorated by place-names such as Beaminster and Sturminster (Dorset) or Axminster (Devon). Minsters were mother churches to which people over an extensive district paid dues, and they remained significantly larger units than the neighbouring parishes that were carved from them by local lords in late Anglo-Scandinavian or Norman times.

The creation of numerous small manors from the later ninth century onwards prompted local lords to build their own churches. The boundaries of the new parishes often conformed to those of the manors, but sometimes churches and parishes were joint foundations. In a few cases in eastern England, such as Swaffham Prior (Cambridgeshire), two churches stand in the same churchyard because local lords insisted on separate places of worship. The shapes and sizes of these new parishes varied across England, according to the nature of the terrain and the size of the population. The leading towns had numerous parishes, whose boundaries wound along the streets and lanes and the backs of gardens. Yet towns such as Leeds or Manchester that were small before the Industrial Revolution were contained in single, enormous parishes that stretched over the neighbouring countryside. The medieval parish of Sheffield covered 22,370 acres until it was divided into 23 new parishes in the early Victorian period.[9]

The characteristic features of churches that were erected before the Norman Conquest include double belfry windows with a mid-wall shaft supporting a through-stone slab, triangular windows or doorways, strip-work panelling of wall surfaces, and the use of large stones arranged in a 'side-alternate' or 'long-and-short' manner. An outstanding example is the tower of All Saints, Earls Barton, which was erected on an earlier fortified site about a thousand years ago and which still dominates a large Northamptonshire village beside the river Nene. The round-headed windows, the striking belfry window with five openings, and long-and-short quoins in the Mercian style immediately suggest late Anglo-Saxon work below the battlements that were added in the late Middle Ages. The tower is about 60 feet high and is divided into four stages by string-courses. The masonry and plaster are bound together by elaborate pilaster strips in a decorative pattern that might have emulated those of earlier timber towers. The entrance to the tower is through a western doorway. The rest of the church was built later in Norman and Gothic styles.[10]

The strip-work patterns and long-and-short quoins on the lower part of the late tenth-century tower of St Peter, Barton-on-Humber (Lincolnshire), are reminiscent of those at Earls Barton. The plaster masks the roughly coursed rubble, in contrast to the ashlar stone of the later upper stage. The door on the southern side of the tower was the principal entrance to the church, for the ground floor of the tower served as a nave. The western annexe was used as a baptistery (the only one to survive in England), but the similar-sized chancel on the eastern side was removed when the late-medieval nave was built. Barton-on-Humber, a port on the banks of the Humber, contained two large medieval churches. St Peter's was closed in 1970, thus allowing Warwick Rodwell's team to undertake an extensive programme of excavations and repairs and to discover 2,800 burials. It is now in the care of English Heritage and is the major centre for research into medieval disease and diet, and medical and burial practices.[11]

Parish churches were often built near a lord's castle or manor house. Some now stand alone in the countryside because the lord's residence, and even the village that lay alongside it, have disappeared. In some deserted villages, the church has subsequently been incorporated within the manorial complex. Derbyshire provides a medieval example at Haddon Hall, and an eighteenth-century one at Kedleston. Seen today, a church standing oddly in relation to a village or town immediately suggests that the main focus of settlement may have altered over the centuries.

The simplest timber-framed churches rarely survive. The north and south walls of the nave of St Andrew, Greensted-juxta-Ongar, form part of the oldest surviving wooden church in England, tucked away in a quiet part of Essex. It was built on low walls with vertical oak trees that were cleft down the middle, so that the flat surface formed the inner wall and the rounded part of the trunks faced outwards. The timbers are grooved and tongued together. It used to be thought that the nave was built about 850, but dendrochronology samples now suggest a mid-eleventh-century date.[12]

Norman lords built hundreds of new churches and chapels-of-ease and re-designed most of the existing ones. Very many parish churches, in all parts of the land, still contain some Norman work. The parish church was usually the only stone or brick building in a medieval village, for even most manor houses were timber framed. But many lowland counties were without good-quality stone and so the masons had to make do with flints, cobbles, old Roman bricks and other materials picked up in the local fields. In Essex, for example, the walls of the Norman nave and chancel of the rural parish church of St Andrew, Sandon, were built of flint, pebbles, pudding stone conglomerate, and re-used Roman bricks (which were used especially for the quoins), all set in a thick lime mortar. The use of whatever building materials were available locally gives English parish churches their distinctive appearances and separates one 'country' from another.

The earliest Norman churches had thick walls, filled with rubble and cemented by poor-quality mortar, and naves supported by low, rounded arches and sturdy piers, but by the middle years of the twelfth century masons were building churches in a more confident and decorative style.

Most of the existing smaller churches and chapels-of-ease built in the late Norman period date from the 1140s and 1150s onwards. In parishes that remained poor and sparsely populated in succeeding centuries, churches were altered only in minor ways and therefore much of their original work survives. The appearance of the single-cell Norman church of St Andrew, Winterborne Tomson (Dorset), with an apsidal east end supported by shallow buttresses, has not been changed since it was built in the early twelfth century, for the local population declined subsequently. The walls were built with flints (some of them knapped) and with many different local stones set in a thick lime mortar.

During the middle and later years of the twelfth century, Norman parish churches, large and small alike, became much more decorative, both externally and internally. Characteristic mouldings, such as beakhead, chevron or zigzag patterns, were used on doorways, windows, capitals and arches. The strangest carvings to modern eyes are the serpents and other grotesques that were carved as a tympanum over the main door on the south side of the nave or which formed a corbel table running around the external walls under the eaves. The most famous collection of such carvings, inspired by the moralizing illustrations in contemporary bestiaries, is at Kilpeck in Herefordshire, the county that also has the finest group of carved Norman fonts. The font in the little church of St Michael, Castle Frome, is supported at the base by three crouching men with beards; the central scene shows the baptism of Christ by St John the Baptist, and the other carvings depict the symbols of the four writers of the gospels. It is thought that the Herefordshire sculptures were the work of perhaps just two teams of craftsmen who were inspired by what they had seen in France, Italy and Spain. At least one local lord is known to have gone on pilgrimage to the shrine of St James at Compostella.[13]

Elsewhere, the semi-circular apse at the eastern end of the church, which had gone out of fashion in Anglo-Scandinavian England, was revived in late Norman churches such as Birkin in Yorkshire, or Steetley in Derbyshire. The characteristic features of Romanesque architecture on display inside a parish church are a rounded chancel arch with a series of decorated orders and the rows of circular piers supporting the arcade between the nave and its aisles, which by the last quarter of the twelfth century had capitals carved with scallop or waterleaf designs. The most elaborate chancel arch is that composed of six orders, each of a different design, at St Peter's, Tickencote, in Rutland. The meaning of Norman sculptures is often lost to us, but they were originally used for teaching the Christian message to illiterate congregations.

The sturdy appearance of Norman church towers does not imply a defensive function, as is sometimes thought, except perhaps in a few cases on the northern and Welsh borders, such as Clun in west Shropshire, where the church marks the site of the old settlement before a new market town was planned; or at Great Salkeld in Cumberland, where the internal door of

FIGURE 14 *The font at Castle Frome is one of the finest examples of the Herefordshire School of Romanesque sculpture. This side depicts the angel of St Matthew.*

the tower is strongly barred and iron-plated on the nave side and the village has a large medieval dyke around it to keep out cattle raiders. The flint round towers of East Anglia were constructed in their distinctive manner not for defence but because of the lack of suitable building stones for quoins. By far the majority of those that survive are found in Norfolk (120) and Suffolk (42), with seven in Essex, three in Sussex and two each in Cambridgeshire and Berkshire.[14] Late Norman towers did not have spires and were usually capped with low pyramidal roofs of timber and shingles, most of which were replaced or hidden by battlements in the later Middle Ages. A more ambitious plan involved the construction of a central tower between an aisleless nave and a square-ended chancel, as at Studland

(Dorset), Stewkley (Buckinghamshire) and Iffley (Oxfordshire), where the west front is decorated as lavishly as that of an abbey church. The largest Norman churches with central towers had aisles and transepts. Outstanding examples include St Kyneburgha, Castor (near Peterborough) and St Nicholas, Old Shoreham (Sussex). More than any other building, an ancient parish church gives a place its sense of identity.

The rebuilding of parish churches in Gothic styles

In towns and villages across England, the parish church was the focal point of local life. Services were held much more regularly than now; the nave occasionally served as a public hall; and the porch was used as a social and business meeting place. Thousands of churches were enlarged to accommodate the rising population in the years before the Black Death, though in many cases the adoption of the Early English Gothic style is evident only in minor architectural features, such as the replacement of the splayed windows of Norman churches by lancets or simple Y-tracery. A fine example of the new style can be seen at St Mary's, West Walton in the Norfolk Marshland, which dates from the second quarter of the thirteenth century. The tower that forms the entrance to the churchyard is detached from the church (as in some other Fenland parishes) because of the fear that if it subsided in the soft soils it would drag the whole building down. The design of the tower suggests the influence of churches in the Isle de France, but the south porch has 'pepper pot' turrets that are decidedly East Anglian. Inside, the nave arcades have Purbeck marble shafts, pointed arches, sharp-edged mouldings, and stiff-leafed foliage on the capitals instead of the monsters that the Norman sculptors preferred.[15]

Geometric tracery, produced by the compass, was replaced at parish church level in the first half of the fourteenth century by a variety of Decorated styles. In small churches the designs were often modest and plain, for local masons often lacked the technical skills, and stones that were suitable for carving were not always available. The changes consisted of little more than the introduction of some new windows, with perhaps an ogee arch over a piscina or cinquefoil arcading on the font. But in the wealthier parishes the flowing and sinuous lines of reticulated or curvilinear tracery in ogee-shaped windows gave a church such as St Mary's, Higham Ferrers (Northamptonshire), a wonderful new appearance. The ogee arch, enriched with crockets, finials and ball-flower ornamentation, was used in church interiors for features such as a canopy, a niche, a piscina or a sedilia, while capitals overflowed with naturalistic foliage, until in the end this love of luxury and display at every point provoked a reaction in favour of a much plainer style.

Those parts of England where large new churches were built in the Decorated manner flourished in the first half of the fourteenth century. The East Riding of Yorkshire, for example, has an impressive collection of great parish churches from this time, most famously that at Patrington, a manor of the Archbishop of York, a haven on the banks of the Humber, and a small town with two weekly markets and annual fairs. The church was built of creamy Magnesian Limestone that was brought down the river, with stone-vaulted aisles and transepts and with delicate carvings on the font and every capital and gargoyle. The spire was added in the fifteenth century.[16]

Spires are a feature of the Gothic styles of the thirteenth or early fourteenth century, but they are notoriously difficult to date precisely. The most-attractive ones are those that catch the eye in parish after parish on the Oolitic Limestone as it curves through Northamptonshire up into Rutland and Lincolnshire and those that follow the narrow Magnesian Limestone belt through central Yorkshire, reaching a height of 189 feet at Hemingborough. Decorated 'lights', ranged in two or three tiers on the cardinal sides, were inserted in the spires to relieve heaviness and to act as gabled windows or ventilation openings. These spires look so fine because limestone takes a thin ashlar; on churches built of sandstone, spires can look bulky. Builders solved the problem of how to fit an eight-sided spire on top of a four-sided tower by designing half-pyramids or broaches, but in later times spires were recessed and an ornamental parapet masked the junction with the tower.

In a group of Essex parishes, the lack of suitable stone meant that carpenters were engaged to construct wooden spires. The great vertical posts that rise from ground level had to be braced at the base to take the wind and the swing of the bells. At Stock, the late thirteenth-century spire has to be re-shingled every 70 years or so; the tower is clad with clap board; and the outshots that hide the supporting braces, except in the east where the nave wall provides stability, have tiled pent roofs. St Lawrence, Blackmore, which was originally an Augustinian priory church, has a fifteenth-century tower of local oak in three diminishing, rectangular stages, linked by splayed pent roofs, and anchored in outshots. Similar wooden belfries survive nearby at Magdalen Laver, Mountnessing, Navestock, and East and West Hanningfield. They are confined to a particular part of Essex.[17] A few medieval timber-framed towers can be visited in other parts of England, notably at Bromsbarrow and Pembridge in Herefordshire, Upleadon in Gloucestershire, and Lower Peover and Marton in Cheshire. Much further south, in Hampshire, the entire early fourteenth-century west wall at Hartley Wespall is framed with large timbers and cusped braces.

The importance of the parish church in the daily lives of the people of late-medieval England is revealed by the ready willingness of parishioners to contribute towards rebuilding and furnishing. Between a third and a half of the 11,000 or so English parish churches that are of architectural importance are mainly or wholly in the Perpendicular Gothic style, a purely native development that inspired church builders for over 200 years. Most of them date from the later fifteenth and early sixteenth centuries. The emphasis placed on magnificent towers, which had no liturgical purpose, demonstrates how local pride drove parishioners to emulate or outdo their neighbours.[18] The contract for building the church tower at Walberswick in Suffolk in 1426, for instance, stipulated that it should be modelled on that of nearby Tunstall, and that the west door and the window above should be as good as those at Halesworth.[19]

Like their predecessors, England's finest late-medieval churches are strikingly different in appearance because of the use of local building materials. The Cotswold cloth merchants were lucky to have first-class Oolitic Limestones to choose from, whereas their counterparts in East Anglia had to make do with flint. This hardest, most intractable of all building materials needed thick mortar that was slow to set, so towers rarely went up at the rate of more than ten feet a year. The technique of knapping, whereby a flint was broken in half with a straight, smooth cleft if it was hit a skilful blow with a hammer, became widespread from the fourteenth century onwards. Irregular surfaces were plastered over, but a shiny, black surface of knapped flints produced an attractive finish. Limestone was brought by sea and river from Caen in Normandy or from English quarries such as Barnack (Northamptonshire) and was often combined with knapped flints to make flushwork patterns, such as chequers, lozenges, or the letter 'M' to signify the Virgin Mary.

Suffolk has many outstanding examples of churches constructed in this manner, notably at Blythburgh, Dedham, Hadleigh, Lavenham, Long Melford, Southwold and Stoke-by-Nayland.[20] They are rivalled by contemporary Cotswold churches, led by Burford, Chipping Camden, Cirencester and Northleach, and by a magnificent group of towers in Somerset, notably those at Huish Episcopi and Taunton, paid for out of the profits of the cloth industry. Meanwhile, splendid Perpendicular churches were erected in the wealthiest towns. Two of the very best are St Mary Redcliffe at Bristol and St Mary's at Beverley at the opposite end of the town to the collegiate church known as Beverley Minster. They are amongst England's chief medieval glories.

The parish church of St John the Baptist, Bere Regis (Dorset), was completely rebuilt in the second half of the fifteenth century. The magnificent nave roof that was paid for by Cardinal Morton, Archbishop of Canterbury and Lord Chancellor to King Henry VII, provides an outstanding display of medieval carpentry techniques, using tie beams, arched braces, hammer beams, curved struts, king posts, queen posts, and cusped struts supporting the ridge and the purlins. The bosses depict foliage, a male head, a shield with a modern or restored painting of the arms of Morton, a Tudor rose, a knot, and the shield of St George, and the ends of the hammer beams are carved with full-length representations of the Apostles.[21]

In the two or three generations before the Reformation, parish churches throughout England benefited from bequests and other gifts to improve the fabric and to provide gilded or painted images, stained-glass windows, pulpits, screens and wall paintings. Southwold's screen is an outstanding example whose panels depict the Apostles, the prophets and the nine orders of angels. In the fifteenth and sixteenth centuries images of saints, with lights before them, filled the churches; some were placed on altars housed in their own chapels. The blaze of colour in a late-medieval parish church created a very different atmosphere from the plain interiors of today. Horrific paintings of the Day of Judgement hung over the chancel arch; wall-paintings and stained-glass windows illustrated the seven deadly sins, the seven corporal works of mercy, the Ten Commandments, Christ wounded by sabbath-breaking, the figures of the three living and the three dead, and the *danse macabre* of the figure of Death.[22] The late-medieval belief that the souls of the dead had to rely on the prayers of the living if they were to reach Heaven from Purgatory was the driving force behind the creation of chantry chapels, which were erected by rich families or guilds at the end of an aisle or alongside the chancel and served by their own priests. Parish churches and chantries now attracted the funds that had once gone to the monasteries or the military orders.[23]

Religious guilds or devout fraternities, dedicated to a saint or to some aspect of the veneration of Christ, such as Corpus Christi, also grew in number from the second half of the fourteenth century, and new foundations were made well into the 1530s, shortly before such institutions were dissolved. They were particularly popular in the towns; London had about 150, King's Lynn over 70. Although many urban guilds were craft organizations, the overwhelming majority were primarily religious fraternities. In the late Middle Ages parish guilds were also founded in rural churches, where they maintained lights before the images of saints and provided extra priests to help the rector in his duties. Their social activities included convivial feasts and provision for brethren and sisters who fell upon hard times. Parish guilds also had economic roles in providing credit, leasing property and creating commercial networks. Donations by members made some of the rural guilds major local landowners. The Guild of St Mary and St John the Baptist at Dronfield (Derbyshire), for instance, owned about 520 acres within the central township and more than 200 acres beyond. It had over 100 members and its Alderman and Wardens were drawn from the leading families in the parish.[24]

Eamon Duffy has revised a longstanding view by emphasizing the popularity and durability of late-medieval religious attitudes and perceptions and insisting that no substantial gulf existed between the religion of the clergy and the educated elite on the one hand, and that of the people at large on the other. Far from being a failing religion, medieval English Catholicism was, up to the very moment of its dissolution, a highly successful enterprise, with a remarkable degree of lay involvement and doctrinal orthodoxy.[25]

On the eve of the Reformation over 50,000 Books of Hours or Primers were probably in circulation among the English laity. No other form of book commanded anything like such a readership.[26] Yet illiterate people, too, commonly attended short or 'low' Masses that were celebrated at side altars, on weekdays as well as Sundays, and it was not unusual for them to worship daily. Others were content to cross themselves upon passing the image of St Christopher and the Christ child painted on the north wall of the nave opposite the open main door. Most parishioners confessed their sins to their priest just once a year, usually in Holy Week. The invention of printing in the late fifteenth century enabled the publication of manuals that were designed to assist parish clergy in their pastoral work.

The survival of more than 200 pre-Reformation pulpits, most of them dating from the fifteenth century, suggests that many parish priests were capable of preaching, at least from the texts that were prepared for them, but there is no doubt that other clergymen were not competent to perform such a task.[27] In the late fourteenth and early fifteenth centuries, the interior walls of churches were covered with wall-paintings to illustrate the Scriptures and to act as visual aids to the teachings from the pulpit, but when windows became larger and the wall-space was reduced, paintings in glass were used instead. Another device, much favoured in East Anglia during the last three generations before the Reformation, was to portray the Seven Sacraments around the bowl of the font.[28] In the West Country they were depicted in stained-glass windows.

Sunday was not the only day of worship; more than 50 days a year were official feasts dedicated to a saint, when all except the most essential agricultural work, such as milking, was forbidden. In the late Middle Ages the cults of St Anne and of St George became increasingly popular, alongside that of England's most important native saint, Thomas Becket, but there was much regional variation in such observances. Towards the end of the Middle Ages the Palm Sunday procession became the most elaborate and eloquent of the processions, and the greatest feast was that of Corpus Christi.

The liturgical calendar was the one that late-medieval people observed in the conduct of their everyday business. Saints' days were used in legal documents; anniversaries and birthdays were reckoned by the religious festivals on which they occurred; and rents and leases fell in at Lady Day, Lammas or Michaelmas. Marriage was forbidden during the four weeks of Advent and the 40 days of Lent. Everyone was expected to abstain from meat and other animal products such as eggs and cheese during Lent, on the vigils of the feasts of the Twelve Apostles, and at some other feasts. Altogether, adults were obliged to fast on nearly 70 days each year. The seasonal observances of the liturgical calendar affected everyone.

Yet the imagery of the Middle Ages was not confined to religious subjects. Malcolm Jones has estimated that at least 75 per cent of surviving iconography, in the form of illustrations, carvings, jewellery, textiles, tableware and lead badges worn as cheap souvenirs from pilgrimages, is concerned with non-religious subjects. This popular or folk art presented human relations and emotions in a variety of imaginative, vivid, comic and often crude, nasty and brutish ways. Medieval artists were not solely concerned with the charming and the uplifting.[29]

The impact of the Reformation

In 1521 Henry VIII ordered a nationwide search for heretical books, which were then burned outside St Paul's Cathedral in a great bonfire that lasted two days. Three years later, William Tyndale, an Oxford scholar, left Henry's repressive state for Cologne, where he began to translate the New Testament into English from the original Greek and Hebrew. In 1526, six thousand copies of his translation were published abroad. Many of them were confiscated at the English ports and others were burned publicly, but many others got through. English people now had access to a Bible that they could understand. The clarity and beauty of Tyndale's writing has had a lasting effect on the English language, for many of his words and phrases were later incorporated into the authorized King James Bible of 1611 and they have passed into common speech. We still use expressions such as 'fight the good fight', 'eat, drink and be merry', 'broken-hearted', 'clear-eyed', 'the spirit is willing but the flesh is weak', and words such as 'stumbling-block' and 'taskmaster'. Many more could be quoted.[30]

The Protestant Reformation of the English Church began in 1532–4 when Henry VIII, who was determined to divorce Catherine (the first of his six wives) in order to re-marry and produce an heir to the throne, renounced the authority of the Pope and declared himself the head of the Church of England. The story is well known.[31] Henry did not at first intend to go further, but prompted by his chief minister, Thomas Cromwell, and the new Archbishop of Canterbury, Thomas Cranmer, he turned from being the man whom the Pope had once proclaimed 'Defender of the Faith' for his attacks on Martin Luther, to the instigator of major changes in the conduct of worship. In April 1534 Thomas More, a great supporter of traditional Catholicism, was sent to the Tower for voicing his opposition to the divorce, and by the early summer of 1535 Cromwell was openly criticizing Catholic doctrines and forms of devotion. The following year, royal injunctions, somewhat tentatively, attacked abuses connected with pilgrimages and the cult of images and relics. Then in 1538 new injunctions instructed churchwardens to remove any images which had been 'abused with pilgrimages or offerings', to forbid the veneration of holy relics, and to extinguish the lights which had been placed before the images of saints by guilds and pious individuals in churches and chapels throughout the land. Only the candles before the high altar, in the rood-loft, and by the Easter sepulchre were spared. Heavy penalties ensured compliance with these orders. The cult of saints never recovered, and the number of feast days was reduced. An official English bible was issued in 1539, but during the last years of Henry's reign most of the traditional Catholic rituals continued as before.

The pace of change quickened considerably when the young Edward VI came to the throne upon his father's death in 1547. Under the leadership of Archbishop Thomas Cranmer and Lord Protector Somerset's government, prominent ecclesiastics and laymen advanced the views of the Protestant reformers of Germany and Switzerland: Luther, Calvin and Zwingli. They ordered the destruction of all shrines and pictures of saints and of all images to which offerings had been made or before which candles had burned. They limited the number of lights in the church to two upon the high altar, they banned the blessing of wooden crosses, and they forbade processions in and around the church when Mass was celebrated, thus cancelling one of the principal Palm Sunday ceremonies. They ordered churchwardens to buy the *Paraphrases* of Erasmus, a work much admired by the reformers, and they enforced these injunctions by dividing England into six circuits, each with four to six visitors who were carefully selected for their commitment to the Protestant cause.

In the autumn of 1547 the government dissolved chantry chapels, religious guilds, and endowed masses known as perpetual obits, and confiscated their properties on the grounds that the doctrine of purgatory was false and so dedicated prayers for the dead were unnecessary. The dissolution of religious guilds brought popular forms of religion to an end, notably the Corpus Christi celebrations, which had become a particular target of the most zealous Protestants, and it destroyed the social organizations that had long played an important role in binding local societies together. In February 1548 a royal proclamation forbade four of the major ceremonies of the religious year: the blessing of candles at Candlemas, of ashes upon Ash Wednesday, of foliage upon Palm Sunday, and the 'Creeping to the Cross' on Good Friday.[32] About a fortnight later, the Privy Council ordered the removal of all the remaining images in parish churches throughout the land. *The Book of Common Prayer* of 1549, revised in 1552, set out a new liturgy: services were now held entirely in English, prayers to individual saints and for intercession on behalf of the dead were prohibited, and many old feast days, fasts and ceremonies, including the Rogationtide processions, were abolished. The churchwardens' accounts that survive suggest that every parish obtained a copy of the book. Some parishes also purchased the *Book of Homilies*, an official collection of sermons upon important topics and doctrines that could be read to congregations by those clergy who were incapable of preaching.

Robert Parkyn, the conservative curate of Adwick-le-Street, near Doncaster, was typical in complying with the changes, however much he detested them. He noted, for instance, that in December 1550 all the stone altars in churches and chapels north of the river Trent were replaced with wooden communion tables.[33] These changes to the ways in which worship was conducted throughout the land were enforced with remarkably little outward opposition, except for a disastrous rebellion in Devon in 1549 that ended in bloody defeat.

In his classic study of the impact of the Reformation upon Morebath, a remote sheep-farming community on the edge of Exmoor, Eamon Duffy used the accounts kept by the parish priest Sir Christopher Trychay through his long ministry, from 1520 to 1574, to illuminate the background to this rebellion.[34] He tells us:

> By the early summer of 1549 the parish of Morebath had been stripped to the bone. Its images and many of its ritual furnishings were gone, its vestments concealed, its social life was suspended as the church house lay locked and empty, and every one of its parish organizations had been dissolved.

In mid-July 1549 the parishioners reacted by equipping and financing a group of five young men to join an army of rebels at their camp on St David's Down outside Exeter. The rebels were routed, and around 4,000 of them were killed. Duffy noted that a very different story could be told of Suffolk and Essex, particularly the Stour Valley, where ordinary parishioners welcomed the Reformation.

The Protestant reformers came from the ranks of the better educated who had benefited from the growing number of schools and colleges which shared a common constitution, curriculum, aims and facilities. Most late-medieval parish priests were men of simple faith, low incomes and limited learning. In Yorkshire, for example, on the eve of the Reformation, lowly curates served over 100 parish churches. Before the dissolution of the chantries, colleges and hospitals the West Riding of Yorkshire had nearly 900 clergymen, but by the end of Henry VIII's reign their number had been reduced to less than 550; by the time that Mary came to the throne in 1553 only 250 were left. A Pontefract man claimed that the town had once had an abbey, two colleges, a friary, an ancress, a hermit, four chantry priests and a guild priest, but now all they had was an unlearned vicar who hired two curates to serve a living that was worth under £3 a year. The sweeping changes to the forms of worship during the reign of Edward VI had a profound effect on the city of York, which lost about 100 chantries and nearly all its religious guilds. The Crown suppressed the colleges of St William and St Sepulchre, and the Corporation closed 13 of the smaller parish churches. Together with the dissolution of the city's abbeys, friaries and hospitals, this devastation brought not only spiritual bafflement but also economic disaster.[35]

The progress of the Protestant Reformation came to a sudden end in July 1553 with the accession of the Catholic queen, Mary Tudor, who immediately declared a temporary tolerance of both creeds, but who then began to persecute Protestants. In Mary's five-year reign some 250 Protestants were burned for heresy, and some 800 others fled into exile on the Continent. Her brother's statutes concerning altars and lights were soon repealed, and seasonal processions and ceremonies returned. The Corpus Christi processions and mystery plays were revived in the major urban centres, and church ales and other seasonal festivities reappeared everywhere. Within nine months of her accession, the rhythm of the late-medieval ecclesiastical year had been revived, except for the minor feasts that had been abolished in 1536. Churchwardens' accounts show that Catholic forms of worship were restored quickly, even though this meant considerable expense. Ronald Hutton concluded from his study of surviving churchwardens' accounts across the country that professed Catholics at the end of Mary's reign outnumbered the Protestants at the death of Edward VI.[36]

Late-medieval Catholicism had been vigorous and strong and had the support of the majority of English people, but when Mary died in November 1558 her Protestant sister Elizabeth came to the throne. The Protestant reforms provoked much popular discontent but no uprising. The governing classes adopted a new culture of Prayer Book piety, preaching and teaching, associated with virulent anti-Popery, but it had no widespread appeal. Protestants remained a minority of the national population until well into the Elizabethan era. The Reformation is best regarded as a series of disparate and at the time reversible events that were influenced as much, if not more, by political as by theological considerations. The real turning points came with the excommunication of Queen Elizabeth I in 1570 and the defeat of the Spanish Armada 18 years later.

The Church of England

How far the Elizabethan church settlement of 1559, with a liturgy based on the 1552 version of *The Book of Common Prayer*, accorded with the new queen's wishes has been a matter of much debate, but it was not clear at the time that the settlement would last. The impact was immediate, but the removal of the physical surroundings of Catholic worship was done slowly, for churchwardens were naturally reluctant to destroy the images and fittings that had been paid for so recently and when the survival of the new authority was not certain. Ecclesiastical visitation and court records and churchwardens' accounts show that many altars were not taken down until well into the 1560s.

Elizabeth and her chief minister, Lord Burghley, proceeded cautiously on religious matters. In 1559 the Church of England was declared the one true form of religion and church furnishings associated with Catholicism were banned once again. Church interiors were made bare, the walls were whitewashed and adorned with biblical texts, and the Royal Arms, replete with the Tudor griffin (and later with the Stuart unicorn), replaced the medieval doom paintings over the chancel arch. Pews were installed in the nave, their arrangement reflecting the social structure of the community, with the rich families at the front, the middling townsfolk or the rural yeomen, craftsmen and husbandmen in the middle, and the labourers and cottagers squashed together at the sides and the rear. The state and the ecclesiastical authorities expected everyone to attend church services and enforced this aim as far as possible through the ecclesiastical courts, but attendance at Sunday worship never approached the legal ideal, and court records reveal that during services parishioners sometimes jostled for pews, nudged, spat, knitted, made coarse remarks, told jokes and fell asleep. Preaching was popular only with the educated classes, the godly who saw themselves as a tiny minority or the elect.[37]

The ignorance of ministers at the time of the Reformation was widespread. For example, in 1551 only 168 of the 311 clergy in the diocese of Gloucester could recite the Ten Commandments, 34 did not know the author of the Lord's Prayer, and 10 could not repeat it. The reading of homilies as official sermons was therefore insisted upon until a greatly increased proportion of ministers were trained at university. In the diocese of Canterbury in 1571, for example, only 18 per cent of clergymen were graduates, but by the end of Elizabeth's reign in 1603 the number had risen to 60 per cent, and by the 1630s the ministers of parish churches throughout the land had become a married, resident, graduate group of higher professional standing than ever before.[38]

The Elizabethan government soon faced opposition to its religious policy from zealous Protestants who thought the reforms had not gone far enough. The term 'Puritan' was used widely though loosely from the late 1560s, by which time these Calvinists formed a well-educated, influential and vocal group.[39] The main Puritan strength was in the towns and in large moorland parishes such as Halifax where settlements were dispersed and industry was taking hold. Contrasting religious adherences were formed at local levels that were much smaller than that of a county. For instance, as Andrew Hopper has observed, Yorkshire cloth towns such as Halifax and Bradford had far more in common in religious, cultural and socio-economic terms with adjacent areas in Lancashire than they did with the Vale of York.[40]

Puritan influence began to grow towards the end of Elizabeth's reign, though some ardent believers despaired and emigrated across the Atlantic, and those who stayed remained a minority well into the seventeenth century. The Protestant emphasis on prayer and reading the Bible nevertheless became deeply imprinted on the minds of congregations throughout the land. Studies of Shakespeare's plays, for instance, have revealed quotations from, or references to, 42 books of the Bible – eighteen from the Old Testament, eighteen from the New, and six from the books gathered together in the *Apochrypha* – and other phrases have been traced to the official homilies and *The Book of Common Prayer*.[41]

The break with Catholicism was the principal factor in England's international affairs. Pressure on the government to revert to Catholicism came especially from Spain, the leading power in Europe, whose empire extended menacingly as far north as the Low Countries across the English Channel. Relations with Spain had worsened when Elizabeth encouraged

Sir Francis Drake, the first English commander to sail around the world, in his piratical attacks on Spanish ships ladened with gold and silver from the Caribbean and his destructive raids on their colonies. His heroic status among English people rose to new heights with his audacious attack on the Spanish fleet in Cadiz harbour in 1587 and the naval battle in the following year when unseasonably severe weather forced the battered Armada up the North Sea and round Scotland and Ireland, hotly pursued by the English fleet. England was safe and had become a force to be reckoned with. The defeat of the Spanish Armada was celebrated ever afterwards as a key point in the nation's history, when an invasion from a dominant European power was thwarted.

Elizabeth's successor, King James VI of Scotland, ensured the continuity of the Protestant settlement. It was James who invented the name Great Britain (so called to distinguish the mainland from Little Britain, or Brittany), and he used it on his coinage, but it did not receive statutory authority until the 1707 Act of Union. The King took a great interest in theological matters, and the conference of bishops and leading Puritans that he arranged at Hampton Court in 1604 commissioned a new translation of what became known as the King James Bible. It lasted well into the twentieth century as the version authorized by the Church of England and its phrases and cadences remain well known to this day. The following year, a frustrated group of young Catholic gentlemen planned an audacious attempt to destroy the entire English government at the state opening of Parliament on the 5th of November. The plot was betrayed, the conspirators tortured and executed, and the image of Guy Fawkes has been burned on Bonfire Night ever since. Yet in the north of England, particularly in Lancashire, North Yorkshire and parts of Derbyshire, Catholic gentry families held fast to their faith and long provided chapels and priests to maintain discreet congregations.[42]

The Civil War which broke out in 1642 brought several years of misery, in which buildings were destroyed, churches were vandalized when troops were billeted there or when Puritan zealots smashed the stained glass windows, trade was greatly disrupted, and ordinary householders were forced to accommodate soldiers of either side without payment. Families were sometimes deeply divided, and minor battles, numerous skirmishes and the unruly behaviour of soldiers who stole horses, bedding and food, made life unpleasant and sometimes unbearable. An anonymous letter, dated 1 October 1642, complained about the ill discipline of Royalist soldiers in Shropshire during the opening weeks of the war:

> Our Country is now in a woful condition, by reason of the multitude of soldiers daily billeted upon us, both of horse and foote . . . All the Country over within 12 or 14 miles of Shreswbury are full of Souldiers . . . we heare one outrage or other committed daily, they ride armed up and down, with swords, muskets and dragoones, to the great terror of the people, that we scarce know how in safety to go out of doors; they take

men's horses, breake and pillage men's houses night and day in an unheard of maner, they pretend quarrel with the Roundheads as they call them, but for aught I see they will spare none if they may hope to have good bounty.[43]

According to Richard Gough, 20 of the humblest men from the Shropshire parish of Myddle went to fight for the Royalists. Thirteen of them were killed in action, and one of the survivors, Thomas Ash of Marton, 'brought nothing home but a crazy body and many scars'. The sufferings endured by some of the parishioners who stayed were very real. Richard Wicherley of Houlston

was troubled in the time of the wars with the outrages and plunderings of soldiers on both parties (as all rich men were) and seeing his goods and horses taken away, and his money consumed in paying taxes, hee tooke an extreme greife and dyed.

Gough regarded the Civil War as a landmark, and his numerous references show that he was fully acquainted with the issues and the course of national events. Nevertheless, the wars had little lasting effect upon his local society.[44]

The key battle that was fought at Naseby (Northamptonshire) on 14 June 1645 resulted in a resounding victory for the Parliamentarian New Model Army. By May 1646 most of the Royalist troops had surrendered. On 30 January 1649 King Charles II was executed on a scaffold leading from the Banqueting House in Whitehall. For 11 years England was without a monarch, though Oliver Cromwell served for five of these with the title of Lord Protector of the Commonwealth of England, Scotland and Ireland as well as Captain-General of the Army. Upon his death in 1658, the restoration of Charles II to the throne of England soon appeared inevitable.

Upon the restoration of Charles II the Church of England was re-instated as the Established Church and those ministers who refused to conform to the Act of Uniformity of 1662 were ejected from their livings. After its position as the official religion of the state had been confirmed in 1689, the Anglican Church entered a long period of stability and eventually of slumber. Beyond the capital city, relatively few new churches were built in this period, but the Great Fire of London in 1666 had destroyed St Paul's Cathedral and most of the City's numerous parish churches. Sir Christopher Wren and Nicholas Hawksmoor, followed by James Gibbs and others, seized the opportunity to design new places of worship in an innovative manner and to build them mostly with Portland stone brought by sea from Dorset. Their sites were usually small and cramped, but an ingenious series of spires gave them a distinctive character adorning the London skyline. Wren's design for the new St Paul's was rooted in the tradition of ancient Rome and the Renaissance, especially St Peter's Basilica at the Vatican, and the choir was decorated in a sumptuous manner with woodcarving by Grinling Gibbons and ironwork by Jean Tijou.

During the later seventeenth and eighteenth centuries the interiors of England's ancient parish churches were filled with box pews and galleries. The present internal appearance of most ancient parish churches dates from the period 1840–90, when many of these furnishings were removed. Only about 140 Georgian interiors survive reasonably intact.[45] The most famous example is St Mary, Whitby, on the cliffs high above the town, where the church is crammed with pews and galleries, the squire's pew across the chancel arch, a three-decker pulpit, chandeliers, and a stove with flue rising through the ceiling. Churches at that time were often cold and damp. Tobias Smollett wrote satirically in *Humphry Clinker* (1771):

> When we consider our ancient churches ... may we not term them so many magazines of rheums, created for the benefit of the medical faculty? And may we not safely aver that, in winter especially (which may be said to engross eight months in the year), more bodies are lost, than souls saved, by going to church?[46]

The religious radicalism of the 1640s and 1650s and an outbreak of millenarian beliefs amongst the Fifth Monarchy Men were confined to minority groups. Respectable Protestant Nonconformity congregations survived the years of repression between 1662 and 1689 because of the support of members of the rural gentry and urban tradesmen who dominated their local societies and who were able to defy the Acts of Parliament. Ejected ministers often continued to serve tiny congregations in a discreet manner. In the moorland parish of Penistone in South Yorkshire, the leading families ensured that Henry Swift remained their vicar, despite his refusal to conform to the new laws, up to his death in 1688. When the Crown appointed a conformist as the next vicar in the following year, Elkanah Rich of Bullhouse took advantage of the new law of toleration and registered his hall as a Nonconformist meetinghouse. The plain, sturdy chapel that he built alongside his hall in 1692 became a popular alternative to the parish church, and its congregation remains Independent to this day.[47]

The term 'chapel' had been used in the Middle Ages for a chapel-of-ease in a large parish or for a chantry chapel attached to the parish church or a medieval bridge, but during the seventeenth century it became associated with the new places of worship that were erected by Puritan landowners and which, after the restoration of King Charles II in 1660, were classified as Nonconformist. These seventeenth-century chapels were plain, rectangular single-storey buildings whose interiors were focused on the pulpit so that their congregations could hear the Preaching of the Word. The Loughwood Meeting House, which was erected by the Baptists at Dalwood (Devon) in 1655, consists of a single room with a west gallery. It has a rubble wall and a thatched roof. A small stable was built alongside the chapel, for

Nonconformists often travelled long distances to reach a chapel of which they approved. The interior of the chapel, including the plastered barrel vault ceiling, is painted white, and the pews and fittings are in untreated pine.

Prosperous congregations built more-substantial chapels in the towns. At York, the red brick chapel that the city's Presbyterians built in St Saviourgate in 1692–3 was designed in the rare form of a Greek cross with a central tower-like structure. The congregation later turned to Unitarianism. The Congregational Chapel at Frome (Somerset), which has a 1707 datestone at the centre of its broad pediment, is two storeys high and seven bays wide. Its classical appearance is enhanced by fine architectural details. The hipped roof allowed space for the insertion of a large gallery.

Religious dissent was suppressed readily in estate villages where families remained dependent upon an Anglican squire for their tenancies and employment. An ecclesiastical census of 1676 arranged by Bishop Compton revealed that Dissenters comprised only 4 per cent of the national population. However, they had a much stronger presence in certain towns and extensive parishes. In South Yorkshire, for example, only eight of the estimated 3,000 communicants in the old market town of Doncaster were Nonconformists, whereas the similar sized industrial town of Sheffield, a few miles away, had 300 Dissenters, many of whom were prominent in the running of the town's affairs.[48]

The most widespread of the old Dissenting sects in the late seventeenth century were the Quakers, who had become quiet, respectable pillars of their communities, pursuing a very different lifestyle from the young radicals of the 1650s. Many Quaker meetinghouses, built in a simple vernacular style, survive from the late seventeenth or early eighteenth centuries. By the second decade of the eighteenth century the membership of the Society of Friends in England and Wales had reached about 50,000, but a generation later Quaker membership was on the decline.[49]

Meanwhile, the Presbyterians and Independents had lost much of their force, and some congregations had drifted into Unitarianism, whose rational approach attracted ministers and merchants but had little appeal to the poor. Neither the Established Church nor the old Dissenting sects had the 'enthusiasm' to attract the growing population in the manufacturing towns and industrial villages. When the first Methodists sought to convert the irreligious in the middle decades of the eighteenth century, they sometimes met with violent opposition. The visits of famous preachers encouraged local people to continue their efforts, but progress was slow and in many places preaching was abandoned. It was chiefly in the traditional dissenting districts that Methodism first flourished. Their national success came later, in the nineteenth and twentieth centuries, when many old local societies were transformed and new industrial ones were created.[50]

CHAPTER EIGHT

Timber-framed houses

It was once widely believed that England's timber-framed buildings, with their sturdy and sometimes sophisticated standards of construction, were mostly sixteenth or seventeenth century in date and that they had all been built by the wealthier inhabitants of local societies. The concept of the 'vernacular threshold' held that the houses and cottages of the middling and poorer ranks of society did not survive from early times. The general opinion was that medieval peasant houses were so insubstantial that they could not have lasted for more than a generation. The more systematic recording of houses by members of the Vernacular Architecture Group and the technique of dendrochronology, the science of tree-ring dating, have overturned these views. We now know that thousands of medieval houses are still standing in many parts of rural England and that many of them belonged to ordinary farming families.

This new conclusion was demonstrated convincingly by the publication of *The Medieval Peasant House in Midland England* (2013), edited by Nat Alcock and Dan Miles, with contributions from other distinguished scholars. They revealed in great detail that most of the several hundred cruck-framed houses in the Midlands are in fact of medieval date and, simply from their numbers, they could not all be of superior status.[1] The new orthodoxy is that medieval peasant houses were substantial and built to last. Their timber frames are exposed to general view in many parts of England, but elsewhere they are often hidden behind later stone or brick walls and slated roofs.

Since the 1970s small groups of archaeologists, who were originally attached to university departments but who now work from independent laboratories, have developed the scientific method known as dendrochronology. This technique is based on the fact that every year a tree adds a growth ring just under its bark. As trees grow at different rates according to the season's weather, some rings are wide and others are narrow, and so distinctive sequences in the patterns of tree rings are formed. These patterns can be detected in other trees, especially those that grew during the same period in the same district. Fortunately, most timber-framed buildings were made from oak, which is the most suitable species of wood for tree-ring dating.[2]

The dendrochronologist begins by selecting timbers within a building that are suitable for drilling by a specially designed bit in order to obtain 12mm diameter cores. The resulting holes are plugged and stained to match the surrounding surface so that no damage is done to the structure or to its appearance. The cores are then dried and sanded so that a careful comparison of their tree-ring patterns can be made with previous samples that are stored in computer databases.

The results are amazingly accurate. Very often, dendro tests (as they are known for short) reveal the exact year in which the timbers were felled. There is plenty of documentary evidence to show that medieval carpenters used 'green' timbers, instead of allowing them to 'season' for a few years, so we can be confident that most timber-framed buildings were constructed in the year of felling or shortly afterwards. However, a precise felling date can be determined only when the last tree ring beneath the bark is present. If the bark and some of the sapwood have been removed, a range of possible dates must suffice. Thus, a cruck barn in Dronfield (Derbyshire) that Robert Howard and Alison Arnold of the Nottingham lab sampled in 2014 has two trusses that can be dated within a year or two of 1460, and three additional trusses that can be placed within the range 1537 to 1562.[3]

The earliest date that has been obtained so far for a timber-framed building is 1205 for part of Sycamore Farm House, Long Crendon (Buckinghamshire). Some of the cruck-framed buildings in south Oxfordshire (originally Berkshire) villages, such as Harwell and Mapledurham, also date from the thirteenth century. The Alcock and Miles study of 83 houses in the counties of Buckinghamshire, Leicestershire, Oxfordshire and Warwickshire whose timbers were suitable for sampling found that nearly all the crucks there were built between the 1260s and the 1550s. The medieval legacy of building is far more evident on the ground than was once supposed.

Previous attempts to date vernacular buildings by the radiocarbon dating of timbers had proved to be too imprecise to be helpful, so suggestions about the dates of buildings had to be based on the interpretation of methods of construction. Dating a building through a typology of styles often worked satisfactorily and many experienced scholars made well-informed estimates of the age of a building, which dendrochronology has subsequently proved correct. The approximate date of a timber-framed building was judged by comparing its style and carpentry techniques with similar buildings that bear date stones or whose date of erection was known from historical records. The most influential study along these lines was Cecil Hewett, *English Historic Carpentry* (1980), which sprang from his work on the famous thirteenth-century barns at Cressing Temple (Essex). Hewett believed that timber-framed buildings could be dated by their methods of jointing and their carpentry techniques, and his publishers claimed that he had 'shown that the methods of assembling timber buildings, particularly the joints used, follow a strict historical sequence, as datable as ceramics'.[4]

Richard Haddlesey has now shown that, where dendro dates can be compared with Hewett's estimates, 'his technique often yielded reasonably accurate results [but] he could, however, be very inaccurate'. Hewett was remarkably close with his Cressing Temple dates, but in several instances he was out by over 100 years and in one case by as much as 350 years. This major error was made at St Mary's church, Sompting (Sussex), which prompted Hewett to claim that carpentry techniques were well established in the Anglo-Saxon era.[5] It now seems likely that these methods were introduced into England about 1180 by the late Normans, and it is clear that a particular type of joint cannot provide firm dating evidence. Some carpenters were very conservative in their methods. One day, perhaps, dendrochronology will provide us with a clearer understanding of the various date ranges for particular techniques in different parts of England.

Another classification system that has been proved wrong by dendrochronology and more extensive fieldwork is that put forward by Ronald Brunskill,[6] which claimed that early carpenters' assembly marks were bold, rather sweeping scratches made with a race knife, whereas marks of the seventeenth century were more carefully made with a gouge and knife or chisel, and those of the eighteenth and nineteenth centuries were small, neat and deep marks made with a chisel. It is now clear that carpenters' assembly marks were much more varied than that and they were not confined to particular periods. English vernacular architecture is marked by its regional diversity and by the idiosyncrasies of local craftsmen. Only London and York had carpenters' and joiners' guilds to enforce certain ways of doing things, and even they were not concerned with marks. A typical team on a building project consisted of just two men and an apprentice, and each team created its own method of numbering. A 2009 report from Oxford Archaeology South on Church Farm, Lawknor (Oxfordshire) concluded that '[u]nfortunately it is very difficult to date carpenters' marks purely on style and execution as they were often individual to the carpenter.'[7]

Marks made by a chisel occurred much earlier than allowed by Brunskill's classification times. A study of marks in 43 Warwickshire houses by S. G. Wallsgrove dealt with six basic types, but he noted that more were found and that combinations of different marks were used.[8] The medieval carpenter's 'paring chisel' was long and thin and for hand use only, but they were capable of making the marks that have survived. Examples of chiselled marks in the form of Roman numerals from various parts of England include those on the Mermaid Inn, Rye (Sussex), dated to c.1525; those on a cruck truss at 29 High Street, Hallaton (Leicestershire), dated to 1465–83; at Bredon Barn (Worcestershire), which has been dendro-dated to 1345–58; and on the timbers in the tower of St Mary's church, Sompting (Sussex), which date from between 1300 and 1330.[9]

Medieval marks were sometimes made with a gouge. Assembly marks were gouged in thirteenth-century roofs at Salisbury Cathedral, using both Roman and Arabic numbers. They show how a team of carpenters could develop their own system of numbering.[10] An early example of gouged marks that can be found in various parts of England is a cruck truss at Church Cottage, Cadeby (Leicestershire), dendro-dated to 1472–3, with two gouged strokes on the eastern face and two strokes with a half-circle on the west.[11] A cruck frame dated 1479–80 at Myndtown (Oxfordshire) has 'heavy gouged assembly marks'. The Tithe Barn at Great Haseley (Oxfordshire), dated to 1494–5, has marks cut with a 9mm gouge that measure about 100mm overall.[12] Other late-medieval examples could be cited.

In their study of a fourteenth-century barn at Middle Littleton (Worcestershire), where the numbering is 'uniquely chaotic', Walter Horn and Freddie Charles concluded that, as all the samples taken from the timbers pointed to one felling date, 'the different numbering styles appear to belong to the same build and may be explained by the assumption that two master carpenters worked together, each with his own style of numbering'.[13]

Detailed investigations of carpenters' assembly marks in Surrey, which have been made by the county's Domestic Buildings Research Group, have led to a more convincing explanation than Brunskill's classification. The wide range of marks that were used, at the same time and in the same building, was necessary because many hundreds of joints were needed in the construction of a house and so carpenters had to devise ways of marking them without the use of large numbers. The members conclude:

> If only scribed marks were used then the frames would be differentiated only by tags, but it is more common to find scribed marks, two different size straight chisels, and a curved chisel being used to create four of the sets before tags were necessary.

The different types of marks do not indicate different periods of time. Rather, it seems likely that 'each carpenter soon developed his own favourite method of numbering' and that 'the ability to sort out the frames would have been a tremendous help when they were moved from the frame plot to their final site; how otherwise could several hundred pieces of timber be efficiently sorted?'[14]

Cruck-framed buildings

The first books to study cruck-framed buildings – S. O. Addy, *The Evolution of the English House* (1898) and C. F. Innocent, *The Development of English Building Construction* (1916) – took most of their examples from the home district of both authors, around Sheffield, so for a long time the A-frame was regarded as the typical method of cruck construction. Dendro tests have shown, however, that the crucks that survive in northern England tend to be later than those in the midland and southwestern counties, where cruck buildings were framed differently. In the Midlands and Welsh Borders, crucks were the characteristic buildings of the fifteenth and early sixteenth centuries, whereas in the West Riding of Yorkshire, although a few date from the late fifteenth century, most date from the sixteenth century, and others continue well into the seventeenth. Even with a common form of construction, we must be prepared to find regional variations.

The carpenters' first task was to find suitable trees with trunks and curving branches of suitable length. They were often able to split the timber lengthways to form two identical blades, the load-bearing members that supported the weight of the roof directly. The practice in the North was to fasten the blades together at mid-level by a tiebeam and higher up by a collar beam; both beams were slotted ('halved') into the blades and secured by pegs. In South Yorkshire, local carpenters used nine different ways to fasten the blades at the apex in order to support a ridge-piece between the two pairs of crucks. In some cases, where the blades did not reach exactly the same height, they used two methods in the same building. The tie-beam extended beyond the blades in order to support long timbers, known as wall-plates, which stretched as far as the next pair of blades. Halfway down the roof, between the ridge-piece and the wall-plate, other long timbers, known as purlins, were fixed to the outer part of the blades in order to carry the rafters that supported the roofing material. As the original walls did not shore up the roof, they were easily replaced in later centuries when stone walls were built to take the weight of the roof. The space between each pair of cruck blades formed a bay. Cruck-framed buildings were commonly only two or three bays in length, but the larger ones reached six bays or more.

The frames were prepared in the workshop or in the wood where the trees were felled before they were assembled at the site according to the sequence of the marks that the carpenter had made. The northern practice was to drill holes near the base of the blades and to thrust poles through them, so that, with the aid of ropes, strong men could lift the frame onto stone footings. These provided a secure foundation and prevented rotting from rising damp. The extra height that was gained was sometimes used to adjust the level of a building on a slope. Some cruck blades rest simply on paving stones or upon a foundation of rubble, however.

Madge Moran has shown that the numerous crucks that are to be found in Shropshire have a different appearance from those in the North. Tie-beams were not used, and the 'spurs' of midland counties, such as Leicestershire and Warwickshire, that were in effect tie-beams without a middle section, were uncommon. She describes the silhouette of a typical Shropshire cruck truss as being more like a pair of inclined boomerangs. Shropshire has examples of 11 different ways of fastening the cruck blades at the apex, and here, too, it is quite common to find variations of these methods within the same building. Documentary evidence shows that crucks were constructed in Shropshire in the thirteenth century. The majority of the surviving buildings date from the fifteenth and early sixteenth centuries, when they were the automatic choice of the wealthier peasants, but they seldom appear to have been used for lowly cottages. The use of crucks in Shropshire houses declined after about 1530, and by the seventeenth century they were used only for outbuildings.[15]

The remarkable national distribution pattern of cruck buildings remains unexplained. Crucks are found in large numbers in southwest and northeast Yorkshire, parts of Lancashire and Cheshire, along the river Severn (Herefordshire, Worcestershire and Shropshire), in southeast and central Wales, and in the midland counties of Leicestershire, Warwickshire and south Oxfordshire. Yet they are conspicuously absent from eastern and southeastern England.[16] A plausible hypothesis is that native pendunculate oak trees, whose shape is ideal for cruck construction, predominate in the areas where crucks are found, whereas the less suitable sessile oaks are the major type in eastern England.

The cruck-framed houses in the Severn-side counties and Wales are mostly late medieval, even though many of them are very elegant, with strikingly decorative carpentry, whereas those in Warwickshire and Leicestershire are the most 'ordinary' in appearance and often lack any distinction in their construction. The medieval houses of Midland England are predominately cruck-framed and three bays in length. Some box-framed houses are medieval, but this style became dominant only after crucks passed out of use. Surprisingly, however, the earliest surviving houses in the Midlands are either aisled, with free-standing posts set within the walls, or they use the more substantial base crucks at ground-floor level.

The dendro dates for cruck buildings in Leicestershire and Warwickshire that have been published show that all but three of these houses were built between 1380 and 1510, with a high proportion in the fifteenth century, reaching a peak between 1430 and 1480. Although the sample is small, it is very much in accord with the dates from cruck buildings in Buckinghamshire and Shropshire, and from Kent for all timber buildings, most of them Wealden houses. Curiously, Oxfordshire has a relatively high proportion of earlier and later buildings, but a substantial minority that belong to the fifteenth century. The Alcock and Miles survey has refuted the old idea that the earliest surviving timber-framed houses were built only by the wealthy. The sheer number of cruck houses in the Midlands confirms that they must be peasant dwellings. Some villages have ten or even twenty such houses.[17]

Box-framed buildings

The chief limitations of cruck-framed buildings are in their height and width, for their dimensions were dependent upon the size of the blades that could be cut from suitable local oak trees. When it became fashionable to insert a ceiling into a hall that had previously been open to the rafters, the space in the upper part was very constricted. This was not a problem with the other major method of constructing a medieval building, whereby posts and beams were used to make a box-like frame that supported a triangular roof, whose weight was distributed throughout the frame and the walls. As box frames provided more space than crucks, they were preferred for buildings of superior status. Yet in some parts of England both types of construction can be found in the same house. It is common to find that an open hall framed with crucks may have one or two box-framed wings.

The roof styles of box-framed buildings vary from region to region. Those parts of the West Riding of Yorkshire and Derbyshire that fringe the Pennines favoured the use of a king post that rises from a tie-beam to the ridge-piece in order to take the weight of the rafters and the heavy stone slates of the roof. The earliest king posts that caught the eye when looking upwards in open halls sometimes had decorative mouldings and a carved boss underneath. Now, they are often hidden from view, left untouched in a loft when a ceiling was inserted. Some surviving examples are earlier in date than neighbouring cruck frames, for their more advanced style of carpentry was within the means of wealthy families, while the simpler cruck technique long continued to provide limited space for cottages, barns and other farm buildings.

Yorkshire gentry houses such as Elland New Hall, Shibden Hall and Thornhill Lees Hall were planned around a central hall that was open to a king-post roof truss and cross-wings that were divided into two storeys. The roof trusses were sturdy enough to support heavy stone slates, while a stone sill provided a firm, damp-proof foundation for the close-studded walls, whose posts were arranged in attractive diagonal patterns, especially in the gable ends. A group of more than 20 houses that were built by the yeomen-clothiers of the Halifax district during the second half of the fifteenth century and the first quarter of the sixteenth were arranged in the normal manner, but they are not easy to recognize from outside, for like most of the county's timber-framed houses they were clad in stone in later times and so are heavily disguised. Their most distinctive feature is the use of aisles to widen the hall, usually in the form of a single aisle to the rear. These 'Halifax houses' were built about the same time as the fine Perpendicular Gothic churches of the West Riding, and together they demonstrate the growing prosperity of the cloth-manufacturing district in contrast to the stagnating economies of the once-prosperous East and North Ridings.[18]

In other areas, notably Kent, Sussex and much of East Anglia, the best medieval houses have sufficient distinctive details (in such features as their roof structure, crown posts, beam mouldings and bracing patterns) to establish a reasonably precise typology, linked to buildings whose date is known from dendrochronology or from documents. Smaller and simple medieval houses have been recorded there, but they are too rare to provide a detailed picture of the houses of more modest peasants.

The most substantial timber-framed buildings in southeastern England are the so-called Wealden houses, which date from the 1380s to the 1530s. Kent alone has over 350 of them, but the same types are found in much smaller numbers up and down the country; Warwickshire, for instance, has a fine collection. They follow a standard form and plan, consisting of an open hall and end bays all in a line, but they vary in size and decoration. The open hall usually has an elaborately carved crown-post roof and, at the front, it is set back between the jettied upper storeys of the two wings. The deep eaves of this recess had to be supported by arched braces so that all the rooms were covered by the same hipped roof.[19]

The late-medieval prosperity of Norfolk, Suffolk, Essex and Kent is reflected in the large numbers of timber-framed buildings that still stand in both towns and the countryside. These counties did not have good-quality building stone, but they had sufficient wood. Oliver Rackham calculated that Grundle House in Suffolk, a timber-framed building constructed about 1500 in the standard form of a hall and two cross-wings, used some 300 trees, mostly oak, but 20 per cent elm, and that such a quantity might have been produced once in every six years from 50 acres of managed woodland. About 40 of the trees in the construction of this small manor house were large ones, but the rest were less than 50 years old. At that time, the woods of Suffolk were capable of producing 70 such houses each year. Late-medieval woodwards divided their woods into sections and felled them on a rotation basis.[20]

The Welsh Border counties were also well wooded and wealthy in late-medieval and Tudor times. In Herefordshire the small towns and villages of Pembridge, Weobley and Eardisland contain remarkable numbers of sturdy houses from this era, many of which have been dendro-dated.[21] They survive because the county ceased to be prosperous in later centuries. In other parts of England, the lack of medieval peasant houses is partly due to lack of wealth at the time and partly to the absence of suitable timber. Many villages did not have access to woods, either because none existed or because the lord restricted access. In the East Midlands peasant families had to build with clay. The longhouses of Devon also had thick walls of clay, known as cob, with stone foundations and overhanging thatch roofs to keep the rain out. The almost total absence of surviving medieval farmhouses in Cornwall, a county with little timber, but with readily available supplies of suitable stone, suggests that the inhabitants were poor at that time. Medieval peasants took advantage of the local materials that were available, such as clay and wattles for wall panels, or earth for mud walls. Although house plans were basically the same throughout England, the use of local materials gave buildings a distinctive regional appearance.

Peasant houses

The evidence from standing buildings and the foundations of those that have been recovered through excavation show that peasant houses were typically arranged around a central hall that was open to the rafters. These halls could be lengthened by the addition of an extra bay or two, but their almost standard width was regulated by the roof span; the better ones gained extra space through the use of aisles. A wood fire in a central hearth provided the heating, with most of the smoke escaping through the roof, but timber and plaster smokehoods attached to an internal wall were starting to replace central hearths in the wealthier districts. The entrance to the building was usually along a cross-passage with opposed doorways at one end of the hall. In the old-fashioned longhouses that remained in vogue in rural districts, this passage often separated humans from their livestock. Alternatively, the low end may have been used as a workshop or as a store for tools and equipment. In time, it became the service end of the building, containing perhaps a kitchen, a dairy or a buttery. At the other side of the hall, the larger peasant houses had a private parlour, which was used as a withdrawing room and a bedroom, sometimes with an upstairs room known as a solar. This basic plan of three units – kitchen, hall, parlour – continued in use well into the post-medieval period.[22]

In midland villages, each house was separate and protected from unwelcome intrusions. The whole property, including a garden or toft, was surrounded by a fence or hedge, or perhaps a dry stone wall, and access was through a gate leading on to the street, and a door with a lock. Windows were small and shuttered. Excavations on village sites show that barns, stables, cowsheds and other outbuildings usually stood close together, around a yard. Kitchens or bakehouses were often detached from the main building to reduce the risk of fire. Christopher Dyer notes that houses designed for living might also store implements and food, especially bacon and grain. The idea of separate living and working spaces would probably not have seemed a meaningful concept to members of a peasant household. It is difficult to draw a firm line between domestic and farm buildings, as their function could change. There is plenty of documentary evidence for the conversion of bakehouses, carthouses and stables into dwellings for retired peasants. The quality of construction of some farm buildings was comparable with the dwellings.

The character of some late-medieval buildings is captured by a few examples from a survey of former parish guild lands at Dronfield (Derbyshire) in 1561.[23] William Mason of Barnes Farm had a two-bay house thatched with straw, a four-bay barn, a detached kitchen and a stable. His neighbour, Robert Hancock, leased a three-bay house that was straw thatched, a three-bay barn that was thatched with broom, a cow house and a wain house of three bays, a one-bay stable that was stone slated, and an orchard and a garden. John Sykes was the tenant of a dwelling house with a barn, both of them two bays wide and thatched with straw, with a bakehouse of one bay and a kiln, surrounded by a garden and a croft. Elizabeth Eyre, a widow, had a three-bay house, a one-bay bakehouse and a one-bay barn 'all straw thacked', and Robert Cawton rented a three-bay house that was thatched with turves, a one-bay smithy, an orchard and a garden.

'Peasant' is still a convenient term to describe a small-scale farmer, the type of person who would have been the head of household in most of the surviving timber-framed houses. In medieval England such farms only occasionally exceeded 30 acres before 1350 or 70 acres in the period 1380–1540. Dyer offers a convincing explanation of the striking paradox that the dates for the Midlands cruck houses coincide almost exactly with the evidence from documents for the decay and destruction of tenant buildings, mostly in the period 1370–1480, though on some manors beginning in the 1350s and 1360s, and sometimes continuing well after 1500. The national population had fallen drastically with the onslaught of the Black Death, so half of the housing stock was made redundant. Excavations support the documentary evidence, because they reveal that over the whole of England hundreds of foundations of houses were abandoned between the mid-fourteenth and the early sixteenth centuries. Individual peasants had accumulated multiple holdings, and the houses and buildings that were surplus to their requirements were not worth repairing. These were times of low land values, low prices for agricultural produce, and a general contraction in the rural economy. Dyer concludes that the documentary sources are not as dramatically opposed to the visual evidence as first appears. Decay and new growth coexisted in late-medieval society. Those who survived the plague were able to grasp opportunities to better themselves by acquiring more land. Wills tell a different story to manor court rolls. The lucky people who were able to increase their incomes built the timber-framed houses that we see today.

We must not assume that peasants built their own houses, for specialist craftsmen might have performed even the least skilled jobs. The large numbers of carpenters and wrights who were recorded in the poll tax returns of 1379 and 1381 could have made a living only if they had worked on a high number of building projects. Unfortunately, surviving buildings cannot easily be linked with the individuals who built and lived in them. Dendrochronology can sometimes point to a likely owner, however. In 2013 Robert Howard took six core samples from the timber frame at Dronfield Woodhouse Hall. Five of the six samples came together as a single group of data, indicating that the trees were all from the same general patch of woodland and from the same phase of felling in 1533. At the time of the survey of former parish guild lands in 1561, the tenant was Mr Robert Barley. The hall was described as a dwelling house of three bays, a kitchen of one bay, a chamber and a parlour, together with an ox house, stable, two barns, a wain house of two bays, an orchard, a garden, and two little crofts. Robert Barley's father, Thomas Barley, was a junior member of the gentry family of Barleys of Barlow Hall. He was described as Mr Thomas Barley of Dronfield Woodhouse in 1520; in 1536 he was said to be of Dronfield Woodhouse; and in the following year he took a lease of the tithes of Dronfield Woodhouse. He can therefore be identified as the man who erected the cruck-framed house there in 1533.[24]

FIGURE 15 *Robert Howard of the Nottingham Tree-Ring Dating Laboratory takes a sample from the cruck frame at Dronfield Woodhouse Hall, which revealed a felling date of 1533.*

It is much more difficult to identify the first owner of a humble cottage. This was possible with The Oaks at Myddlewood (Shropshire) because of a unique parish history, written in 1701–2, by a local inhabitant, Richard Gough, combined with documentary evidence from estate records and parish registers. The original cottage that consisted of just one ground-floor room, possibly open to the rafters, was first recorded in a rental of 1588, shortly after its erection, by John Hughes, the younger son of a local farmer. The cottage was altered by the addition of an extra bay, the insertion of a ceiling to provide an upper storey, and the provision of a chimney stack. The surviving building is still basically the labourer's cottage that belonged to the Hanmer family during the seventeenth century.[25]

Townspeople had much less space in which to build and their houses often had to accommodate shops on the ground floor. A typical arrangement can be seen in a long row of 23 mid-fifteenth-century houses in Church Street, Tewkesbury (Gloucestershire). The front of each property was used as a shop, with a chamber above, and a passage led from the street to a small open hall at the rear. The continuous line of jettied chambers emphasizes the regular appearance of the row. A more substantial group of shops and houses with crown-post roofs still descends the narrow street known as the Shambles in York, where the butchers once plied their trade. Before the fifteenth century most houses in York were only one or two storeys high, but in the late Middle Ages some shopkeepers were able to afford an extra one. The contemporary Butcher Row in Shrewsbury still retains some of its timber-framed buildings, notably Abbot's House, which was erected by the Abbot of Lilleshall as an investment for his abbey. The timbers were felled in 1457–8, and a frame-raising ceremony was recorded in 1459. Three storeys high, with two bold jetties, the house provided living space above the ground-floor shops.[26]

On the whole, townsfolk preferred box frames to crucks. They continued to use timber frames well into the seventeenth century, for they valued the opportunities for display. Yet some important medieval urban buildings were constructed of stone. These included notable inns such as The Angel at Grantham on the Great North Road and The George at Glastonbury.

By the end of the Middle Ages the once-flourishing Cinque Port of Sandwich had been reduced to a mere regional centre as it grappled with the problems of the silting up of its haven and competition from London. Still largely enclosed within its medieval defences, Sandwich retains a remarkable collection of timber-framed buildings. A recent survey led by Sarah Pearson, one of England's most experienced investigators of historic buildings and the leading authority on the houses of Kent, has identified 57 houses that date from the early fourteenth century up to about 1520 and another ten timber-framed buildings that were used for other purposes. Yet the town had only about 380 households in 1513, and this number had declined to about 290 by 1560. The authors of the survey conclude: 'This phenomenal proportion of surviving buildings is matched in no other major towns in England.' Sandwich's houses date mostly from around 1460 and reach a peak about the end of the fifteenth century. They are smaller than the few surviving earlier ones and seem to have been erected by 'the middling sort' rather than the wealthiest townsmen. They survive because they were never replaced when Sandwich went into decline during the reign of Henry VIII.[27]

The character of the small borough of Much Wenlock (Shropshire), with a population of less than 2,500, was also formed in the late-medieval era. Within an area of about 200 square yards, Madge Moran's team was able to find a remarkable collection of timber-framed buildings. Those that have been dendro-dated include a large samson-post in Bastard Hall, which was felled sometime between 1255 and 1289 and whose tree rings go back to the time of Alfred the Great, two base crucks of 1327–30 and 1407–8, and two crucks of 1416 and 1435. The Prior's House, which was traditionally ascribed to about 1500, turns out to be 75 years older. Like other Shropshire towns, there is little evidence of building activity in the first half of the sixteenth century, when recession bit deeply.[28]

In the ancient city of York the sharp decline of the population caused by the Black Death allowed more space for the rebuilding of mansions on a large scale. Most of York's substantial houses were still timber framed, but the quality of neighbouring buildings differed hugely. Wall tiles or thin bricks became a common infill between timber uprights from about 1400 onwards, and by 1450 the risk of fires had ensured that most buildings were roofed with brick tile rather than with thatch. By the second decade of the sixteenth century, domestic glass windows were becoming more common and chimneys were replacing the braziers that had been used to heat the upper rooms.[29]

The great rebuilding

During the reign of Queen Elizabeth, country gentry began to build their halls anew in stone or brick, yet the old timber-framed tradition persisted in some areas, notably in Lancashire, Cheshire and other western counties. Their black-and-white appearance is a Victorian innovation, for old paintings and photographs depict timbers that were generally unstained. The outstanding example is Little Moreton Hall, a standard late-medieval house surrounded by a moat that was enlarged in successive campaigns from 1559 onwards. The long gallery that was added in the 1570s must have been a sensation in the Cheshire countryside, but the weight of its timbers and floors made of lime-ash and gypsum soon caused the structural problems that have produced the eye-catching buckling effect that startles visitors today. In East Anglia, by contrast, the inferior timbers that were available were usually plastered over using a decorative plastering technique known as pargetting.

Throughout England, medieval peasant houses were sparsely furnished and unclean by modern standards. Even in the better houses, floors were often covered with rushes, which accumulated dirt. The poorer husbandmen and labourers lived in humble, one- or two-roomed houses that are known

FIGURE 16 *The Elizabethan Little Moreton Hall, Cheshire.*

to us only through excavation and documentary descriptions. We need not mourn their passing. Evidence from literary sources and probate inventories shows that during the second half of Queen Elizabeth I's reign housing standards improved considerably.

Recent improvements to smaller houses were noted by William Harrison, the rector of Radwinter in Essex, in his *Description of England* (1577).[30] He observed the 'multitude of chimnies latelie erected' and 'a great amendment of lodging', meaning comfortable beds instead of pallets. But he qualified his remarks by saying that these improvements were widespread but not general. For example, the old straw pallets were 'not verie much amended as yet in some parts of Bedfordshire, and elsewhere further off from our southern parts'.

By contrast, in his *Breviary of Suffolk* (1618),[31] Robert Ryece wrote that the

poor cottager . . . doth very well to . . . raise his frame low, cover it with thatch, and to fill his wide panels (after they are well splinted and bound) with clay or culm enough well tempered; over which it may be some, of more ability both for warmth, continuance and comeliness, do bestow a cast of hair lime and sand, made into mortar and laid thereon, rough or smooth as the owner pleaseth.

Harrison also commented on the decorative pargetting designs that are a pleasing feature of timber-framed houses in Suffolk and neighbouring counties:

> In plastering likewise of our fairest houses we use to lay first a line or two of white mortar, tempered with hair, upon laths, which are nailed one by another . . . and finally cover all with the aforesaid plaster, which, beside the delectable whiteness of the stuff itself, is laid on so even and smoothly as nothing in my judgement can be done with more exactness.

William Smith, writing about Cheshire in a similar vein a few years later,[32] remarked:

> For they had their fyer in the middest of the howse against a hob of clay, and their oxen also under the same rouff. But within these 40 yeares it is altogether altred, so that they have builded chemnies, and furnished other partes of their howses accordingly.

In Cornwall, Richard Carew[33] recalled the time when most husbandmen's houses had

> walles of earth, low thatched roofes, few partitions, no planchings or glasse windowes, and scarcely any chimneys, other than a hole in the wall to let out the smoke: their bed, straw and a blanket . . . To conclude, a mazer and a panne or two, comprised all their substance: but now most of these fashions are universally banished, and the Cornish husbandman conformethe himself with a better supplied civilitie to the Easterne patterne.

By the second half of the seventeenth century stone and brick were used for all but the most humble cottages and outbuildings, and in the eastern half of England brick houses were normally roofed with Dutch-style pantiles. At the end of the century a clergyman, Abraham de la Pryme, observed that the houses in Hatfield Chase (South Yorkshire) were formerly: 'All of wood, clay and plaster, but now that way of building is quite left off, for every one now from the richest to the poorest, will not build except with bricks.'[34] During the eighteenth century Norwegian softwoods were imported via the Humber and the Tees, while simple traditional roof designs that were copied from pattern books remained in use well into the nineteenth century.

The general standard of ordinary farmhouses improved through modification or by complete rebuilding from Elizabethan times onwards. Middling families began to install chimneys and window glass and to make their houses more comfortable with window curtains and coverings on the walls, even if they had to make do with painted cloths rather than the tapestries or wainscot panelling of their richer contemporaries. Ceilings were inserted to create upstairs chambers, and if enough money was available parlours and service rooms were provided with wainscotting and boarded floors and fitted with fireplaces and glass windows. The 'iron chimneys' that replaced the old open hearths often got a proud mention in yeomen and husbandmen's wills in the middle years of the sixteenth century. Whereas in earlier times houses were furnished meanly with tables, benches, stools and beds and the minimum essential cooking pots, plates and mugs, by the late Elizabethan and early Stuart period the better farmhouses had a greater range of furniture and household goods, such as pewter drinking vessels and cooking pots made of iron, copper or brass. Food was now more plentiful and varied, and people were better dressed.

The upper floors and chimneys that were new features in the second half of the sixteenth century were sometimes depicted on surveyor's maps, notably those made by John Walker of various places in Essex. His map of 'Newlandes Ende' in Matching parish (1609),[35] for example, shows six single-storey houses, a more substantial dwelling with a gabled, two-storey cross wing, and a four-bay, jettied house of two storeys. These are all of the 'lobby-entrance' type of house where a doorway opened on to a prominent central chimneystack. Fantastic brick stacks became popular in many parts of the South East, when the owners of smaller houses imitated local aristocrats and gentry.

In an influential pioneering article in 1953 on 'The Rebuilding of Rural England, 1570–1640',[36] William Hoskins used contemporary literary evidence, household accounts, probate inventories, and above all the visual evidence of rural buildings with datestones to argue for 'a revolution in the housing of a considerable part of the population' within the 70 years after 1570, though he accepted that in some parts of the country, notably the northernmost four counties, active rebuilding occurred later. His essay was immediately influential and inspired much of the early work of the newly formed Vernacular Architecture Group, but the ideas have now been considerably refined, almost to the point of outliving their usefulness. Hoskins was first challenged by Robert Machin, who emphasized the wide variations in the dates of new buildings in the different regions of England.[37] The period 1570–1640 no longer seems as special as Hoskins had argued, except perhaps in certain restricted areas. As we have seen, the stock of late-medieval houses was not of the poor quality that had been supposed and many of the design features that are found in later houses had already been adopted. The introduction of enclosed fireplaces, for example, occurred much earlier than Hoskins realized. In Hampshire, this happened in the late fifteenth and sixteenth centuries. Edward Roberts has shown that in Hampshire the first two-storeyed halls with enclosed fireplaces were built around 1460, with the numbers increasing during the first half of the sixteenth century. Floors and enclosed fireplaces began to be inserted into open halls from 1520s. Open-hall houses ceased to be built during the 1560s and 1570s.[38] The same pattern has been observed in Kent, with major changes between 1520 and 1580. It is now thought better to speak of a continuum of improvement from the late fifteenth century onwards, with much regional variation.

The use of local stone for farmhouse walls and roofing slates has given England a wonderfully rich tradition of vernacular architecture. The country is so varied geologically that a traveller has to move only a short distance to see a variety of building materials in use. Those villagers who lived away from the coast or a navigable river found it was too expensive to import stone from another region, so they had to make do with whatever was at hand. The lucky ones had high quality Oolitic Limestone; some others had to make do with flints. The stone manor houses and halls and the farmhouses of the yeomen in the Cotswolds or in Northamptonshire and Rutland often bear a sixteenth- or seventh-century datestone and the initials of the proud owners. They are immediately recognizable by their gables and by their mullioned-and-transomed windows with drip moulds or stringcourses above them.

In eastern parts of England, where good local stone was unavailable for building, brick began to be used by yeomen and husbandmen. The towns often led the way in following the new fashions, though the first house in York to be built completely in brick was not erected until 1610.[39] Some house-owners continued to value timber for its decorative effect, even when they used stone for their lower walls, and old timber-framed houses were often given a coat of plaster and a colour wash. In some parts of England the owners of woods found it more profitable to produce coppiced underwood for ironmasters and lead smelters than to grow 'standards' for timber, but changing fashions and fear of fire in populous places were probably as important as the shortage of timber in the general adoption of stone or brick as the normal building materials. By the time of the Civil War only the humblest urban cottages were still being constructed with wood. The timber-framed tradition survived longer in the countryside.

The study of distinctive groups of vernacular houses in particular 'countries' needs to take account of the family and business ties between the various owners. For example, northeast Derbyshire has an impressive collection of seventeenth- and early eighteenth-century stone houses, most of which were erected by lead smelters and merchants at a time when the Derbyshire lead field was the most prosperous in Europe. Lead was mined on the Carboniferous Limestone of what is now known as the White Peak, but it was smelted in the well-wooded river valleys further east and exported through the river port of Bawtry, so the Burtons, Rotherhams and other local families within the large parish of Dronfield were able to rise to the ranks of the minor gentry and to build houses in the latest styles.[40] In 'countries' such as this, wealth obtained from industry was far greater than that gained from farming, though these different activities continued to be profitably combined.

The ancient parish of Halifax has a group of remarkably distinctive stone houses at the top end of the vernacular scale. Here, too, family links and wealth generated by local industry provide the explanation, for the owners were rich clothiers. It is likely that only small groups of craftsmen were at work in this neighbourhood, for although no two 'Halifax houses' are alike, a distinctive style of building and ornamentation is immediately recognizable. This style owed much to the Gothic vernacular tradition, with gables, large mullioned-and-transomed windows arranged symmetrically under string courses, battlements, gargoyles and finials, but it also incorporated classical details in the arches and columns of the spectacular, ornamental porches. Even there, however, the Gothic spirit is triumphant, for the most arresting feature in several of these houses is the rose window in the gable above the entrance. Rose windows, in a variety of styles, are peculiar to the 'Halifax houses' of the second and third quarter of the seventeenth century.[41]

The continuity of building traditions from the late Elizabethan period into the second half of the seventeenth century makes it difficult to date houses for which there is no firm evidence. Even at the same social level, owners sometimes chose to build in the accepted manner two generations later. The quality and dates of English farmhouses and cottages vary considerably from one part of the country to another. In the West Riding of Yorkshire, for instance, the seventeenth-century stone houses of yeomen-clothiers survive in their hundreds in the upper Calder Valley, whereas the East Riding has relatively few surviving vernacular buildings before well into the eighteenth century. The vernacular architecture of one 'country' readily distinguishes it from that of others.

Houses and the hearth tax

One way of comparing the housing stock of the English counties after the Restoration of King Charles II is to analyse the evidence of the hearth tax returns. These are records of a tax that was levied on every householder's hearths twice a year between 1662 and 1689. By that time, fireplaces and elaborate chimneystacks had become a matter of pride in larger houses and were readily identified, and even the humblest houses were usually fitted with a chimney. Hearths had become an obvious target for taxation, 'it being easy to tell the number of hearths, which remove not as heads or polls do'. But, like most taxes, it was unpopular and it was abolished after the Glorious Revolution ousted King James II in favour of William of Orange and Queen Mary.

Historians have come to realize that tables of the percentages of people with, say, one, two, three to five, and six or more hearths within the various counties do not necessarily provide a straightforward comparison of wealth and poverty across the land.[42] The problem of interpretation can be illustrated by comparing the numbers of one-hearth houses in Kent and Westmorland. Kent was one of the richest counties in England, though its wealth was distributed unevenly across its varied landscapes and 'countries', whereas Westmorland was one of the poorest, in what is often held to be the 'backward North'. The survival of numerous ancient buildings in Kent compared with few in Westmorland seems to support this judgement. In 1664 only 36 per cent of Kent's householders were taxed on a single hearth, whereas in Westmorland in 1669 the proportion was as high as 80 per cent. There is no doubt that the inhabitants of Kent were more prosperous than those in Westmorland, but detailed studies of the two counties show that the differences were more nuanced than these figures suggest.

Sarah Pearson observes that at all but the highest social levels in Kent, the first enclosed fireplaces were built between 1520 and 1580 with smoke bays or timber chimneys which had flues of timber and plaster. While this funnelled the smoke away from the hall and allowed an extra chamber to be built on the upper floor, it did not in itself lead to extra fireplaces, since timber flues normally served a single one. Flues began to be built of brick and stone in the later sixteenth and seventeenth centuries, a change that took place slowly. At farmhouse level the introduction of extra hearths almost always seems to have been deferred until the seventeenth century. The difference between pre- and post-1625 probate inventories is striking. Several large medieval farmhouses, updated in the sixteenth century by the insertion of smoke bays or timber chimneys, have brick fireplaces or chimneys inscribed with dates in the first four decades of the seventeenth century. As this change took place mainly before the 1664 hearth tax, but sometimes afterwards, the one-hearth houses in that return included substantial properties that had not been updated. New, small houses in the countryside had two fireplaces, and the new buildings in the ports and dockyard towns had integral stacks and several fireplaces, but that may have been because they were subdivided between different families. As many timber-framed houses in east Kent were totally rebuilt in brick between 1680 and 1750, the implication is that the earlier houses were too poor to keep. The picture is more complicated than it first appears and the differences between the different 'countries' of Kent were significant.[43]

Colin Phillips has brought an historian's expertise to the study of the Westmorland hearth tax returns. In 1669 no less than 80 per cent of householders were living in one-hearth houses. Some improvements occurred during the next few years, for in the winter of 1674–5 that proportion fell to 73 per cent, but this was still twice as high as in Kent. It has long been argued that Westmorland farmhouses had simple plans and few rooms, but Phillips's analysis of contemporary probate inventories suggests otherwise. Where probate inventories can be linked to names in the hearth tax returns, they suggest that internal subdivision and the construction of extra rooms had been underway for some time. Farmhouses were built to more than one type of plan. The survival into the 1660s and 1670s in Westmorland of houses that were planned with only a hearth in the central 'firehouse' and the use of a chimney hood may provide an architectural explanation for the preponderance of one-hearth households. Another point to consider is that, as about 15 per cent of the entries in the hearth tax returns had the same surname as the next householder on the list, buildings may have been sub-divided into multi-hearth properties that were shared between siblings, widows and widowers. One-hearth households may appear superficially similar in the tax returns, but they were in fact a diverse group. To equate one hearth simply with poverty is therefore wrong. The number of householders in Westmorland who were exempted from payment of the tax compares favourably with the lists from other parts of England.[44]

The use of documentary evidence is as crucial to a better understanding of vernacular architecture as the surviving buildings themselves. It is clear that the types and ages of house before the Industrial Revolution varied greatly, not only between town and countryside but also from one 'country' to another.

CHAPTER NINE

Population, family life and society

Population growth, loss and recovery

At the Norman Conquest a foreign aristocracy replaced the previous Anglo-Scandinavian elite, but the genetic stock of the English population remained largely the same as before. We do not have a firm figure for the total population of England at that time, but estimates based on Domesday Book range from 1.5 to 2.25 million. By 1300 it had risen to perhaps as much as 5 million. This long period of growth came to a sudden end in the crisis years of 1315–22, when disease and famine from a series of harvest failures and devastating outbreaks of cattle plague and sheep murrain caused the national population to decline by at least 15 per cent.

A generation later, the Black Death brought disaster on a scale that had never been known before and has never been repeated since. The population of England plummeted almost to its Domesday Book level. On 24 October 1348 the Bishop of Winchester wrote that 'this cruel plague has now begun a ... savage attack on the coastal areas of England'. It coincided with another two dreadful years of harvest failure. By November it had reached London, with devastating effect. In early January 1349 the parliament that had been planned for Westminster was abandoned because 'the plague of deadly pestilence has suddenly broke out ... and daily increases in severity'.[1] Within a couple of years this mysterious disease had killed at least a third and probably around a half of the national population. All other events in English history pale into insignificance compared with the impact of this terrible killer.

The exact nature of the disease remains controversial. In the early twentieth century it became accepted that the Black Death had been bubonic plague, spread by fleas on the backs of black rats in summer time, but contemporary accounts do not mention rats, and modern studies of epidemics in other parts of the world have shown that bubonic plague has a different pattern of development and that mortality rates are much lower. It has been argued that an unidentified haemorrhagic virus that was spread by droplet infection was the culprit,[2] yet DNA analysis of teeth from skeletons in mass graves near Hereford cathedral has confirmed the presence there of the *Yersinia pestis* bacterium, which was passed on by bites from fleas and which causes bubonic plague.

The unpredictable way that the disease spread is hard to follow. We have to rely on unconnected scraps of evidence, for no systematic records of deaths from the 'plague' or 'pestilence' were ever kept. In the country at large, it probably reached its peak in April and May 1349, by which time it had reached as far west as Cornwall and as far north as Yorkshire. The crowded towns perhaps suffered worst, but even in spacious districts such as the Forest of Knaresborough and the upper Calder Valley in Yorkshire manorial records show that about 40–45 per cent of holdings were left empty upon the death of tenants in 1349–50.[3] In most cases where calculations are possible from surviving manor court records, the deaths of tenants clustered between 40 and 60 per cent, but in some English manors only one in five tenants died, while in others the death rate reached two out of three and even three out of four.[4] We have no means of estimating the numbers of poorer people who died, nor how many women and children were affected. When the plague was at its peak, it is quite possible that up to 50 people in a village, and up to 300 in London, died in a day. Death on such a scale had never been experienced before. Laconic entries in contemporary chronicles rarely provide more than the briefest details about people's responses, but clergymen who were as baffled as anyone else tried to answer the question of why God had allowed this horrible disease to kill so many by asserting that it was divine punishment for sinful living. Graffiti roughly scratched in Latin on the north wall of the tower of St Mary's church, Ashwell (Hertfordshire), in 1350 can be translated as 'pitiable, savage and violent. A wicked populace survives to witness.'

Plague remained endemic in England for over 300 years. A major outbreak of the disease in 1361–2, which became known as the children's plague, may have been a mutant form, or perhaps its victims were mostly the young because surviving adults had acquired immunity during earlier attacks. The cumulative effect of repeated local outbreaks was to reduce the national population level dramatically.[5]

The lucky survivors of the Black Death must have been traumatized by their experiences but, in material terms, they were soon able to benefit from the new situation in which they found themselves. Manorial lords had to be flexible and make concessions, otherwise their peasants went to live elsewhere. Families that had previously scratched a living from unsuitable soils at the edges of woods, moors, fens or marshes now seized the opportunity to improve their standard of living on more productive and larger farms. The wealthier and shrewder peasants bought extra property and founded dynasties of yeomen. They were constrained only by the higher

Crowder House.

FIGURE 17 *Crowder House, South Yorkshire, in 1884. The Wilkinson family farmed here, through direct inheritance, from 1402 to 1859.*

wages they had to pay their labourers and by the lower rents that they could charge their sub-tenants. A long-term and dramatic shift in the balance of power between lords and tenants was underway.

Towards the end of the Middle Ages, England had a population of about 2.5 million, of whom nine out of every ten lived in the countryside. The richest and most populous counties were in the South East and East Anglia, though Devon and Somerset, too, had grown prosperous. The northwestern counties of Lancashire, Westmorland and Cumberland were the poorest and the least inhabited. Yet comparisons between counties can be misleading, for the fortunes of the various 'countries' or neighbourhoods within them varied considerably. Foreign visitors regarded England as a rich and agreeable land, apart from its climate, but they commented on the emptiness of the countryside. England had far fewer people in Henry VIII's reign than in the late thirteenth or early fourteenth centuries.

Then, during the reign of Queen Elizabeth I, the population of England, along with that of the whole of west Europe, recovered to the level that had been achieved before the Black Death. By the outbreak of civil war in 1642, England's population had almost doubled to about 5 million. Improved farming practices and a steadily developing economy sustained this growth by providing enough food for almost everyone except in the worst years of harvest failure. The harvests were generally average to good for the first 30 years of Elizabeth's reign, but then England suffered from a series of famines that brought widespread discontent. The harvests of 1586 and 1587, at the time of mounting apprehension about the Spanish Armada, were disastrous, as were the four successive harvests in the barren years between 1594 and 1597. Baltic grain had to be imported from Danzig (Gdansk) on a large scale to avert famine, and many families struggled to survive.[6] The fear of famine remained very real in James I's reign. In 1622 and 1623 the pastoral uplands of Cumberland, Westmorland and neighbouring counties endured a series of harvest failures that weakened human resistance to disease and caused some people to die of hunger.[7] By the middle decades of the seventeenth century, however, widespread starvation had ceased to be a major concern. Malnutrition may have made people less resistant to illness, but infectious disease was the real problem.

Queen Mary's reign had coincided not only with bad harvests but with devastating visitations of 'sweating sickness' in 1551 and in 1557–8, when the queen herself may have been amongst the 8 or 9 per cent of the population who died from it. This mysterious epidemic, which was perhaps a virulent form of influenza, disappeared in 1559, but plague remained endemic, especially in the towns, where outbreaks were unpredictable. Between September 1582 and December 1583 Doncaster lost 747 people to the plague, and between October 1586 and November 1587 about 300 died in Chesterfield. Further north, two-thirds of the inhabitants of Richmond were killed in a visitation of plague between August 1597 and December 1598; the parish register recorded 1,050 deaths by 'pestilence', and an inscription in the parish church of Penrith claimed that altogether 2,200 people died in the deanery of Richmond. Plague continued to strike randomly well into the seventeenth century. For example, 3,512 people died in York in 1604 – that is 30 per cent of the inhabitants – in what turned out to be the city's last major visitation of the disease.[8] Such disasters rarely had long-term effects, however, for local population levels soon recovered when young couples took advantage of opportunities to marry young and thus have more children.

A greater restriction on population growth was the grim reality of the heavy rate of infant mortality. More than one-fifth of all the children who were born in England during Elizabeth's reign and about one-quarter of those born during the seventeenth century died before they reached the age of ten, usually from infectious diseases. Well over half of these deaths occurred during the child's first year, often during the first month. Infant mortality rates were far higher in the crowded, insanitary towns than in the countryside, except for such notoriously unhealthy spots as the Fens. Nevertheless, Tudor and Stuart society was far more youthful than today. Dependent children formed about 40 per cent of the English population.[9]

Plague remained a major killer in the years immediately following the Restoration. London was a notoriously unhealthy place where the pestilence was endemic. The last, and most horrific, outbreak of the disease in 1665 started in the slums of St Giles-in-the-Fields and spread to the parishes inside the northwestern walls of the City. At its peak, over 50 people were buried each day in several of the larger parishes. Unpredictably, and despite the quarantine measures that JPs tried to enforce, this epidemic spread as far north as Eyam, a remote lead-mining community in the Peak District, where 260 of the 1,200 or so parishioners died during the fourteen months of the visitation.[10] Thereafter, plague never returned to England, largely because of the strict quarantine precautions that were imposed in English and other European ports. The chief scourge of the late seventeenth and eighteenth centuries was smallpox, against which inoculation with a milder form of the disease was introduced from the eastern Mediterranean in 1701. This was less effective than vaccination with cowpox, which was first tried by Edward Jenner in the later eighteenth century.[11]

Unpredictable outbreaks of other infections were usually responsible for the sharp increases in the number of burials that were recorded from time to time in parish registers. These local crises occurred throughout the year, but they were much more frequent in late summer and autumn, particularly in the months of August and September. The pattern suggests that dysentery and other diarrhoeal infections were responsible. Children were especially vulnerable. No less than 82.6 per cent of the 224 people whose burials were recorded in the Sheffield parish register between July and October 1715 were children; during the month of August only one of the 54 deaths that were recorded there was that of an adult.[12] The last of the great epidemics that swept the country in the wake of dearth occurred in the 1720s, when harvests were so bad that large quantities of grain had to be imported. During various years between 1723 and 1729 many parishes recorded more burials than baptisms.[13] The vicar in the lowlands northeast of Doncaster wrote in his burial register in 1729, 'The greatest mortality that ever can be remembered, or made out to be in the parish of Arksey.'

The lack of growth in the national population during the second half of the seventeenth century and the first half of the eighteenth, at a time when the economy was growing, ensured that average living standards rose. Nobody predicted the population explosion that was soon to come. Before the Industrial Revolution, three out of every four English people were country folk, and many others lived in small market towns that were not much larger than villages.

English families

Before baptisms, marriages and burials were first recorded in parish registers in 1538, we do not have enough evidence to answer basic questions about families with any certainty. The national poll tax returns of 1377–81 suggest that households rarely contained more than two generations. Charles Phythian-Adams's study of medieval Coventry showed that at the time of a census of the city in 1523 only three of the 1,302 households contained members of more than two generations and that only 1 per cent of all households contained adult relatives of any sort.[14] A list of about 51,000 people in the archdeaconry of Stafford ten years later, which was arranged in family groups, reveals that only about 10 per cent of the families included relatives other than spouses or children. Most of these relatives were the parents of the heads of households, but many of them were no longer alive (for the list was concerned with souls), so this figure should be reduced considerably.[15]

Of course, average figures mask the diversity of experience. A particular household varied in size over time, as new children were born and older ones left home. Wealthier households were larger because they had greater numbers of living-in servants and perhaps more children through earlier marriages. But, in general, late-medieval households seem to have been very similar in composition to those in Tudor and Stuart times, for which we have much more information.

The great majority of English couples in the sixteenth and seventeenth centuries were well into their twenties when they married. Young people chose their own marriage partners. In south Lancashire in the 1660s Roger Lowe walked with girls in the fields, drank with them in the alehouses, went with them on visits to the nearby towns, or spent evenings 'sitting up' with them in a parlour.[16] Parental consent to a marriage was desirable if a 'marriage portion' was to be obtained, but it was not essential. Richard Gough mentions portions for girls ranging from £30 to £100 in north Shropshire.[17] Boys might be provided with land or established as a master craftsman after completing an apprenticeship, and sometimes the death of a parent allowed a child to inherit the family property, but couples usually waited until they had sufficient savings to set up home on their own.

The work of the Cambridge Group for the Study of Population and Social Structure (CAMPOP), founded in 1964 by Tony Wrigley, Roger Schofield and Peter Laslett, led the way in establishing firm statistics for the historical demography of the early-modern period.[18] Thus, we now know that in Elizabethan times one out of every three brides was pregnant before marriage. However, this high figure is partly explained by the widely accepted contemporary belief that marriages could start with witnessed pledges of betrothal before a wedding in church. At least one-sixth of the adult population of early-modern England never married. Together with the relatively late age at marriage, this prevented a steep rise in the national population before the Industrial Revolution. The number of illegitimacies never amounted to more than 3 per cent of recorded baptisms and they were particularly low during the 1650s, during the time of the 'godly revolution' following the Civil War.[19]

Marriage normally lasted for life. The early death of one partner and the subsequent remarriage of the other meant that many households contained stepchildren. Men and women who reached the age of 30 could expect to live, on average, for another 30 years, but sudden death was an ever-present threat for people in middle age. Many children never knew their grandparents. Lists of households that survive for parishes scattered across the land show that between 1550 and 1800 about 20 per cent were headed by widows, or to a far less extent by widowers. Some of these elderly widows feature regularly in parish payments for poor relief. Only 6 or 7 per cent of the population lived beyond 80, compared with a proportion that is three or four times higher today.[20]

The average household in sixteenth- and seventeenth-century England, below the social level of the aristocracy and gentry, consisted of a man and his wife and two or three children. Sometimes an elderly grandparent lived with them, but most widows or widowers lived in their own houses, perhaps with a lodger or an elder grandchild. The biggest difference from modern times was that households often included apprentices and farm or domestic servants. Children commonly left home in their early teens to live and work with another family. A census of the inhabitants of Ealing (Middlesex) taken in 1599 reveals that 109 of the 404 inhabitants were servants of one kind or another; most of them were youngsters.[21] This broad picture suggests an average household size of about 4.75 people, but of course domestic arrangements were often more flexible. The number of people living together at any one time varied according to the stage that had been reached in the family life cycle and according to wealth and social standing.

Unlike primitive societies in the modern world, the medieval and early-modern English did not have strong kinship ties. Keith Wrightson and David Levine showed that in Terling (Essex) in 1671 less than half of the 122 householders had relatives among the other householders, and that most of these had just one.[22] Elsewhere, too, kinship ties seem to have been of limited significance. The aristocracy and upper gentry were deeply preoccupied with ancestry and lineage and so tended to recognize a wide range of kinsmen, but at lower social levels neither wills nor diaries suggest close ties between kin. Instead, they demonstrate that good neighbourliness was regarded as a prime virtue. Studies of wills show that the many practical forms of aid and support for friends included the ready provision of credit.[23]

This tradition of neighbourliness helps to explain how Christian names were passed on from one generation to the next, for during the late-medieval and Tudor periods children were regularly named after their godparents. This custom ensured the continued use of less popular names and some striking regional distributions. For example, the use of Malin as a male first name was largely confined to the neighbouring parishes of Handsworth and Sheffield, especially amongst the Stacy family, who started the practice and continued it long after anyone else.[24] George Redmonds has provided many other examples, including names taken from legend and literature, such as

Lancelot in the four northern counties and Diggory in Cornwall. The new statistical approach, pioneered by Scott Smith-Bannister and developed by Redmonds, highlights regional differences and changes over time and it demonstrates the importance of social networks and the patronage of important local families.[25]

From the 1590s onwards, a new practice of naming a child after his or her parents gradually became dominant. This trend, which started with boys in the South and South East, spread to the South West by 1610–19 and the Midlands and the North by the 1620s, but it did not reach the East until a decade later. From the second decade of the seventeenth century onwards, girls, too, were named in this way. The most popular names remained those that had been introduced by the Normans.

The 'deserving poor' and vagabonds

Many of the poorer husbandmen and cottagers did not share the improved standard of living of their social superiors in the late sixteenth and early seventeenth centuries. Their probate inventories record one-roomed buildings and sparse collections of household goods valued at only a few shillings. Single-storeyed cottages sufficed for many a poor family. In 1578, for instance, the Sheffield manor court noted a few encroachments at Owlerton on the northern edge of the parish, where Robert Shawe had built 'a little house of the lord's waste there containing one bay', and Widow Alfrey lived in a two-bay cottage with a garden. In 1616 Nicholas Shooter rented '1 small cottage 1 bay thatched' in the town centre, and Hugh Milnes had a similar one-bay thatched cottage in Church Lane.[26]

The poor cottager was better off in wood-pasture regions such as Herefordshire and Shropshire, where population levels were still low enough to allow encroachments on the commons. Many of them had the right to keep a couple of cows there and the further right to collect fuel, in the form of underwood, gorse or peat. Opportunities to build new cottages were far more restricted in the nucleated villages of the corn-growing districts.

Charitable provision for the old and the needy had been much reduced by the dissolution of religious houses, especially the hospitals. From the late sixteenth century onwards, as the number of poor people grew, the donations of these public bodies were supplemented by private acts of charity, both large and small. The more substantial benefactions are often recorded on boards inside the church tower. A remarkable number of almshouses that were founded by generous individuals still serve their original purpose. These benefactors were often local people who had made their fortune in London and who remembered their places of birth when they made their wills. Almshouses are often adorned with an inscribed tablet and sometimes with a coat of arms. They vary widely in architectural style and pretension, but the usual arrangement was a series of single-room apartments, often

FIGURE 18 *Archbishop Henry Chichele, a native of Higham Ferrers, Northamptonshire, erected this Bede House in the churchyard in 1422–5 for 12 poor men over the age of 50.*

with a common chapel and dining hall as the visual focus. Southwest England has a particularly fine collection of almshouses, including those at Cheriton Fitzpaine in Devon (1594), Donnington in Berkshire (1602), Newland in Gloucestershire (1615), and Wimborne St Giles in Dorset (1624).[27]

The problem of the poor worsened as the national population grew during Elizabeth's reign. Those who sought opportunities to better themselves were joined on the roads to London or the provincial cities by hundreds of unemployed poor people desperate to find a living. Most of those who were classified as vagabonds were youngsters who travelled alone or in twos or threes, certainly not in the large gangs that gave rise to the fearful verses of 'Hark, hark, the dogs do bark / the beggars are coming to town'. The size of the problem is indicated by local enquiries. At Worcester, in 1556–7, the 'blind, lame, impotent, sick and those that are unable to get their livings without the charitable alms of the people' amounted to 734 individuals.[28] At Norwich, in 1570, no less than 504 men, 831 women and 1,007 children – that is, 25 per cent of the city's inhabitants – were officially classified as in need of assistance.[29] In 1616 about a third of Sheffielders were 'not able to live without the charity of their neighbours'.[30] Rural poverty does not seem to have reached the same scale except during the famine years of the 1580s and 1590s, but seasonal underemployment was a major problem, for the poor were largely dependent on the wages that they could earn on local farms.

The Poor Law Acts of 1597 and 1601 made each parish or township responsible for its own poor. The overseers who were elected at Easter vestry meetings were empowered to raise local rates in order to set the poor on work, apprentice poor children, and relieve the 'lame, impotent, old, blind and such other among them being poor and not able to work'. Begging was forbidden and those who were caught attempting it were whipped. When a small group of 'rogues and vagabonds' were brought before the North Riding quarter sessions at Richmond in 1610, the JPs ordered that the women should be whipped and the men branded with the letter 'R'.[31] The overseers were unpaid officers who were recruited from the ranks of the local farmers and craftsmen on a rotational basis. They had the unenviable task of dealing with the everyday problems of relieving the poor, while being answerable to the ratepayers and to the JPs at quarter sessions.

The most unfortunate of the poor were placed 'on the parish' and given weekly pensions in the church porch after services, or provided with rent-free housing, food, clothes, shoes, fuel or medical care. Surviving overseers' accounts from before the Civil War show that the better-off parishioners were sensitive to the needs of the 'deserving poor', provided that they were locally born and bred. Parish relief was supplemented by much informal charity, starting with the poor box inside the church door, for it was widely accepted that Christians had a duty to provide for their poor neighbours. Nevertheless, individual cases caused endless trouble between the ratepayers and those who claimed relief. The operation of the poor law varied considerably from parish to parish and from one overseer to another, but it worked well enough in providing housing, food and clothing for those who were regarded as the 'deserving' or the 'impotent' poor. Children were expected to maintain their elderly pauper parents wherever possible, but this responsibility did not extend to cousins or to more-distant kin. Grandparents looked after orphaned children if they were able, and they lived as a couple or alone in their own houses or cottages as long as they could.

The hearth tax returns of the 1660s and 1670s show that some English parishes or townships had large numbers of poor people, but that many other places, especially those with a flourishing industry where families could combine a craft with running a small farm, had well below the national average. In Norwich, the contrast between the disadvantaged parishes, which had more than 75 per cent of their inhabitants exempt from payment of the tax, and the richer central parishes around the cathedral and the market place was as marked as it had been in Elizabethan times. Yet most of those who were exempt from the tax were far from destitute; poor relief was granted to less than 4 per cent of the city's population.[32] In normal times able-bodied men and women could usually find work, even if much of it was part time or seasonal, and the wages offered in the industrial parts of England meant that farmers nearby had to pay their labourers more than the abysmally low levels of the South and the East.

As population growth slowed down and agricultural output increased, social problems were brought under control and traditions of neighbourly help and paternalism flourished once more. Steve Hindle has shown that only a small minority of the population were 'on the parish', for the poor were expected to 'shift for themselves' as long as possible, by improvising a living from whatever work was available, by depending on the pity of their neighbours and the kindness of their relatives, and often by casual pilfering. The old, the sick, the infirm and dependent youngsters, who together constituted the 'genuine poor', were on the whole treated sympathetically by their neighbours, but idlers and the poor of other parishes met with a hard-hearted response.[33]

The proportion of men, women and children who received regular relief in the late seventeenth and eighteenth centuries averaged 5 or 6 per cent, but with substantial differences between parishes, even between neighbouring ones, and with considerable rises when trade was bad. A significant proportion of those who were given relief were young married couples with several children and no regular work. Some elderly people remained 'on the parish' for two or three decades and were buried at the expense of their neighbours.

The Settlement Acts of 1662, 1685, 1691 and 1697 codified legal practices about who was entitled to receive relief from parish officers. The poor were made the responsibility of the parish or township where they were last legally settled, and the various ways in which a settlement could be obtained were defined. At meetings of the quarter sessions, JPs were increasingly occupied with settlement cases as contending parishes engaged lawyers to try to prove that paupers were legally settled elsewhere. The poor clung to the certificates that showed which parishes were legally responsible for their care under the old poor law.

As the population began to rise in the eighteenth century, many parishes adopted the power to build workhouses that had been given them by the Workhouse Test Act of 1723. Ratepayers were increasingly concerned to put the poor to work in order to deter the idle, even if their schemes rarely turned out to be profitable. By the middle of the eighteenth century at least 600 workhouses had been built and almost 3,000 people had been housed in them and set to work. Spinning, knitting, brewing and baking were the jobs that were most commonly provided. In the short and medium term these workhouses succeeded in lowering the numbers of people on relief by over 50 per cent, but most parishes managed without a workhouse. The poor were not yet the burden on the local rates that they became when the national population exploded in the late eighteenth and early nineteenth centuries.[34]

Most of the migrants who looked for employment in the growing industrial towns travelled only short distances. Throughout provincial England, the labour force remained overwhelmingly local in origin even as the population started to grow rapidly. A good deal of the population mobility within the restricted area of a 'country' involved adolescent servants and apprentices. Although farm servants usually moved when their year's contract expired at Martinmas, they rarely went far. Their movements were also restricted to May Day (western counties) and especially to Michaelmas in the eastern counties. These movements occurred within a temporary phase of the life cycle, which came to an end in adulthood.

The first 650 apprentices who were recorded in the Southampton registers in the early seventeenth century were mostly from the town and its neighbourhood: 56 per cent came from the town itself, 4 per cent from adjacent parishes, 26 per cent from other parts of Hampshire, and 4 per cent from the Isle of Wight. The rest came from other southern counties or the Channel Islands; and in 6 per cent of cases the place was not stated. In 85 of the first 100 entries in the Southampton Poor Child Register between 1609 and 1632, the father was dead and a few other children were illegitimate. Poor boys were normally apprenticed to a definite trade, but it seems that poor girls were treated as domestic servants.[35] The archives of the Cutlers' Company of Hallamshire record the names of 282 poor boys who entered the cutlery trades as parish apprentices between 1624 and 1781. Many of these pauper apprentices were not born and bred in Hallamshire, but came (with a premium) from outside. In all, 41 poor boys came from beyond Sheffield, especially from Cheshire and the High Peak of Derbyshire, with premiums ranging from £1 from Glossop to £25 from the Friends' Workhouse in London. Only 50 of the 282 pauper apprentices eventually took out their freedom.[36]

In practice, large numbers of apprentices of all kinds either failed to complete their training or did not become masters at the end of their term. The dropout rate of London apprentices throughout the sixteenth and seventeenth centuries was about 50 per cent. In Bristol only about a third of the apprentices in the sixteenth and most of the seventeenth century eventually became citizens, a privilege to which they were entitled upon taking out their freedom.[37] Many boys did not take out their freedoms but remained journeymen, working for wages. Apprentices frequently ran away from their masters, perhaps to London or to join the Army.

The core families of local communities

One of the earliest findings of the generation of social historians in the 1960s and 1970s was that the population of England was surprisingly mobile. Peter Laslett and John Harrison's pioneering article on 'Clayworth and Cogenhoe' in 1963 demolished the old idea of isolated, self-sufficient communities by showing that people often crossed their parish boundaries in search of a better life.[38] We now realize, however, that much of this movement did not affect the stability of the groups of families that formed the core of so many local societies. Historians who have examined Tudor and Stuart rural parishes in detail have stressed the importance of the people who stayed put. Back in 1965, W.G. Hoskins noted that 36 (44 per cent) of the 161 households that were recorded in the hearth tax return of 1670 for Wigston Magna (Leicestershire) had lived in the village for at least a century, and 15 or 16 (20 per cent) had been there for 200 years or more. The Freers and the Boulters had established eight branches; the Smiths, Vanns and Wards, six; the Johnsons, five; the Langtons, Holmses, Noones and Abbotts, four; and several other families had three. They provided Wigston with a real sense of continuity.[39]

Wigston was a populous Midland village at the heart of open-field England. Eighty miles or so to the west, the Shropshire parish of Myddle was a very different type of rural community, where beef and dairy cattle grazed the woodland pastures, settlement was scattered, and poor immigrants could still find land on which to squat. Yet here again certain families amongst the 91 who paid hearth tax in 1672, notably the Lloyds, Goughs, Braynes, Groomes, Tylers, Juxes and Formstons, had occupied the same farms for several generations. Nathaniel Reve was probably expressing a common sentiment when he desired to be a tenant of Bilmarsh Farm 'because his grandfather and father had been tenants to it before'. The yeoman, husbandmen and village craftsmen were the ones who were most likely to stay, and those below them on the social scale were the most likely to leave.[40]

Stable families also formed the core of industrial rural communities such as the scythe-making parish of Norton in north Derbyshire. Between January 1560 and December 1653 the Norton register recorded 1,319 burials. Twenty-seven surnames accounted for 48 per cent of the entries, whereas the remaining 52 per cent included 258 different surnames, of which 125 were recorded just once and 45 twice. Here again, the contrast between the stable core of families and the mobile, short-term residents is marked.[41]

A seating plan of Norton church, which can be dated to about 1640, shows that pews were occupied by six branches of the Bartens, six Stevens, five Bates, four Mores, three Atkins, three Blythes, three Greens, three

Rollinsons and 51 others. Many of these families were already well established when the parish register began to be kept early in Elizabeth's reign. The hearth tax return of 1670 confirms their continued importance. The 118 entries for Norton included 48 householders with the 27 most common surnames (41 per cent) in the burial register of 1560–1653. The seven most prosperous householders were relative newcomers to the parish. Continuity of residence was most pronounced amongst the families whose standards of living ranged from the modest to the middling, above the level of the poor cottagers. They included the numerous scythe-making families who remained in Norton because their trade was profitable (they were the wealthiest of the local metalworkers) and because their investment in capital and craft skills was passed on from generation to generation. Scythe makers are just one example of craft families that remained in the same place over several generations.

Having demonstrated the great amount of movement out of the parish of Clayworth between 1676 and 1888, Peter Laslett concluded that

> it might be easy to exaggerate the importance of the rate of *structural* change which these figures imply. A 60 per cent turnover of persons in 12 years is after all only 5 per cent a year . . . At Clayworth in 1688 something like 23 of the 91 households were new since 1676, and 10 of these were entirely novel.

This leaves a large number of households that were present both in 1676 and 1688. If we analyse the two lists in terms of households rather than individuals, the picture that emerges is similar to that of Wigston, Myddle and Norton. Just under half the heads of households recorded in 1676 were still alive and living in Clayworth 12 years later. If we add to these the 18 who had been succeeded by a widow, a son or a close relation, we see that two out of every three families were stable during this period. As some of the incomers may also have had a previous family connection, this figure is a minimum one. When we look at the two lists in this way, the underlying stability of the community is made clear.

The hearth tax return of 1664 for Clayworth confirms this picture. Though it is impossible to provide a firm statistic, we are safe in asserting that throughout the period 1664–76 at least two out of every three families remained in the parish. A wider view is made possible by the survival of a protestation return of 1642 for Clayworth, which lists all males aged 16 or above. A few families may have had no adult males at that point in time, but the 78 different surnames probably included the great majority of households. The 75 householders in the 1676 list included 44 with surnames that were used by the previous generation. The 90 householders in the 1688 list included 27 who had surnames that had belonged to families in the parish 46 years earlier. It is possible that some of the families with common surnames were unconnected, but a careful consideration of all four lists made between 1642 and 1688 suggests that the links were firm. We may conclude that a core of stable families formed the core of the community of Clayworth. Peter Laslett expressed his findings with suitable caution. Others who have followed the trail that he blazed have not been as circumspect.

Other evidence of the limited distances within which most people moved is provided by two Derbyshire court cases. In 1615 John Land of Brassington said that while he 'hath knowen the mannor of Wirkesworth threescore yeares ... [he] doth not know the manor of Ashburne [lying four miles distant], because he hath had little to do there'. In 1640 some Wirksworth men thought that the county town of Derby, lying only eight miles away, was a 'remote place'.[42]

Yet, despite this restricted mobility, ordinary families were connected to a much wider social world. In Shropshire, Richard Gough had numerous contacts with people beyond his parish boundary and was aware of national events and issues. Roger Lowe was familiar not only with the inhabitants of his native Ashton-in-Makerfield, but with people in many of the towns and villages in south Lancashire. And in Essex, the villagers of Terling had a core social area of friends within ten miles, but their contacts frequently extended much further.

Plantations across the seas

Queen Elizabeth I and King James I actively promoted the establishment of new settlements or 'plantations', first in Northern Ireland and then across the Atlantic Ocean in Virginia, New England and the West Indies. Planned settlements and the imposition of English rule, law, religion, landholding systems, and a commercial organization based on market towns were seen as the way of dealing with Irish unrest, but they provoked a major revolt. James I raised funds for the war by forcing the London livery companies to pay a loan and, in 1611, by elevating those who were prepared to pay a hefty fee to join the newly created, hereditary rank of baronet, a 'cash for honours' system of its time. The transfer of land from Irish Catholic families to Protestant immigrants was the largest change of landownership in any European country during the seventeenth century. In 1600 more than 80 per cent of Ireland was still held by Catholic owners, but by 1700 this proportion had declined to 14 per cent. The main group of Protestant settlers in Ulster came from southwest Scotland, though others were from western and southwestern England, and later from parts of northern England. This is how the religious divide that plagued Northern Ireland in the twentieth century began.[43]

At the beginning of Elizabeth's reign, England was a small and backward country on the northwestern edge of Europe, whose overseas possessions consisted only of the Channel Islands. The success of the Spanish and the Portuguese ventures to the New World across the Atlantic and the lure of silver and gold prompted the Crown and courtiers to sponsor an age of expansion. In 1584 Raleigh sent a reconnaissance voyage to Chesapeake Bay, and in 1585–6 he established the first English colony with a seven-strong fleet under Sir Richard Grenville at Roanoke, an island in the territory that they named Virginia in honour of 'the Virgin Queen' Elizabeth. Their efforts failed ignominiously, but in 1607 the newly formed Virginia Company sent three ships across the ocean to Chesapeake Bay and 40 miles up the James River. Only 38 of the original 105 settlers at Jamestown survived the first two years, but the colony eventually prospered through the cultivation of the Native American crop, tobacco. Most of the earliest migrants to Virginia migrated from southwestern England via the port of Bristol.

A different type of colony was established in 1620, when the Mayflower arrived at Plymouth, 200 miles to the north of Virginia. Free to practise their religion as they wished, the new settlers quickly developed a Puritan stronghold. The early migrants to New England came from scattered places in the eastern counties, stretching from Yorkshire to Kent, with smaller numbers from Somerset, Dorset and Wiltshire. In the following decades settlers were attracted to the West Indies, Chesapeake Bay and New England, in that order of popularity, but although the 'Great Migration' of the 1630s was important from an American perspective it accounted for less than 0.5 per cent of the population of England and made little impact in the home country. Most emigrants travelled in family groups, especially from the middling ranks of the yeomen and artisans. The Chesapeake colony attracted numerous indentured servants who worked for a fixed term on the tobacco plantations in order to pay for their passage and board, before obtaining their freedom. Others were deported to the New World as convicts. A substantial number of those who sailed across the Atlantic eventually returned to England, for they had never thought of emigration as a permanent move.[44]

During the century after 1650 England prospered from its growing naval and military power and its involvement in foreign trade. Between the 1660s and the 1680s imports from Asia increased fourfold, and by 1700 America and Asia were providing nearly a third of all English imports. In the next 20 years English ships overtook those of the Dutch in command of global ventures. By 1700 the English were twice as rich as they had been in 1600.[45]

Speech and literacy

The language that was commonly spoken in medieval England would have been largely unintelligible to us. Middle English grew out of a mixture of the speech of the Anglo-Saxons, Vikings and Normans, and administrators, clergymen and scholars used Latin. Once English became the language of the Court, especially from the reign of Henry IV onwards, it gained respectability, and the dialect that was used in London and the southeast

Midlands became accepted as the new standard speech amongst the leaders of the nation.[46]

The first great works of English literature that were written in the second half of the fourteenth century included the use of regional forms of speech. William Langland (c.1332–c.1400), who was probably born at Ledbury in Herefordshire, wrote *The Vision Concerning Piers Plowman*, an allegorical poem in unrhymed alliterative verse, which was both a social satire and a vision of the simple Christian life; the anonymous author of *Sir Gawain and the Green Knight*, an alliterative romance, was steeped in the speech and folklore of a region extending from the Peak District west into Cheshire and north Wales and north into the West Riding; while Geoffrey Chaucer, the greatest of all the medieval poets of England, wrote *The Canterbury Tales* and *Troilus and Cressida* for sophisticated courtly audiences who shared his knowledge of European literature. Even the earliest Robin Hood ballads, which satirized the corruption of the legal and the administrative system, were first told in aristocratic and knightly households. They were set in thirteenth-century Barnsdale in the Vale of York, a dangerous place for travellers, where the Great North Road split into two branches; the Nottinghamshire tales, centred on Sherwood Forest and the county's sheriff, seem to have come from a separate, later tradition.

In 1387 John of Trevisa (Cornwall) commented on the sharp differences in speech between one region and another: 'All the language of the Northumbrians, and specially at York, is so sharp, cutting, and abrasive, and ugly, that we southern men may scarcely understand that language.' Northerners were well aware that they spoke differently from people who lived south of the Trent. When the first shepherd in the Wakefield mystery plays said, 'But Mak, is that truth? Now take out that southern tooth', his meaning must have been clear to his audience. Within these broad regions, local speech varied considerably between one district or 'country' and another. When William Caxton set up the first printing press in England in 1476, he was concerned about the lack of a common standard that could be read and understood by everybody.

During the sixteenth and seventeenth centuries England became a semi-literate society, where even some of the humblest people could read. The spread of printing was a great encouragement to this accomplishment. Whereas only 46 books were published in England in 1500, the number rose to 259 in 1600 and to 577 by 1640. The practice of reading aloud helped to spread the flow of information; those who were unable to read could always find someone to help them, though many felt no need to read or write because it was of little practical benefit to them. Printing played a large part in the enormous expansion and enrichment of the English language. It has been estimated that between 1570 and 1630 over 30,000 new words were either coined or borrowed from Latin and European languages.[47]

Most medieval grammar schools seem to have survived the dissolution of the chantries, and many more schools were opened in the late sixteenth and early seventeenth centuries.[48] They were erected in the vernacular style of their district and were commonly adorned with the coat of arms of the founder and with a suitable inscription. They survive even in remote parts of the countryside, such as Burnsall in Wharfedale, where Sir William Craven, a native of the parish who had become a wealthy merchant and Mayor of London, founded a school in 1602, with a master's house attached. The grammar school at Hawkshead in Cumbria, which was founded in 1585 by a local man, Edwin Sandys, Archbishop of York, provided free education, clothing and accommodation for 12 'charity boys' and attracted fee-payers from many parts of northwest England. Its rules and its curriculum were the standard ones of the times. The schoolmasters who obtained licences from the Church of England were low in status compared with men in other professions. Many of them taught no more than reading, writing and simple accounts in unendowed village schools, but in the grammar schools the emphasis was on the classics and the Latin language. This enabled even poor boys to go on to the Universities of Oxford or Cambridge to qualify as clergymen or perhaps to pursue a legal career at one of the Inns of Court in London.

Pronunciation changed significantly at the same time, undergoing what linguists refer to as the 'great vowel shift', that is, the shortening of most of the long vowel sounds implied by late-medieval scripts. Though Sir Walter Raleigh, according to John Aubrey, 'spake broad Devonshire to his dyeing day', regional accents were unusual amongst the Court circle, and in many parts of England gentry families spoke a standardized or authorized English by the end of the century. In *The Arte of English Prose* (1589) George Puttenham advised authors not to copy

> the termes of northern-men, such as they use in dayly talke, whether they be noble men or gentlemen, or of their best clarkes, all is a matter: nor in effect any speach used beyond the river of Trent, though no man deny that theirs is the purer English saxon at this day, yet it is not so courtly nor so currant as our Southerne English is, no more is the far westerne mans speech: ye shall therefore take the usuall speach of the court, and that of London and the shires lying above London within [60] myles, and not much above.

Yet Elizabethan and Stuart England had far greater linguistic diversity than today. The richly varied popular speech that was heard up and down the kingdom made it hardly possible to speak of a native English tongue. At the beginning of the seventeenth century Richard Verstegan commented: 'Some Englishmen discoursing together, others being present and of our own nation, and that naturally speak the English toung, are not able to understand what the others say, notwithstanding they call it English that they speak.' When three soldiers from Norfolk visited Westmorland in 1634, they asked for directions from 'rude, rusticall, and ill-bred people' only to find that they 'could not understand them, neither would they understand us'.

Language was a sure indicator of the identity of local neighbourhoods, or 'countries', centred on the nearest market towns. The tone and diction of local accents were distinctive even if the words looked the same in print, while dialects varied in their vocabulary not only between localities but also between particular trades and crafts. As Adam Fox has pointed out, 'Part of learning any trade was to be initiated into its unique linguistic system, to be apprenticed in its terms of art and specialized nomenclature no less than in its skills and techniques'.[49]

Most English people lived in small rural communities where the seasonal cycle of work, local customs, the lore and tradition of the district, and gossip about their neighbours were their principal concerns. In wintertime, families and friends gathered around the hearth to listen to old stories or to sing ballads. Many of the surviving ballads that were sold by pedlars throughout the land can be dated to the second half of the sixteenth century and the first half of the seventeenth. They were commonly inspired by historical events in the neighbourhood and by visual features in the local landscape. Local speech was sprinkled with distinctive proverbial lore and adages. Some 12,000 proverbs and proverbial phrases were in regular use, many more than today. Modern clichés often turn out to have a long ancestry: 'one man's meat is another man's poison', 'make hay as the sun shines', 'cool as a cucumber', 'fit as a fiddle', even 'sick as a parrot' were in use by Elizabethan times.

Despite the twentieth-century spread of 'Received Pronunciation' and 'Estuary English' and the disappearance of much of the old dialects, the way that a modern person speaks often places him or her within a particular district or 'country'. In George Eliot's novel *Adam Bede*, Mr Cassor, the landlord of the Donnithorne Arms, says: 'I'm not this countryman, you may tell by my tongue, sir. They're curious talkers i' this country, sir; the gentry's hard work to hunderstand 'em.' If local populations changed as rapidly as some historical demographers, who have studied parishes but have not looked at the wider neighbourhood, or 'country', have supposed, it is hard to see how dialects and accents could remain so intensely local. The way that newcomers adapted not only to the speech but also to local customs is suggested by another of Eliot's characters, Silas Marner, who resolved that 'whatever's right for i' this country, and you think 'ull do it good, I'll act according, if you tell me'.

The core groups of local families were the ones who set the patterns to which incomers eventually conformed. In Tudor and Stuart times, old people who had lived in a neighbourhood all their lives were the ones whom contending parties turned to whenever a dispute over local customs or practices arose. Customs concerning tenure and common rights were rooted in particular localities. Andy Wood has concluded that, 'While there existed broad, regional characteristics to local custom, it was unusual to find customary regulations in any manor or parish that were exactly the same as another.'[50]

The distinctive characters of the numerous 'countries' of England were formed not only by local speech, customs, beliefs and attitudes, but by their styles of vernacular architecture, the nature of their crafts and their farming systems. The most obvious evidence of the continuity of their core families is immediately apparent in the surnames that were recorded in the poll tax returns of 1377–81, the hearth tax returns of 1662–74, and the census returns of 1841–1911. To this day, Ackroyd, Barraclough and Sutcliffe are instantly recognizable as names from the heart of the West Riding, whereas Greenhalgh, Sowerbutts and Scarisbrick are found across the Pennines in Lancashire. Derbyshire has its Heathcotes, Greatorexes and Ollerenshaws; Leicestershire its Freers, Herricks and Noones; and Dorset its Loders, Sturmys and Squibbs. And so it remains true today, as it did in the seventeenth century: 'By Tre-, Pol-, and Pen-, ye shall know Cornish men'. Before the great changes of the modern era, the English nation was composed of hundreds of local societies that had contacts beyond their parish boundaries as far as the nearest market towns, but which remained mostly unaware of the people in distant parts of the realm.

NOTES

Chapter One

1 Defoe (1962), II, 94.

2 Phythian-Adams (2000), 236.

3 Hey (1997a); Hey (2000), 126–30.

4 Hey (1981); Hey (2002b), 53–4.

5 Bain (1981), 52.

6 Hey (1998).

7 Aubrey (1988), 210.

8 Defoe (1962), II, 181; Hey (1991), 75–80.

9 Tucker (2008).

10 McKinley (1975); (1977); (1981); (1988); (1990).

11 Redmonds (1973); (1997).

12 Redmonds, King and Hey (2011).

13 www.archersoftware.co.uk.

14 Hey (1998).

15 Kettle (1976).

16 Wrottesley (1886).

17 Yates (1775).

18 The Staffordshire hearth tax returns are printed in the volumes of *Collections for a History of Staffordshire* (Staffordshire Record Society) for the years 1921, 1923, 1925, 1927 and 1936.

19 Barnwell and Airs (2006); Arkell (2003); Hey and Redmonds (2002).

20 Marshall (1990), 16; Edwards (1982); Webster (1988).

21 Fenwick (1998–2005).

22 Ferguson, Thornton and Wareham (2012).

23 Hall (1930).

24 Cox (1908).

25 Garnett (1997).

26 Sheffield Telegraph (1905).

27 Hall (1939), 4.

28   Glasscock (1975); Palliser (2001).

29   Barron (2004).

30   Beier and Finlay (1986); Clark and Slack (1976); Hinde (2003).

31   Boulton (2000).

32   Slack (1985), 145–51.

33   Slack (2015), 147–8.

34   Wrigley (1987).

35   Earle (1989), 86.

36   Hey (2010a), 44–7.

37   Earle (1989), 91–2.

38   Hey (1974), 191–4.

39   Hopper (2013).

40   Hey (1991), 302–3.

41   The National Archives, WO/30/48.

42   Printed for John Trundle and sold at Christ Church Gate, London, 1614.

43   Hey (2001), 68–75.

44   Everitt (1973), 91–137; Taylor (1888).

45   Gerhold (2005), xii, 3–7.

46   Hey (2014a).

47   Goose and Luu (2005).

48   Browning (1936), 376.

49   Plomer (1984), 75.

Chapter Two

1   Cunliffe (2013); Oppenheimer (2006); Sykes (2006).

2   Bahn and Pettit (2009).

3   Balaresque et al. (2010).

4   Salway (1993), 29.

5   Bédoyere (2006), 20–31.

6   Tacitus, *Agricola*, Book 1 [11].

7   Bowman (2003).

8   Wiseman and Wiseman (1980), chapter 12.

9   Tacitus, *Agricola*, Book 1 [11].

10   Wilson (2009) (Lullingstone Villa guidebook).

11   Collingwood and Wright (1995).

12   Higham and Ryan (2013), chapter 2.

13   Pryor (2004), chapter 2.

14 Higham and Ryan (2013), chapter 2.

15 Jones and Semple (2012).

16 www.peopleofthebritishisles.org/

17 Carver (1998).

18 Gelling (1978); Gelling and Cole (2000).

19 Dodgson (1966).

20 Defoe (1962), I, 89.

21 Mawer (1929); Gelling and Cole (2000), 180–2.

22 Higham and Ryan (2013), chapter 3.

23 Brooks (2000), 34.

24 Green (2012).

25 Todd (1987), 267.

26 Cameron (1959), 53.

27 Higham and Ryan (2013), chapter 4.

28 Rollason (2003).

29 Hey (2008), 61–4.

30 Rodwell and Hey (2010).

31 Blair (2013), 12–19.

32 Richards (2001).

33 Gelling (1978), 215–37; Cullen, Jones and Parsons (2011).

34 Fellows-Jensen (1968); (1972); (1978).

35 Gelling (1978), chapter 9.

36 Higham and Ryan (2013), chapter 5.

37 Hall (1989).

38 Wood, M. (2013).

39 Cameron (1959), 50–60.

40 Higham and Ryan (2013), chapter 8.

41 Camp (1990).

42 Keats-Rohan (1999); Henry of Huntingdon (1879).

43 Forrester (1859).

44 Sanders (1960); Wagner (1976); Green (1997).

45 Reaney (1967), 98–127.

46 McKinley (1990), 25–8.

47 Clay and Douglas (1951), 103.

48 Fenwick (1998; 2001; 2005).

49 Hey (2013a).

50 www.englandsimmigrants.com/

51 Redmonds, King and Hey (2011), 41–61.

Chapter Three

1   Hey (1991), 36–43.
2   http://www.uppakra.se/backup/docs/uppakra6/20_Blackmore_U6.pdf.
3   Palliser (2014), 23–40.
4   Hill and Rumble (1996).
5   http://poppy.nsms.ox.ac.uk/woruldhord/contributions/675.
6   James (1997).
7   http://www.buildinghistory.org/towns.shtml.
8   Barber (1994).
9   Roberts and Whittick (2013).
10 Rowley (1972), 182–6.
11 Rawcliffe and Wilson (2004).
12 Beresford and St Joseph (1979), 215–17.
13 Dymond (1985), 88–91.
14 Hill (2008).
15 Dobson (1974).
16 Hoskins (1984), 277–8.
17 Quiney (2003); Brooke, Highfield, and Swaan, (1988), 56 and 62.
18 Beresford and St Joseph (1979), 182–3.
19 Platt (1973).
20 Scarfe (1972), 98–101.
21 Hoskins (1967), 26–8.
22 Scarfe (1972), 162–3.
23 Parker (1970).
24 Beresford and St Joseph (1979), 217–19.
25 Allison (1969), 81–5.
26 Allison (1976), 239.
27 Crouch and Pearson (2001).
28 McCord and Thompson (1998), 22–4 and 130–5.
29 Higham (2004), 168–70 and 194–6.
30 Beresford and St Joseph (1979), 238–41.
31 Phythian-Adams (1979).
32 Blomefield (1806), 182–3.
33 Hey (2015a), 20–30.
34 Palliser (2014), 240–93.
35 Lander (1988), 19; Carus-Wilson (1937).
36 Betterton and Dymond (1989).
37 Nicholls (1842).

38 Hoskins (1984), 275–8.

39 Toulmin Smith (1964), 60.

40 Hoskins (1964), 68–85.

41 Thirsk (1967), 467.

42 Blyton (2014), 76.

43 Palliser (1979), 260–87.

44 Camden (1607), 692.

45 Hey (1981).

46 See, for example, Porter (1984).

47 Hoskins (1984), 278.

48 Borsay (1989).

49 Hembry (1990).

50 Morris (1982), 86–7, 116, 132 and 145.

51 Dugdale (2011), 318.

52 Defoe (1962), II, 36, 250–1 and 255–6.

53 Hey (1991), 62.

54 Clark and Slack (1972), 31.

55 Barker and Jackson (1990).

56 Linebaugh (1981).

Chapter Four

1 West (2001).

2 Haughton and Powlesland (1999).

3 Blair (2014).

4 Sheppard (1974).

5 Wrathmell (2012); Jones and Page (2006).

6 Aston and Gerrard (2013).

7 Roberts and Wrathmell (2000).

8 Orwin and Orwin (1954).

9 Harvey (1983).

10 Hall (1995).

11 Williamson (2003).

12 Jones and Page (2006).

13 Allison (2003).

14 Hey (2008), 132.

15 Fox (1994).

16 Herring (2006).

17   Rippon (2006).

18   Turner (2006), 24–43.

19   Hey (2013a), 216–38.

20   Redmonds (1985).

21   Hey (2014b).

22   Hey (1974), 29–31.

23   Everitt (1986).

24   Warner (1987).

25   Lewis, Mitchell-Fox and Dyer (1997).

26   Hey (2013b).

27   Linebaugh (2008), 34.

28   Scarfe (1968), 9.

29   Langton and Jones (2010).

30   Hey (2002a), 16 and 98–101.

31   Hey (2008), 105–9, 138–9 and 192–3.

32   Taylor (2000).

33   Hey (2008), 318–19.

34   Liddiard (2007); Mileson (2009).

35   Hey (2006).

36   Rackham (1976) and (2003).

37   Bettey (1986), 112.

38   Beresford (1954): Dyer and Jones (2010), 6.

39   Fox (2012), 140–5.

40   Wrathmell (2012).

41   Neave (1993); Wrathmell (1980).

42   Hoskins (1964), 121–3.

43   Wood, A. (2013), 69.

44   Woodward (1984).

45   Dyer, Hey and Thirsk (2000).

46   Hoskins (1965).

47   Dyer, Hey and Thirsk (2000). p. 51.

Chapter Five

1   Dyer (2002); Campbell (2000); Britnell (1993).

2   Holt (1988).

3   Kershaw (1973).

4   Cook, Stearne and Williamson (2003); Hey and Rodwell (2006).

5 Wiltshire et al. (2005).

6 Hey (2011a), 169–70.

7 Dyer (2002), chapter 8.

8 Ryder (1983).

9 Rackham (2003), chapters 9 and 10.

10 Wood (1999), 245.

11 Ibid., 176–8.

12 Newman (2006).

13 Hatcher (1993).

14 Tylecote (2013).

15 Cleere and Crossley (1995), 79–84.

16 Carus-Wilson (1941).

17 Dyer (2012).

18 Heaton (1965).

19 Hey (2001), 110–15.

20 Dyer (2008).

21 Hey (2002a), 112–25.

22 Gardner (2011), 5.

23 Fox (2001).

24 Harrison (2004).

25 Blair (2007).

26 Thirsk (1967).

27 Allen (1992).

28 Cook and Williamson (2007).

29 Thick (1984).

30 Spufford (1979).

31 Hey (1984b).

32 Broad (1983).

33 Hey (1984a).

34 Bettey (1986), 121–6.

35 Eddison (2000).

36 Thirsk (1978).

37 Hey (2011a), 257–8.

38 Kerridge (1985).

39 Hey (2011a), 331–4.

40 Jennings (1967); Hartley and Ingleby (2001).

41 Defoe (1962), I, 61–2, 189, 266, 279–80.

42 West Yorkshire Archive Service, Wakefield, D1.

43 Millington and Chapman (1989).

44 Page (1911), 132–7; Glover (1833), 423.

45 Palliser (1979), 273.

46 Levine and Wrightson (1991).

47 Crossley (1990), 226–42.

48 Weatherill (1971).

49 Crossley (1990), 153–69.

50 Trinder (1973), 25.

51 Hey (1991), 182–3.

52 Hey (1972).

53 Barraclough (1984), 40.

54 Wood (1999), chapter 3.

55 Hey (2008), 304–9.

56 Clarkson (1966).

57 Hussey (2000).

58 Verey (2008), 8 April 1833.

Chapter Six

1   Swanton (2000).

2   Thompson (2008); Renn (1973).

3   Coulson (2003).

4   Liddiard (2005), 7–10.

5   Ibid., 98.

6   Brindle (2012).

7   Liddiard (2005), 34.

8   Jewell (1994), 40.

9   Cannon (2007).

10 www.gatehouse-gazetteer.info/English%20sites/1835.html.

11 Clifton-Taylor (1967), 42.

12 Cannon (2007), 415–22.

13 Wood (2012).

14 Palliser (2014), 150.

15 Luxford (2008).

16 Burton (1994); Butler and Given-Wilson (1979).

17 Lawrence (1994).

18 Coppack (2000).

19 Coppack (2003).

20 Platt (1969).

21 Colvin (1951).

22 Burton (1979).

23 Hey, Liddy and Luscombe (2011).

24 Rawcliffe (2013).

25 Nicholson (2001); Nicholson (2013).

26 Hewett (1962).

27 Bond (2004).

28 Hoyle (2001).

29 Dickens (1959).

30 Sewell (1846), 46–7.

31 Howard (1987).

32 Clifton-Taylor (1972), chapter 9.

33 Girouard (1983).

34 Girouard (1993).

35 Beckett (1986).

Chapter Seven

1 Clifton-Taylor (1974).

2 For example, Butler (2007).

3 Hey (2002a), 9.

4 Taylor and Taylor (1980), 135–48.

5 Cameron (1996), 130.

6 Cramp (1970); www.british-history.ac.uk/vch/durham/vol2/pp79-85.

7 Taylor and Taylor (1980), 234–8.

8 Parsons and Sutherland (2013).

9 Hey (2010b), 22.

10 Taylor and Taylor (1980), 222–6.

11 Rodwell (2012), 292–5.

12 www.vag.org.uk/dendro-tables/england/county/essex.pdf.

13 Thurlby (1999).

14 http://greatenglishchurches.co.uk/html/norfolk_round_tower_churches.html.

15 Pevsner and Wilson (2002), 771–3.

16 Hey (2011a), 153–7.

17 Clifton-Taylor (1974), 53–4.

18 Harvey (1978).

19 British Library, Additional Charter 17634.

20 Clifton-Taylor (1974), 62–3.

21 RCHM (1970), 13–18.

22 Duffy (1992), 155–99.

23 Wood-Legh (1965).

24 Westlake (1919); Tearle (2012); Hey (2015b).

25 Duffy (1992).

26 Hindman and Marrow (2013).

27 Barnard (2012).

28 Nichols (1997).

29 Jones (2002).

30 Bragg (2011).

31 Duffy (1992); Haigh (1987).

32 Hutton (1994); Whiting (1969).

33 Dickens (1947).

34 Duffy (2001).

35 Smith (1970), 88 and 92.

36 Hutton (1994), 69–110.

37 Thomas (1971), 159–66.

38 Heath (2013), 74–5; O'Day (1979).

39 Collinson (1982).

40 Hopper (2007), 130–3.

41 Dobson and Wells (2005), 45.

42 Bossy (1975).

43 Quoted by Mrs Stackhouse Acton (1867), *The Garrisons of Shropshire during the Civil War, 1642–48*, 9.

44 Hey (1974), 194–8.

45 Chatfield (1979).

46 Smollett (2008), 2.

47 Hey (1995).

48 Whiteman (1986).

49 Hey (1973).

50 Everitt (1972).

Chapter Eight

1 Alcock and Miles (2013).

2 Miles (1997).

3 Arnold and Howard (2014).

4 Hewett (1980).

5 www.scribed.com/doc/51055232/Calibrating-the-Work-of-Cecil-Hewitt.

6   Brunskill (1994).

7   http://library.thehumanjourney.net/170/1/LEWCFO9.pdf.

8   Wallsgrove (1989).

9   www.vag.org.uk/dendro-tables.

10   Miles (2005).

11   Alcock and Miles (2013) (attached CD).

12   www.oxford-dendrolab.com/oxfordshire.asp.

13   Horn and Charles (1966).

14   www.dbrg.org.uk/Marks/Cmarks.pdf.

15   Moran (2003).

16   See the distribution map in Alcock and Miles (2013), 8.

17   Ibid., 11–24.

18   Giles (1986).

19   Pearson (1994); Jones and Smith (1960–1).

20   Rackham (1972).

21   www.vag.org.uk/dendro-tables/county/herefordshire.pdf?.

22   Alcock and Miles (2013), 105–17.

23   Nottinghamshire Archives, DD/P/70/28.

24   Hey (2015b).

25   Hey (1974), 167–9.

26   Moran (2003), 238–40.

27   Clarke, Pearson, Mate and Parfitt (2010).

28   Moran (2003), 277–98.

29   Palliser (2014).

30   Harrison (1577).

31   Ryece (1618).

32   Smith and Webb (1656).

33   Carew (1602).

34   British Library MS Lansdowne 897.

35   Essex Record Office: John Walker's map of Newlandes Ende.

36   Hoskins (1964).

37   Machin (1977).

38   Roberts (2003).

39   Palliser (1979), 32.

40   Hey (2011b).

41   Giles (1986).

42   Barnwell and Airs (2006).

43   Ibid., 46–54.

44   Ibid., 164–74.

Chapter Nine

1   Hatcher (2008), 93.

2   Scott and Duncan (2004).

3   Hey (2011a), 171–3.

4   Dyer (2002), 233–4 and 271–81.

5   Slack (1985).

6   Hindle (2004), 81–92.

7   Appleby (1977).

8   Slack (1985), 70–71; Hey (2011a), 238–9.

9   Houlbrooke (1984), 136–40.

10   www.lse.ac.uk/economicHistory/pdf/FACTSPDF/FACTS2-Wallis.pdf.

11   Smith (1987).

12   Hey (1991), 71–4.

13   Gooder (1972).

14   Phythian-Adams (1979).

15   Kettle (1976).

16   Sachse (1938).

17   Hey (1974), 213.

18   Wrigley and Schofield (1981); Wrigley, Davies, Oeppen and Schofield (1997).

19   Houlbrooke (1984), 82–3.

20   Prior (1985).

21   Allison (1962); The National Archives, E 163/24/35.

22   Wrightson and Levine (1997).

23   Arkell, Evans and Goose (2000).

24   Hey (1997b).

25   Redmonds (2004); Smith-Bannister (1997).

26   Hey (2010b), 71–2.

27   Brown (1981), 58–72.

28   Dyer (1973), 166.

29   Pound (1971).

30   Hey (1991), 62–3.

31   Fieldhouse and Jennings (1978), 290.

32   Seaman, Pound and Smith (2001).

33   Hindle (2004).

34   Snell (1985).

35   Merson (1968).

36   Binfield and Hey (1997), 26–39.

37   Ben Amos (1991).

38 Laslett and Harrison (1963).

39 Hoskins (1965), 194–204.

40 Hey (1974), 119–42.

41 Hey (2003).

42 Wood (1999), 33.

43 Bardon (2012).

44 Clark and Souden (1987), chapters 5 and 6.

45 Slack (2015).

46 Blake (1986).

47 Fox (2000), 14–16.

48 Orme (2006).

49 Fox (2000).

50 Wood, A. (2013), 13.

BIBLIOGRAPHY

Airs, M. (1998), *The Tudor and Jacobean Country House: A Building History* (Stroud: Sutton).

Alcock, N. and Miles, D. (2013), *The Medieval Peasant House in Midland England* (Oxford: Oxbow Books).

Allen, R.C. (1992), *Enclosure and the Yeoman: The Agricultural Development of the South Midlands, 1450–1850* (Oxford: Clarendon Press).

Allison, K.J. (1962), *Elizabethan 'Census' of Ealing* (Ealing Local History Society).

Allison, K.J. (1969), ed., *A History of the County of York East Riding: 1, the City of Kingston Upon Hull* (London: Victoria County History).

Allison, K.J. (1976), *The East Riding of Yorkshire Landscape* (London: Hodder and Stoughton).

Allison, M. (2003), *History of Appleton-le-Moors* (Easingwold: privately published).

Appleby, A.B. (1977), *Famine in Tudor and Stuart England* (Stanford: Stanford University Press).

Arkell, T. (2003), 'Identifying Regional Variations from the Hearth Tax', *The Local Historian*, 33:3, 148–74.

Arkell, T., Evans, N. and Goose, N. (2000), eds, *When Death Do Us Part: Understanding and Interpreting The Probate Records Of Early Modern England* (Oxford: Leopard's Head Press).

Arnold, A. and Howard, R. (2014), *7–12 Church Street, Dronfield, Derbyshire: Tree-Ring Analysis of Timbers* (English Heritage, Research Report Series, no. 55).

Aston, M. and Gerrard, C. (2013), *Interpreting the English Village: Landscape and Community at Shapwick, Somerset* (Oxford: Windgather).

Aubrey, J. (1988), *The Natural History of Wiltshire*, ed. R. Barber (London: The Folio Society).

Bahn, P. and Pettit, P. (2009), *Britain's Oldest Art: The Ice Age Cave Art of Creswell Crags* (London: English Heritage).

Bain, I. (1981), ed., T. Bewick, *My Life* (London: The Folio Society).

Balaresque, P., Bowden, G.R., Adams, S.M., Leung, H-Y, King, T.E., et al. (2010), 'A Predominantly Neolithic Origin for European Paternal Lineages'. *PLoS Biology*, 8(1): e1000285. doi:10.1371/journal.pbio.1000285.

Barber, B.J. (1994), ed., *Doncaster: A Borough and its Charters* (Doncaster: The Waterdale Press).

Bardon, J. (2012), *The Plantation of Ulster* (London: Gill and Macmillan, reprint).

Barker, F. and Jackson, P. (1990), *The History of London in Maps* (London: Barrie & Jenkins).

Barley, M.W. (1986), *Houses and History* (London: Faber).

Barnard, G.W. (2012), *The Late Medieval English Church: Vitality and Vulnerability before the Break with Rome* (London: Yale University Press).

Barnwell, P.S. and Airs, M. (2006), eds, *Houses and the Hearth Tax: The Later Stuart House and Society* (York: Council for British Archaeology Research Report, 150).

Barraclough, K. (1984), *Steelmaking Before Bessemer: 1. Blister Steel, The Birth of an Industry* (London: The Metals Society).

Barron, C.M. (2004), *London in the Later Middle Ages: Government and People, 1200–1500* (Oxford: Oxford University Press).

Beckett, J.V. (1986), *The Aristocracy in England, 1660–1914* (Oxford: Blackwell).

Bédoyere, G. de la (2006), *Roman Britain: A New History* (London: Thames & Hudson).

Beier, A.L. and Finlay, R. (1986), eds, *London, 1500–1700: The Making of the Metropolis* (Harlow: Longman).

Ben Amos, I.K. (1991), 'Failure to Become Freemen: Urban Apprentices in Early Modern England', *Social History*, 16:2, 155–72.

Beresford, M.W. (1954), *The Lost Villages of England* (London: Lutterworth Press).

Beresford, M.W. and St Joseph, J.K. (1979), *Medieval England: An Aerial Survey* (Cambridge: Cambridge University Press).

Betterton, A. and Dymond, D. (1989), *Lavenham: Industrial Town* (Lavenham: Dalton).

Bettey, J.H. (1986), *Wessex from AD 1000* (Harlow: Longman).

Binfield, C. and Hey, D. (1997), eds, *Mesters to Masters: A History of the Company of Cutlers in Hallamshire* (Oxford: Oxford University Press).

Blair, J. (2005) *The Church in Anglo-Saxon Society* (Oxford: Oxford University Press).

Blair, J. (2007), ed., *Waterways and Canal-Building in Medieval England* (Oxford: Oxford University Press).

Blair, J. (2013) 'Redating Early England', *Current Archaeology* (December 2013), 12–19.

Blair, J. (2014), 'Exploring Anglo-Saxon Settlement: In Search of the Origins of the English Village', *Current Archaeology*, XXV: 3, 12–22.

Blake, N.F. (1986), *A History of the English Language* (London: Macmillan).

Blomefield, F. (1806), *An Essay towards a Topographical History of the County of Norfolk*, III.

Blyton, P. (2014), *Changes in Working Time (Routledge Revivals): An International Review* (London: Routledge).

Bond, J. (2004), *Monastic Landscapes* (Stroud: Tempus).

Borsay, P. (1989), *The English Urban Renaissance: Culture and Society in the Provincial Town, 1660–1770* (Oxford: Oxford University Press).

Bossy, J. (1975), *The English Catholic Community* (London: Darton, Longman & Todd).

Boulton, J. (2000), 'London 1540–1700' in P. Clark, ed., *The Cambridge Urban History of Britain, II: 1540–1840* (Cambridge: Cambridge University Press), 316–17.

Bowman, A.K. (2003), *Life and Letters on the Roman Frontier: Vindolanda and its People* (British Museum).

Bragg, M. (2003), *The Adventure of English: The Biography of a Language* (London: Hodder and Stoughton).

Bragg, M. (2004), *The Adventure of English: The Biography of a Language* (London: Sceptre).

Bragg, M. (2011), *The Book of Books: The Radical Impact of the King James Bible 1611–2011* (London: Hodder and Stoughton).

Brindle, S. (2012), *Dover Castle* (English Heritage).

Britnell, R.H. (1993), *The Commercialisation of English Society, 1000–1500* (Cambridge: Cambridge University Press).

Broad, J. (1983), 'Cattle Plague in Eighteenth-Century England', *Agricultural History Review*, 31:2, 104–15.

Brooke, C. Highfield, R. and Swaan, W. (1988), *Oxford and Cambridge* (Cambridge: Cambridge University Press).

Brooks, N. (2000), *Anglo-Saxon Myths: State and Church, 400–1066* (London: A & C Black).

Brown, P. (1981), *Buildings of Britain, 1550–1750: South West England* (Ashbourne: Moorland).

Browning, A. (1936), ed., *The Memoirs of Sir John Reresby* (Glasgow: Jackson).

Brunskill, R. (1994), *Timber Building in Britain* (London: Gollanz).

Burton, J.E. (1979), *The Yorkshire Nunneries in the Twelfth and Thirteenth Centuries* (York: Borthwick Papers, 56).

Burton, J. (1994), *Monastic and Religious Orders in Britain, 1000–1300* (Cambridge: Cambridge University Press).

Butler, L. (2007), *The Yorkshire Church Notes of Sir Stephen Glynne (1825–1874)* (Yorkshire Archaeological Society Record Series, CLIX).

Butler, L. and Given-Wilson, C. (1979), *Medieval Monasteries of Great Britain* (London: Michael Joseph).

Camden, W. (1607), *Britannia* (London).

Cameron, K. (1959), *The Place-Names of Derbyshire*, 3 vols (Cambridge).

Cameron, K. (1996), *English Place-Names* (London: Batsford).

Camp, A.J. (1990), *My Ancestors Came with the Conqueror: Those Who Did and Some of Those Who Probably Did Not* (London: Society of Genealogists).

Campbell, B.M.S. (2000), *English Seigniorial Agriculture, 1250–1450* (Cambridge: Cambridge University Press).

Cannon, J. (2007), *Cathedral* (London: Constable).

Carew, R. (1602), *The Survey of Cornwall,* reprinted in 2012 by RareBooksClub.com.

Carver, M.O.H. (1998), *Sutton Hoo: Burial Ground of Kings?* (Philadelphia: University of Pennsylvania Press).

Carus-Wilson, E.M. (1937), *The Overseas Trade of Bristol in the Later Middle Ages* (Bristol Record Society).

Carus-Wilson, E.M. (1941), 'An Industrial Revolution of the Thirteenth Century', *Economic History Review*, Old Series, 11:1, 39–60.

Chatfield, M. (1979), *Churches the Victorians Forgot* (Ashbourne: Moorland).

Clark, P. (2000), ed., *The Cambridge Urban History of Britain: ii (1540–140)* (Cambridge: Cambridge University Press).

Clark, P. and Slack, P. (1972), eds, *Crisis and Order in English Towns, 1500–1700* (London: Routledge and Kegan Paul).

Clark, P. and Slack, P. (1976), eds, *English Towns in Transition, 1500–1700* (Oxford: Oxford University Press).

Clark, P. and Souden, D. (1987), eds, *Migration and Society in Early Modern England* (London: Hutchinson).

Clarke, H., Pearson, S., Mate, M., and Parfitt, K. (2010), *Sandwich: The 'Completest Medieval Town in England'* (Oxford: Oxbow Books).

Clarkson, L.A. (1966), 'The Leather Crafts in Tudor and Stuart England', *Agricultural History Review*, 14:1, 25–39.

Clay, C.T. and Douglas, D.C. (1951), eds, *L.C. Lloyd, The Origins of Some Anglo-Norman Families* (Harleian Society).

Cleere, H. and Crossley, D. (1995), *Iron Industry of the Weald* (Cardiff: Merton Priory Press).

Clifton-Taylor, A. (1967), *The Cathedrals of England* (London: Thames & Hudson).

Clifton-Taylor, A. (1972), *The Pattern of English Building* (London: Faber and Faber).

Clifton-Taylor, A. (1974), *English Parish Churches as Works of Art* (London: Batsford).

Collingwood, R.G. and Wright, R.P. (1995), *The Roman Inscriptions of Britain*, I (Stroud: Sutton).

Collinson, P. (1982), *The English Puritan Movement* (London: Methuen).

Colvin, H.M. (1951), *The White Canons in England* (Oxford: Oxford University Press).

Cook, H. and Williamson, T. (2007), eds, *Water Meadows: History, Ecology and Conservation* (Oxford: Windgather).

Cook, H., Stearne, K. and Williamson, T. (2003) 'The Origin of Water Meadows in England', *Agricultural History Review*, 51:1, 155–62.

Coppack, G. (2000), *The White Monks: The Cistercians in Britain, 1128–1540* (Stroud: The History Press).

Coppack, G. (2003), *Fountains Abbey: the Cistercians in Northern England* (Stroud: The History Press).

Coulson, C.L.H. (2003), *Castles in Medieval Society: Fortresses in England, France, and Ireland in the Central Middle Ages* (Oxford: Oxford University Press).

Cox, J.C. (1908), 'Derbyshire in 1327: Being a Lay Subsidy Roll', *Journal of the Derbyshire Archaeological and Natural History Society*, 30, 23–96.

Cramp, R. (1970), 'Decorated Window-Glass and Millefiori from Monkwearmouth', *The Antiquaries Journal*, 50:2, 327–35.

Crossley, D.W. (1990), *Post-Medieval Archaeology in Britain* (Leicester: Leicester University Press).

Crouch, D. and Pearson, T. (2001), eds, *Medieval Scarborough: Studies in Trade and Civic Life* (Yorkshire Archaeological Society Occasional Paper No. 1).

Cullen, P., Jones, R. and Parsons, D.N. (2011), *Thorps in a Changing Landscape* (Hatfield: University of Hertfordshire Press).

Cunliffe, B. (2013), *Britain Begins* (Oxford: Oxford University Press).

Defoe, D. (1962), *A Tour through the Whole Island of Great Britain* (London: Dent, Everyman edition), 2 vols.

Dickens, A.G. (1947), 'Robert Parkyn's Narrative of the Reformation', *English Historical Review*, 62, 58–83.

Dickens, A.G. (1959), ed., *Tudor Treatises* (Yorkshire Archaeological Record Series, 125), 123–6.

Dobson, M. and Wells, S. (2005), eds, *The Oxford Companion to Shakespeare* (Oxford: Oxford University Press).

Dobson, R.B. (1974), *The Jews of Medieval York and the Massacre of March 1190* (York: Borthwick Papers, 45).

Dodgson, J. McN. (1966), 'The Significance of the Distribution of the English Place-Name in -ingas, -inga- in South-East England', *Medieval Archaeology*, 10, 1–29.

Duffy, E. (1992), *The Stripping of the Altars: Traditional Religion in England, 1400–1580* (London: Yale University Press).

Duffy, E. (2001), *The Voices of Morebath* (London: Yale University Press).

Dugdale, J. (2011), *The New British Traveller: Or, Modern Panorama of England*, 3 (Charleston: Nabu Press).

Dyer, A.D. (1973), *The City of Worcester in the Sixteenth Century* (Leicester: Leicester University Press).

Dyer, C. (2002), *Making a Living in the Middle Ages* (London: Yale University Press).

Dyer, C. (2007), ed., *The Self-Contained Village?: The Social History of Rural Communities, 1250–1900* (Hatfield: University of Hertfordshire Press).

Dyer, C. (2008), 'Place-names and Pottery' in O. J. Padel and D. N. Parsons, eds, *A Commodity of Good Names: Essays in Honour of Margaret Gelling* (Donnington: Shaun Tyas), 44–54.

Dyer, C. (2012), *A Country Merchant, 1495–1520: Trading and Farming at the End of the Middle Ages* (Oxford: Oxford University Press).

Dyer, C. and Jones, R. (2010), eds, *Deserted Villages Revisited* (Hatfield: University of Hertfordshire Press).

Dyer, C., Hey, D. and Thirsk, J. (2000), 'Lowland Vales' in J. Thirsk, ed., *The English Rural Landscape* (Oxford: Oxford University Press), 78–96.

Dymond, D. (1985), *The Norfolk Landscape* (London: Hodder and Stoughton).

Earle, P. (1989), *The Making of the English Middle Class: Business, Society and Family Life in London, 1660–1730* (London: Methuen).

Eddison, J. (2000), *Romney Marsh: Survival on a Frontier* (Stroud: The History Press).

Edwards, D.G. (1982), ed., *The Derbyshire Hearth Tax Assessments, 1662–70* (Derbyshire Record Society, VII).

Everitt, A. (1972), *The Pattern of Rural Dissent in the Nineteenth Century* (Leicester: Leicester University Press).

Everitt, A. (1973), ed., *Perspectives in English Urban History* (London: Macmillan).

Everitt, A. (1986), *Continuity and Colonization: The Evolution of Kentish Settlement* (Leicester: Leicester University Press).

Fellows-Jensen, G. (1968), *Scandinavian Personal Names in Lincolnshire and Yorkshire* (Copenhagen: Akademisk Forlag).

Fellows-Jensen, G. (1972), *Scandinavian Settlement Names in Yorkshire* (Copenhagen: Akademisk Forlag).

Fellows-Jensen, G. (1978), *Scandinavian Settlement Names in the East Midlands* (Copenhagen: Akademisk Forlag).

Fenwick, C.C. (1998), ed., *The Poll Taxes of 1377, 1379 and 1381: I Bedfordshire-Leicestershire*; (2001) *II Lincolnshire to Westmorland*; (2005); *III Wiltshire to Yorkshire* (Oxford: Oxford University Press for The British Academy).

Ferguson, C., Thornton, C. and Wareham, A. (2012), eds, *Essex Hearth Tax Return Michaelmas 1670* (The British Record Society, Hearth Tax Series, VIII).

Fieldhouse, R. and Jennings, B. (1978), *A History of Richmond and Swaledale* (Chichester: Phillimore).

Forrester, T. (1859), ed., *Orderic Vitalis, The Ecclesiastical History of England and Normandy*, 3 vols (London: Bohn).

Fox, A. (2000), *Oral and Literate Culture in England, 1500–1700* (Oxford: Oxford University Press).

Fox, H.S.A. (1994), 'Medieval Dartmoor as Seen through its Account Rolls', *The Archaeology of Dartmoor: Perspectives from the 1990s* (Devon Archaeological Society Proceedings, 52).

Fox, H. (2001), *The Evolution of the Fishing Village: Landscape and Society along the South Devon Coast, 1086–1550* (Oxford: Leopard's Head Press).

Fox, H. (2012), *Dartmoor's Alluring Uplands* (Exeter: University of Exeter Press).

Gardiner, M. and Rippon, S. (2007), eds, *Medieval Landscapes* (Bollington: Windgather).

Gardner, A. (2011), *Alabaster Tombs of the Pre-Reformation Period in England* (Cambridge: Cambridge University Press).

Garnett, H.J.H. (1997), ed., *Eckington: The Court Rolls, V, 1694–1804* (Huddersfield: privately published).

Gelling, M. (1978), *Signposts to the Past: Place-Names and the History of England* (London: Dent).

Gelling, M. and Cole, A. (2000), *The Landscape of Place-Names* (Stamford: Shaun Tyas).

Gerhold, D. (2005), *Carriers and Coachmasters: Trade and Travel before the Turnpikes* (Chichester: Phillimore).

Giles, G. (1986), *Rural Houses of West Yorkshire, 1400–1830* (London: HCHM).

Girouard, M. (1983), *Robert Smythson and the Elizabethan Country House* (London: Yale University Press).

Girouard, M. (1993), *Life in the English Country House: A Social and Architectural History* (London: Yale University Press).

Glasscock, R. E. (1975), ed., *The Lay Subsidy of 1334* (Records of Social and Economic History, New Series II, The British Academy).

Glover, S. (1833), The *History and Gazetteer of the County of Derby*, 2 (Derby).

Gooder, E.A. (1972), 'The Population Crisis of 1727–30 in Warwickshire', *Midland History*, I, 1–22.

Goose, N. and Luu, L. (2005), eds, *Immigrants in Tudor and Early Stuart England* (Brighton: Sussex Academic Press).

Green, J.A. (1997), *The Aristocracy of Norman England* (Cambridge: Cambridge University Press).

Green, T. (2012), *Britons and Anglo-Saxons: Lincolnshire AD 400–650* (Lincoln: Studies in the History of Lincolnshire, 3).

Haigh, C. (1987), ed., *The English Reformation Revised* (Cambridge: Cambridge University Press).

Hall, D. (1995), *The Open Fields of Northamptonshire* (Northamptonshire Record Society).

Hall, R.A. (1989), 'The Five Boroughs of the Danelaw: A Review of Present Knowledge', *Anglo-Saxon England*, 18, 149–206.

Hall, R.A. (1994), *Viking Age York* (London: Batsford).

Hall, T.W. (1930), *A Descriptive Catalogue of . . . the Bosville and the Lindsey Collections* (Sheffield: Northend).

Hall, T.W. (1939), ed., *A Descriptive Catalogue of Land-Charters and Muniments relating to Vills and Burghs of North Derbyshire* (Sheffield: Northend).

Harrison, D. (2004), *The Bridges of Medieval England: Transport and Society, 400–1800* (Oxford: Oxford University Press).

Harrison, W. (1577), *Description of England*. A modern edition (with modernized spelling) is W. Harrison, *The Description of England*, ed. G. Edelen (New York: Ithaca, 1968).

Hartley, M. and Ingleby, J. (2001), *The Old Hand-Knitters of the Dales* (Skipton: Dalesman Publshing).

Harvey, J. (1971), *The Master Builders: Architecture in the Middle Ages* (London: Thames & Hudson).

Harvey, J. (1978), *The Perpendicular Style, 1330–1485* (London: Batsford).

Harvey, M. (1983), 'Planned Field Systems in Eastern Yorkshire: Some Thoughts on Their Origin', *Agricultural History Review*, 31:2, 91–103.

Hatcher, J. (1993), *The History of the British Coal Industry, I* (Oxford: Oxford University Press).

Hatcher, J. (2008), *The Black Death: An Intimate History* (London: Weidenfeld & Nicolson).

Haughton, C. and Powlesland, D. (1999), *West Heslerton: The Anglian Cemetery* (Yedingham: Landscape Research Centre, 2 vols).

Heath, P. (2013), *The English Parish Clergy on the Eve of the Reformation* (London: Routledge).

Heaton, H. (1965), *The Yorkshire Woollen and Worsted Industries from the Earliest Times up to the Industrial Revolution* (Oxford: Oxford University Press).

Hembry, P. (1990), *The English Spa, 1560–1815: A Social History* (London: The Athlone Press).

Henry of Huntingdon (1879), *Historia Anglorum*, ed. T. Arnold (London: Rolls Series, IV).

Herring, P. (2006), 'Cornish Strip Fields' in S. Turner, ed., *Medieval Devon and Cornwall: Shaping an Ancient Countryside* (Bollington: Windgather Press), 44–77.

Hewett, C.A. (1962), 'Structural Carpentry in Medieval Essex', *Medieval Archaeology*, 6, 240–70.

Hewett, C.A. (1980), *English Historic Carpentry* (Chichester: Phillimore).

Hey, D. (1972), *The Rural Metalworkers of the Sheffield Region* (Leicester: Leicester University Press).

Hey, D. (1973), 'The Pattern of Nonconformity in South Yorkshire, 1660–1851', *Northern History*, VIII, 86–118.

Hey, D. (1974), *An English Rural Community: Myddle Under the Tudors and Stuarts* (Leicester: Leicester University Press).

Hey, D. (1981), ed., *Richard Gough: The History of Myddle* (Harmondsworth: Penguin).

Hey, D. (1984a), 'Yorkshire and Lancashire' in J. Thirsk, ed., *Agrarian History of England and Wales, V* (Cambridge: Cambridge University Press), 59–88.

Hey, D. (1984b), 'The North-West Midlands: Derbyshire, Staffordshire, Cheshire, and Shropshire' in J. Thirsk, ed., *Agrarian History of England and Wales, V* (Cambridge: Cambridge University Press), 129–58.

Hey, D. (1991), *The Fiery Blades of Hallamshire: Sheffield and its Neighbourhood, 1660–1740* (Leicester: Leicester University Press).

Hey, D. (1995), 'The Riches of Bullhouse: A family of Yorkshire Dissenters', *Northern History*, XXXI, 178–93.

Hey, D. (1997a), 'The Local History of Family Names', *The Local Historian*, 27:4, i–xx.

Hey, D. (1997b), 'Mahlon Stacy: An Early Sheffield Emigrant' in M. Jones, ed., *Aspects of Sheffield, I: Discovering Local History* (Barnsley: Wharncliffe), 39–47.

Hey, D. (1998), 'The Distinctive Surnames of Staffordshire', *Staffordshire Studies*, 10, 1–28.

Hey, D. (2000), *Family Names and Family History* (London: Hambledon and London).

Hey, D. (2001), *Packmen, Carriers and Packhorse Roads: Trade and Communications in North Derbyshire and South Yorkshire* (Ashbourne: Landmark).

Hey, D. (2002a), *Historic Hallamshire* (Ashbourne: Landmark).

Hey, D. (2002b), *How Our Ancestors Lived: A History of Life a Hundred Years Ago* (Kew: The Public Record Office).

Hey, D. (2003), 'Stable Families in Tudor and Stuart England' in D. Hooke and D. Postles, eds, *Names, Time and Place: Essays in Memory of Richard McKinley* (Oxford: Leopard's Head Press), 165–81.

Hey, D. (2006), 'A Manorial Landscape at Holmesfield' in P. Riden and D.G. Edwards, eds, *Essays in Derbyshire History Presented to Gladwyn Turbutt* (Derbyshire Record Society, XXX), 3–22.

Hey, D. (2008), *Derbyshire: A History* (Lancaster: Carnegie).

Hey, D. (2010a), *The Worshipful Company of Blacksmiths* (Lancaster: Carnegie).

Hey, D. (2010b), *A History of Sheffield* (Lancaster: Carnegie).

Hey, D. (2011a), *A History of Yorkshire: 'County of the Broad Acres'* (Lancaster: Carnegie).

Hey, D. (2011b), 'The Houses of the Dronfield Lead Smelters and Merchants, 1600–1730' in C. Dyer et al., eds, *New Directions in Local History since Hoskins* (Hatfield: University of Hertfordshire Press), 114–26.

Hey, D. (2013a), 'Townfields, Royds and Shaws: The Medieval Landscape of a South Pennine Township', *Northern History*, L:2, 216–38.

Hey, D. (2013b), 'The Commons of the Ancient Parish of Sheffield' in I. Rotherham, ed., *Cultural Severance and the Environment* (Dordrecht: Springer), 263–74.

Hey, D. (2014a), 'Immigration, Surnames and the London Hearth Tax' in M. Davies et al., eds, *London and Middlesex 1666 Hearth Tax* (The British Record Society, Hearth Tax Series, IX:1), 154–8.

Hey, D. (2014b), 'The Medieval Origins of South Pennine Farms: The Case of Westmondhalgh Bierlow', *Agricultural History Review*, 62:1, 23–39.

Hey, D. (2015a), *A History of the South Yorkshire Countryside* (Barnsley: Pen & Sword), 20–30.

Hey, D. (2015b), *Medieval and Tudor Dronfield* (Dronfield Heritage Centre).

Hey, D. and Redmonds, G. (2002), *Yorkshire Surnames and the Hearth Tax Returns of 1672–73* (York: Borthwick Papers, 102).

Hey, D. and Rodwell, J. (2006), 'Wombwell: The Landscape History of a South Yorkshire Coalfield Township', *Landscapes*, 7:2, 24–47.

Hey, D., Liddy, L. and Luscombe, D. (2011), eds, *A Monastic Community in Local Society: The Beauchief Abbey Cartulary* (Cambridge: Cambridge University Press).

Higham, N.J. (2004), *A Frontier Landscape: The North West in the Middle Ages* (Bollington: Windgather Press).

Higham, N. and Ryan, M.J. (2013), *The Anglo-Saxon World* (London: Yale University Press).

Hill, D. and Rumble, A.R. (1996), eds, *The Defence of Wessex: The Burghal Hidage and Anglo-Saxon Fortifications* (Manchester: Manchester University Press).

Hill, F. (2008), *Medieval Lincoln* (Cambridge: Cambridge University Press).

Hinde, A. (2003), *England's Population: A History since the Domesday Survey* (London: Arnold).

Hindle, S. (2004), *On the Parish? The Micro-Politics of Poor Relief in Rural England, c.1550–1750* (Oxford: Oxford University Press).

Hindman, S. and Marrow, J. (2013), eds, *Books of Hours Reconsidered (Studies in Medieval and Early Renaissance Art History)* (Washington, DC: Harvey Miller).

Holt, R. (1988), *The Mills of Medieval England* (Cambridge: Cambridge University Press).

Hooke, D. and Postles, D. (2003), eds, *Names, Time and Place: Essays in Memory of Richard McKinley* (Oxford: Leopard's Head Press).

Hopper, A. (2007), *'Black Tom': Sir Thomas Fairfax and the English Revolution* (Manchester: Manchester University Press).

Hopper, A. (2013), 'Social Mobility during the English Revolution: The case of Adam Eyre', *Social History*, 38:1, 26–45.

Horn, W. and Charles, F.W.B. (1966), 'The Cruck-Built Barn of Middle Littleton in Worcestershire, England', *Journal of the Society of Architectural Historians*, XXV, 4, 221–39.

Hoskins, W.G. (1964), *Provincial England: Essays in Social and Economic History* (London: Macmillan).

Hoskins, W.G. (1965), *The Midland Peasant: The Economic and Social History of a Leicestershire Village* (London: Macmillan).

Hoskins, W.G. (1967), *Fieldwork in Local History* (London: Faber and Faber).

Hoskins, W.G. (1984), *Local History in England* (London: Longman, third edition).

Houlbrooke, R.A. (1984), *The English Family, 1450–1700* (Harlow: Longman).

Howard, M. (1987), *The Early Tudor Country House: Architecture and Politics, 1490–1550* (London: George Philip).

Hoyle, R.W. (2001), *The Pilgrimage of Grace and the Politics of the 1530s* (Oxford: Oxford University Press).

Hussey, D. (2000), *Coastal and River Trade in Pre-Industrial England: Bristol and its Region, 1680–1730* (Exeter: University of Exeter Press).

Hutton, R. (1994), *The Rise and Fall of Merry England: The Ritual Year, 1400–1700* (Oxford: Oxford University Press).

James, T.B. (1997), *Book of Winchester* (London: Batsford / English Heritage).

Jennings, B. (1967), ed., *A History of Nidderdale* (Huddersfield: Advertiser Press).

Jewell, H. (1994), *The North-South Divide: The Origins of Northern Consciousness in England* (Manchester: Manchester University Press).

Jones, M. (2002), *The Secret Middle Ages* (Stroud: Sutton).

Jones, R. and Page, M. (2006), *Medieval Villages in an English Landscape: Beginnings and Ends* (Bollington: Windgather Press).

Jones, R. and Semple, S. (2012), eds, *Sense of Place in Anglo-Saxon England* (Donnington: Shaun Tyas).

Jones, S.R. and Smith, J.T. (1960–1), 'The Wealden houses of Warwickshire and their Significance', *Transactions and Proceedings of the Birmingham Archaeology Society*, 79, 24–35.

Keats-Rohan, K.S.B. (1999), *Domesday Book: A Prosopography of Persons Occurring in English Documents, 1066–1166, I, Domesday Book* (Woodbridge: Boydell Press).

Kerridge, E. (1985), *Textile Manufacturers in Early Modern England* (Manchester: Manchester University Press).

Kershaw, I. (1973), *Bolton Priory: The Economy of a Northern Monastery, 1286–1325* (Oxford: Oxford University Press).

Kettle, A.J. (1976), ed., 'A List of Families in the Archdeaconry of Stafford, 1532–3', *Collections for a History of Staffordshire* (Staffordshire Record Society).

Lander, J.R. (1988), *Government and Community: England, 1450–1509* (Cambridge, MA: Harvard University Press).

Langton, J. and Jones, G. (2010), *Forests and Chases of England and Wales, c.1000-c.1500* (Oxford: Oxbow Books).

Laslett, P. (2004), *The World We Have Lost: Further Explored* (London: Routledge).

Laslett, P. and Harrison, J. (1963), 'Clayworth and Cogenhoe' in H.E. Bell and R.L. Ollard, eds, *Historical Essays, 1600–1750: Presented to David Ogg* (London: A and C Black), 157–84.

Lawrence, C.H. (1994), *The Friars: The Impact of the Early Mendicant Movement in Western Society* (Harlow: Longman).

Levine, D. and Wrightson, K. (1991), *The Making of an Industrial Society: Whickham, 1560–1765* (Oxford: Clarendon Press).

Lewis, C., Mitchell-Fox, P. and Dyer, C. (1997), *Village, Hamlet and Field: Changing Medieval Settlements in Central England* (Bollington: Windgather Press).

Liddiard, R. (2005), *Castles in Context: Power, Symbolism and Landscape, 1066 to 1500* (Bollington: Windgather Press).

Liddiard, R. (2007), *Medieval Parks: A New Perspective* (Bollington: Windgather Press).

Linebaugh, P. (1981), *The London Hanged: Crime and Civil Society in the Eighteenth Century* (Cambridge: Cambridge University Press).

Linebaugh, P. (2008), *The Magna Carta Manifesto* (Oakland: University of California Press).

Luxford, J.M. (2008), *The Art and Architecture of English Benedictine Monasteries, 1300–1540: A Patronage History* (Woodbridge: Boydell Press).

McCord, N. and Thompson, R. (1998), *The Northern Counties from AD 1000* (Harlow: Longman).

McKinley, R. (1975), *Norfolk and Suffolk Surnames in the Middle Ages* (Chichester: Phillimore).

McKinley, R. (1977), *The Surnames of Oxfordshire* (London: Leopard's Head Press).

McKinley, R. (1981), *The Surnames of Lancashire* (London: Leopard's Head Press).

McKinley, R. (1988), *The Surnames of Sussex* (Oxford: Leopard's Head Press).

McKinley, R. (1990), *A History of British Surnames* (Harlow: Longman).

Machin, R. (1977), 'The Great Rebuilding: A Reassessment', *Past and Present*, 77:1, 33–56.

Marshall, L.M. (1990), ed., *The Bedfordshire Hearth Tax Return for 1671* (Bedfordshire Historical Record Society).

Mawer, A. (1929), *Problems of Place-Name Study* (Cambridge: Cambridge University Press).

Merson, A.L. (1968), *Apprentices at Southampton in the Seventeenth Century* (Southampton: Southampton University Press).

Miles, D.H.W. (1997), 'The Interpretation, Presentation and use of Tree-Ring Dates', *Vernacular Architecture*, 28, 40–56.

Miles, D.W.H. (2005), 'The Tree-Ring Dating of the Nave Roof at Salisbury Cathedral, Wiltshire' (English Heritage, Centre for Archaeology Reports, 58).

Mileson, S.A. (2009), *Parks in Medieval England* (Oxford: Oxford University Press).

Millington, J. and Chapman, S. (1989), eds, *Four Centuries of Machine Knitting* (Leicester: Leicester University Press).

Moran, M. (2003), *Vernacular Buildings of Shropshire* (Little Logaston: Logaston Press).

Morris, C. (1982), ed., *The Illustrated Journeys of Celia Fiennes, c.1682–c.1712* (London: Webb & Bower).

Neave, S. (1993), 'Rural Settlement Contraction in the East Riding of Yorkshire between the Mid-Seventeenth and Mid-Eighteenth Centuries', *Agricultural History Review*, 41, 124–36.

Newman, P. (2006), 'Tinworking and the Landscape of Medieval Devon' in S. Turner, ed., *Medieval Devon and Cornwall: Shaping an Ancient Countryside* (Bollington: Windgather Press), 123–43.

Nicholls, J. (1842), ed., *T. Fuller: The Church History of Britain from the Birth of Jesus Christ until the year MDCXLVIII*, I (London: Thomas Tegg).

Nichols, A.E. (1997), *Seeable Signs: The Iconography of the Seven Sacraments, 1350–1544* (Woodbridge: Boydell Press).

Nicholson, H. (2001), *The Knights Templar: A New History* (Stroud: Sutton).

Nicholson, H. (2013), *The Knights Hospitaller* (Woodbridge: Boydell Press).

O'Day, R. (1979), *The English Clergy: The Emergence and Consolidation of a Profession, 1558–1642* (Leicester: Leicester University Press).

Oppenheimer, S. (2006), *The Origins of the British: A Genetic Detective Story* (London: Constable & Robinson).

Orme, N. (2006), *Medieval Schools from Roman Britain to Renaissance England* (London: Yale University Press).

Orwin, C.S. and Orwin, C.S. (1954), *The Open Fields* (Oxford: Clarendon Press, second edition).

Page, W. (1911) ed., *The Victoria County History of Middlesex* (London: VCH).

Palliser, D.M. (1979), *Tudor York* (Oxford: Oxford University Press).

Palliser, D.M. (2001), ed., *The Cambridge Urban History of Britain: I (600–1540)* (Cambridge: Cambridge University Press).

Palliser, D.M. (2014), *Medieval York, 600–1540* (Oxford: Oxford University Press).

Parker, V. (1970), *The Making of King's Lynn* (Chichester: Phillimore).

Parsons, D. and Sutherland, D.S. (2013), *The Anglo-Saxon Church of All Saints, Brixworth, Northamptonshire: Survey and Excavation, 1972–2010* (Oxford: Oxbow Books).

Pearson, S. (1994), *The Medieval Houses of Kent: An Historical Analysis* (London: RCHM).

Pevsner, N. and Wilson, B. (2002), *Norfolk 2: North-West and South* (London: Yale University Press).

Phillips, C., Ferguson, C. and Wareham (2008), eds, *Westmorland Hearth Tax* (British Record Society).

Phythian-Adams, C.V. (1979), *Desolation of a City: Coventry and the Urban Crisis of the Late Middle Ages* (Cambridge: Cambridge University Press).

Phythian-Adams, C.V. (1993), ed., *Societies, Cultures and Kinship 1580–1850: Cultural Provinces in English Local History* (Leicester: Leicester University Press).

Phythian-Adams, C. (2000), 'Frontier Valleys' in J. Thirsk, ed., *The English Rural Landscape* (Oxford: Oxford University Press).

Platt, C. (1969), *The Monastic Grange in Medieval England: A Reassessment* (New York: Fordham University Press).

Platt, C. (1973), *Medieval Southampton: The Port and Trading Community* (London: R & K Paul).

Plomer, W. (1984), ed., *Kilvert's Diary, 1870–1879* (Harmondsworth: Penguin).

Porter, S. (1984), 'The Oxford Fire of 1644', *Oxoniensia*, 49, 289–300.

Pound, J.F. (1971), ed., *The Norwich Census of the Poor, 1570* (Norfolk Record Society, XL).

Prior, M. (1985), *Women in English Society, 1500–1800* (London: Routledge).

Pryor, F. (2004), *Britain AD: A Quest for Arthur, England and the Anglo-Saxons* (London: Harper Collins).

Quiney, A. (2003), *Town Houses of Medieval Britain* (London: Yale University Press).

Rackham, O. (1972), 'Grundle House: On the Quantities of Timber in Certain East Anglian Buildings in Relation to Local Supplies', *Vernacular Architecture*, 3, 3–8.

Rackham, O. (1976), *Trees and Woodland in the British Landscape* (London: Phoenix Press).

Rackham, O. (2003), *Ancient Woodland: Its History, Vegetation and Uses in England* (Colvend: Castlepoint).

Rawcliffe, C. (2013), *Urban Bodies: Communal Health in Late Medieval English Towns and Cities* (Woodbridge: Boydell Press).

Rawcliffe, C. and Wilson, R. (2004), eds, *Medieval Norwich* (London: Hambledon & London).

RCHM (1970), *An Inventory of the Historical Monuments in the County of Dorset, II, South-East, part I* (London: Royal Commission on Historical Monuments in England).

Reaney, P.H. (1967), *The Origin of English Surnames* (London: Routledge and Kegan Paul).

Reaney, P.H. and Wilson, R.M. (1997), *A Dictionary of English Surnames* (Oxford: Oxford University Press).

Redmonds, G. (1973), *Yorkshire, West Riding: English Surnames Series* (Chichester: Phillimore).

Redmonds, G. (1985), 'Personal Names and Surnames in Some West Yorkshire Royds', *Nomina*, 9, 73–9.

Redmonds, G. (1997), *Surnames and Genealogy: A New Approach* (Boston: New England Historic Genealogical Society).

Redmonds, G. (2004), *Christian Names in Local and Family History* (Kew: The National Archives).

Redmonds, G., King, T. and Hey, D. (2011), *Surnames, DNA and Family History* (Oxford: Oxford University Press).

Renn, D. (1973), *Norman Castles in Britain* (London: A and C Black).

Richards, J. (2001), *Blood of the Vikings* (London: Hodder and Stoughton).

Rippon, S. (2006), *Landscape, Community and Colonisation: The North Somerset Levels during the 1st to 2nd millennia AD* (York: Council for British Archaeology Research Report 152).

Rippon, S. (2008), *Beyond the Medieval Village: The Diversification of Landscape Character in Southern Britain* (Oxford: Oxford University Press).

Roberts, B.K. and Wrathmell, S. (2000), *An Atlas of Rural Settlement in England* (London: English Heritage).

Roberts, E. (2003), *Hampshire Houses 1250–1700: Their Dating and Development* (Winchester: Hampshire County Council).

Roberts, I. and Whittick, C. (2013), 'Pontefract: A Review of the Evidence for the Medieval Town', *Yorkshire Archaeological Journal*, 85, 68–96.

Rodwell, J. and Hey, D. (2010), 'The King's Wood in Lindrick', *Landscapes*, II: I, 47–66.

Rodwell, W. (2012), *The Archaeology of Churches* (Stroud: Amberley).

Rollason, D. (2003), *Northumbria, 500–1100* (Cambridge: Cambridge University Press).

Rowley, T. (1972), *The Shropshire Landscape* (London: Hodder and Stoughton).

Ryder, M.L. (1983), *Sheep and Man* (London: Duckworth).

Ryece, R. (1618), *Breviary of Suffolk*, re-printed (London: Murray, 1902).

Sachse, W.K. (1938), ed., *The Diary of Roger Lowe of Ashton-in-Makerfield, Lancashire, 1663–74* (London: Yale University Press).

Salway, P. (1993), *The Oxford Illustrated History of Roman Britain* (Oxford: Oxford University Press).

Sanders, I.J. (1960), *English Baronies: A Study of their Origins and Descent* (Oxford: Oxford University Press).

Scarfe, N. (1968), *Essex: A Shell Guide* (London: Faber and Faber).

Scarfe, N. (1972), *The Suffolk Landscape* (London: Hodder and Stoughton).

Scott, S. and Duncan, C. (2004), *Return of the Black Death: The World's Greatest Serial Killer* (Chichester: Wiley).

Seaman, P., Pound, J. and Smith, R. (2001), eds, *Norfolk Hearth Tax Exemption Certificates, 1670–1674* (British Record Society).

Sewell, R.C. (1846), ed., *Gesta Stephani* (Oxford: Sumptibus Societatis).

Sheffield Telegraph (1905), *Sheffield and District Who's Who* (Sheffield), 223.

Sheppard, J. (1974), 'Metrological Analysis of Regular Village Plans in Yorkshire', *Agricultural History Review*, 22, 118–35.

Slack, P. (1985), *The Impact of the Plague in Tudor and Stuart England* (London: Routledge and Kegan Paul).

Slack, P. (1990), *The English Poor Law, 1531–1782* (London: Macmillan).

Slack, P. (2015), *The Invention of Improvement: Information and Material Progress in Seventeenth-Century England* (Oxford: Oxford University Press).

Smith, J.R. (1987), *The Speckled Monster: Smallpox in England, 1670–1970, with Particular Reference to Essex* (Chelmsford: Essex Record Office).

Smith, R.B. (1970), *Land and Politics in the England of Henry VIII: The West Riding of Yorkshire, 1530–1546* (Oxford: Oxford University Press).

Smith, W. and Webb, W. (1656), *The Vale-Royal of England or County Palatine of Cheshire*, reprinted with an introduction by P.T. Smith (Congleton: Heads, 1990).

Smith-Bannister, S. (1997), *Names and Naming Patterns in England, 1538–1700* (Oxford: Clarendon Press).

Smollett, T. (2008), *The Expedition of Humphry Clinker* (Harmondsworth: Penguin Classics).

Snell, K.D.M. (1985), *Annals of the Labouring Poor: Social Change and Agrarian England, 1660–1900* (Cambridge: Cambridge University Press).

Snell, K.D.M. (2006), *Parish and Belonging: Community, Identity and Welfare in England and Wales, 1700–1950* (Cambridge: Cambridge University Press).

Spufford, M. (1979), *Contrasting Communities: English Villagers in the Seventeenth and Eighteenth Centuries* (Cambridge: Cambridge University Press, second edition).

Spufford, M. (1981), *Small Books and Pleasant Histories: Popular Fiction and its Readership in Seventeenth-Century England* (Cambridge: Cambridge University Press).

Spufford, M. (1985), ed., *The World of Rural Dissenters, 1520–1725* (Cambridge: Cambridge University Press).

Swanton, M. (2000), ed., *The Anglo-Saxon Chronicles* (London: Phoenix).

Sykes, B. (2006), *Blood of the Isles: Exploring the Genetic Roots of Our Tribal History* (London: Bantam Press).

Taylor, C. (1983), *Village and Farmstead: A History of Rural Settlement in England* (London: George Philip).

Taylor, C. (2000), 'Fenlands' in J. Thirsk, ed., *The English Rural Landscape* (Oxford: Oxford University Press), 179–82.

Taylor, H.M. and Taylor, J. (1980), *Anglo-Saxon Architecture*, 3 vols (Cambridge: Cambridge University Press).

Taylor, J. (1888), 'The Carriers' Cosmographie' in *Early Prose and Poetical Works of John Taylor, the Water Poet, 1580–1653* (Manchester: Spenser Society).

Tearle, B. (2012), ed., *The Accounts of the Guild of the Holy Trinity, Luton, 1526/7–1546/7* (Bedfordshire Historical Record Society).

Thick, M. (1984), 'Market gardening', in J. Thirsk, ed., *The Agrarian History of England and Wales, V. 1640–1750* (Cambridge: Cambridge University Press), 503–75.

Thirsk, J. (1967), ed., *The Agrarian History of England and Wales, IV* (Cambridge: Cambridge University Press).

Thirsk, J. (1978), *Economic Policy and Projects: The Development of a Consumer Society in Early Modern England* (Oxford: Oxford University Press).

Thirsk, J. (1984), *The Rural Economy of England: Collected Essays* (London: Hambledon).

Thirsk, J. (1985), ed., *The Agrarian History of England and Wales, v: 1640–1750* (Cambridge: Cambridge University Press).

Thirsk, J. (2000), ed., *The English Rural Landscape* (Oxford: Oxford University Press).

Thirsk, J. (2007), *Food in Early Modern England: Phases, Fads, Fashions, 1500–1760* (London: Hambledon Continuum).

Thomas, K. (1971), *Religion and the Decline of Magic* (London: Weidenfeld and Nicolson).

Thompson, M.W. (2008), *The Rise of the Castle* (Cambridge: Cambridge University Press).

Thurlby, M. (1999), *The Herefordshire School of Romanesque Sculpture* (Little Logaston: Logaston Press).

Todd, M. (1987), *The South West to 1000AD* (Harlow: Longman).

Toulmin Smith, L. (1964), ed., *Leland's Itinerary in England and Wales* (London: Centaur Press), vol. 5.

Trinder, B. (1973), *The Industrial Revolution in Shropshire* (Chichester: Phillimore).

Tucker, D.K. (2008), 'Reaney and Wilson Redux: An Analysis and Comparison with Major English Surname Sets', *Nomina*, 31, 5–44.

Turner, S. (2006), *Medieval Devon and Cornwall* (Bollington: Windgather).

Tylecote, R.F. (2013), *A History of Metallurgy* (Leeds: Maney Publishing).

Verey, D. (2008), ed., *The Diary of a Cotswold Parson: Reverend F. E. Witts, 1783–1854* (Stroud: Amberley).

Wagner, A.R. (1976), *Pedigree and Progress: Essays in the Genealogical Interpretation of History* (Chichester: Phillimore).

Wallsgrove, S.G. (1989), 'Carpenters' Marks', *Vernacular Architecture*, 20, 9–11.

Warner, P. (1987), *Greens, Commons and Clayland Colonization* (Leicester: Leicester University Press).

Weatherill, L. (1971), *The Pottery Trade and North Staffordshire, 1660–1760* (Manchester: Manchester University Press).

Webster, W.F. (1988), ed., *Nottinghamshire Hearth Tax, 1664: 1674* (Thoroton Society Record Series, XXXVII).

West, S. (2001), *West Stow Revisited* (Bury St. Edmunds: St. Edmundsbury Borough Council).

Westlake, H.F. (1919), *The Parish Gilds of Medieval England* (London: SPCK).

Whiteman, A. (1986), *The Compton Census of 1676. A Critical Edition* (London: The British Academy).

Whiting, R. (1969), *The Blind Devotion of the People: Popular Religion and the English Reformation* (Cambridge: Cambridge University Press).

Whyte, I. and Winchester, A.J.L. (2005), eds, *Society, Landscape and Environment in Upland Britain* (Birmingham: The Society for Landscape Studies).

Willan, T.S. (1976), *The Inland Trade* (Manchester: Manchester University Press).

Williamson, T. (2002), *The Transformation of Rural England: Farming and the Landscape, 1700–1870* (Exeter: University of Exeter Press).

Williamson, T. (2003), *Shaping Medieval Landscapes: Settlement, Society, Environment* (Bollington: Windgather Press).

Wilson, P. (2009), *Lullingstone Roman Villa* (London: English Heritage Guidebook).

Wiltshire, M., Woore, S., Crisp, B. and Rich, B. (2005), *Duffield Frith: History and Evolution of the Landscape of a Medieval Derbyshire Forest* (Ashbourne: Landmark).

Winchester, A.J.L. (2000), *The Harvest of the Hills: Rural Life in Northern England and the Scottish Borders, 1400–1700* (Edinburgh: Edinburgh University Press).

Wiseman, A. and Wiseman, T.P. (1980), *Julius Caesar: The Battle for Gaul* (London: Chatto & Windus).

Wood, A. (1999), *The Politics of Social Conflict: The Peak Country, 1520–1770* (Cambridge: Cambridge University Press).

Wood, A. (2013), *The Memory of the People: Custom and Popular Senses of the Past in Early Modern England* (Cambridge: Cambridge University Press).

Wood, M. (2013), 'Searching for Brunanburgh: The Yorkshire Context of the "Great War" of 937', *Yorkshire Archaeological Journal*, 85, 138–59.

Wood, R. (2012), *Romanesque Yorkshire* (Yorkshire Archaeological Society, Occasional Paper, 9).

Wood-Legh, K.L. (1965), *Perpetual Chantries in Britain* (Cambridge: Cambridge University Press).

Woodward, D. (1984), ed., *The Farming and Memorandum Books of Henry Best of Elmswell, 1642* (Oxford: Oxford University Press/British Academy).

Wrathmell, S. (1980), 'Village Depopulation in the 17th and 18th Centuries: Examples from Northumberland', *Post-medieval Archaeology*, 14, 113–26.

Wrathmell, S. (2012), ed., *Wharram: A Study of Settlement on the Yorkshire Wolds XIII – A History of Wharram Percy and its Neighbours* (York University Archaeological Publications, 15).

Wrightson, K. and Levine, D. (1997), *Poverty and Piety in an English Village: Terling, 1525–1700* (Oxford: Clarendon Press).

Wrigley, E.A. (1987), 'A Simple Model of London's Importance in Changing English Society and Economy, 1650–1750' in E. A. Wrigley, *People, Cities and Wealth: The Transformation of Traditional Society* (Oxford: Blackwell).

Wrigley, E.A. and Schofield, R.S. (1981), *The Population History of England, 1541–1871: A Reconstruction* (Cambridge: Cambridge University Press).

Wrigley, E.A., Davies, R.S., Oeppen, J.E. and Schofield, R.S. (1997), *English Population History from Family Reconstitution, 1580–1837* (Cambridge: Cambridge University Press).

Wrottesley, G. (1886), ed., 'The Exchequer Subsidy of AD 1327', *Collections for a History of Staffordshire* (William Salt Archaeological Society, VII:1).

Yates, W. (1775), *A Map of the County of Stafford* (London).

INDEX